PUNA WAI KŌRERO

PUNA WAI KŌRERO

AN ANTHOLOGY OF MĀORI POETRY IN ENGLISH

EDITED BY REINA WHAITIRI
AND ROBERT SULLIVAN

AUCKLAND
UNIVERSITY
PRESS

First published 2014
Reprinted 2021

Auckland University Press
University of Auckland
Private Bag 92019
Auckland 1142
New Zealand
www.press.auckland.ac.nz

Introduction and selection © Reina Whaitiri and Robert Sullivan, 2014
Poems © the contributors

ISBN 978 1 86940 817 6

Publication is kindly assisted by

A catalogue record for this book is available from
the National Library of New Zealand

This book is copyright. Apart from fair dealing for the purpose of private study,
research, criticism or review, as permitted under the Copyright Act, no part may
be reproduced by any process without prior permission of the publisher.
The moral rights of the authors have been asserted.

Cover design: Spencer Levine
Cover image: Reuben Paterson, *Whakapapa: get down upon your knees* (detail), 2009.
Glitter and synthetic polymer on canvas, 4000 x 4000 mm. Photo: Schwere Webber.
Image courtesy of the artist and Gow Langsford Gallery, Auckland.

Printed in China through Asia Pacific Offset Limited

CONTENTS

Introduction *Reina Whaitiri and Robert Sullivan*		1
APIRANA NGATA	A scene from the past	5
HIRIA ANDERSON	Forked tongue	10
	Mate kite	11
TE AWHINA ARAHANGA	Evening high	11
HINEMOANA BAKER	Te tangi a te rito	12
	Urupā	13
	Liver	14
	Matariki, e	15
	My life part II: I think you're on your own with that one, bro	15
ROIMATA BAKER	Koro	17
HILARY BAXTER	Reminiscence	19
	I am going back . . .	20
	October 1972	20
ARAPERA HINEIRA BLANK	Expression of an inward self with a linocut	21
	Dreamtime	22
	After watching father re-uniting with sons in prison	23
	Auē, taukuri ē!	24
	What can I?	25
	Rangitukia, soul place	27
MARINO BLANK	Childhood	31
	Minstrel	32
	What to wear to a gynaecology examination	33
PEARL DE VERE BOYED	The changed land	34
	Moonrise in January	36
	Freedom of choice	37
	Still clearing the land	38

BUB BRIDGER	Summer's coming	39
	At the conference	40
	Enigma	41
	Johnny come dancing	42
	Ode to jokers	46
	Wild daisies	47
BEN BROWN	I am the Māori Jesus	48
	Chur bro	54
	Moko	55
TANIA HINEHOU BUTCHER	Māori Bay	56
	In memory of: Hone Tuwhare	57
	Seaweed chaplet	58
	Muriwai	59
JACQ CARTER	If I am the river and the river is me	60
	Our tūpuna remain	61
	E noho rā	62
	To the statue of Wairaka at the mouth of Ōhinemataroa	63
	Comparatively speaking, there is no struggle	64
	Me aro koe ki te hā o Hineahuone!	66
SAMUEL CRUICKSHANK	Pākiri: midnight sea	67
HARRY DANSEY	The old place	68
SHELLY DAVIES	four haiku for chris	70
HENARE DEWES	Tihei mauriora!	71
	Te ao hou	72
KIM EGGLESTON	On the beach	73
	Before the rains	74
AMBER ESAU	Numiamatumua	75
	Crushes	77
	Pray to be wrong	78
	Tongue	79
	Horoi	81

RANGI FAITH	Spring star	83
	Official opening	83
	Losing our mana	85
	The stones stand	85
	The cage	86
	Catch & release, catch & release	87
	A measured tread	88
	Karakia to a silent island	89
MIRIA GEORGE	Still	90
MAREWA GLOVER	Pounamu	91
	Ngāwhā	91
	The shame of Tāneroa	92
	Waitangi II	94
	Te rerenga kēhua (white flight)	94
	Māori women's hui	95
BRIAR GRACE-SMITH	How I got my name	96
ROWLEY HABIB (RORE HAPIPI)	Mother and sons	97
	Tame Iti (behind the tattooed face)	98
	Ōrākau	99
	Composed on a summer's evening	100
	Early morning meeting	101
AROHA HARRIS	Kina	103
JOHN HOVELL	Pāua tide	104
KERI HULME	Pā mai tō reo aroha	106
	He hōhā	109
	Hōkioi	112
	E ngā iwi o ngāi tahu	113
	Winesong 15	115
	Ends and beginnings	116
WITI IHIMAERA	My heart beats strongly	117
	Our watch now	118
	O numi tutelar	119
	Una storia semplice	121
SAM JACKSON	Being Māori	122

PHIL KAWANA	Rūaumoko, my lovely	125
	Songs for my children	132
	Scenes from a council tenancy	134
	Granville requiem	136
	Urupā	139
HINEWIRANGI KOHU	Fried bread	140
	Barriers	141
	In ritual	142
	Expectations	143
	Weep not for me	144
PAULA KORA	Te aute tē whawhea	145
	[It wasn't your smile]	146
ROBIN KORA	Suffrage	147
	Been fishing, Billy?	149
	Tāne's zoo	152
	Visit the sins	153
DORA ROIMATA LANGSBURY	My father's footsteps	156
	The night they knocked the doors down (26/02/2011)	157
MARAMA LAURENSON	Tahu Brown Parata – ol' rolly eyes	157
	Hana Te Hemara – Muru Raupatu	160
KATERINA MATAIRA	Restoring the ancestral house	162
ABIGAIL McCLUTCHIE	Go to the mountains	164
LARISSA McMILLAN	Idle	165
	Hotere	165
TRIXIE TE ARAMA MENZIES	Kōauau	167
	Climber	168
	Ki āku tipuna Māori	168
	Manuhiri	169
	Māui steals time	170
	Uenuku	170
	Watercress	171
	Ocean of tongues	172

KELLY ANA MOREY	Ture te haki	173
	Ordinary clothes	174
	Sticky ending	175
	Mother's Day	176
PAULA MORRIS	English grandmother	177
	Pontefract	178
	Where	179
JUSTINE MURRAY	Staunch	180
	To dream	181
DEIRDRE NEHUA	The abyss	182
MOANA NEPIA	Ka tangi te ruru	183
	Kihikihi	184
	I held you	185
MICHAEL O'LEARY	He waiatanui kia Aroha	189
	Kia Aroha – rua	197
	Hone Tuwhare: a personal memoir	198
	Bastion Point – Koha 22/5/88	199
	For my father in prison, 1965	200
	Poem to your grandmother	201
TRU PARAHA	Knowing entirely everything on Earth that is	202
	Northern territory of my bone-trail dream walking	204
	Elegy	206
	Core subjects	207
	In the belly of the paradox	208
EVELYN PATUAWA-NATHAN	Summer in the Kaihu Valley	210
	Old man and his dog	211
	Waikato lament	212
	Aboriginal on the last train home	213
	Opening doors	213
PARE PAUL	Game on Punk!	214
	On court	216

KIRI PIAHANA-WONG	Hinerangi	217
	Tidelines	219
	Four paintings	220
	On the day you left me it was raining	222
BRIAN POTIKI	jill	224
	hone	224
	down at bluff	225
	dutch portrait	226
	it's all about feel	226
	hiroki's song	227
ROMA PŌTIKI	Bound to	228
	Te kōkā, te whare tangata	229
	A cloak and taiaha journey	230
	The decision of the taniwha	231
	Toetoe turn	233
	Flight	234
	Speaking out	235
MARAEA RAKURAKU	Aunties are Boss	236
VAUGHAN RAPATAHANA	Aotearoa blues, baby	239
JEAN RIKI	A third migration	242
	Last stations	247
REIHANA ROBINSON	Thinking of my father	255
	Humility	256
	Noa Noa makes breakfast for Caroline and me, or, The tea ceremony is introduced to Samoa	257
	How it all began	258
	God of ugly things	260
	Pāua	261
	Ninety Mile Beach	262
TE KAHU ROLLESTON	The Rena	263
	Forget about Guy Fawkes (Parihaka)	265
ZANE SCARBOROUGH	[The world was your oyster]	267
	Tāmati (inspired by JKB)	268
KATE SHAW	To Vaughan	269
MICHAEL STEVENS	Let the moon and the sea . . .	270

BRUCE STEWART	Pono	271
GEORGINA STEWART	Kitchen stool	272
J. C. STURM	At Red Rocks	273
	The last night at Collingwood	274
	Memo for my 70th birthday	275
	Coming of age	277
	A tricky business	278
	As the godwits fly	281
	Urgently	283
	He waiata tenei mo Parihaka	284
	History lesson	286
	At times I grieve	287
	Splitting the stone	288
ROBERT SULLIVAN	Ahi kā – the house of Ngā Puhi	291
	Voice carried my family, their names and stories	292
	Ocean birth	293
	Captain Cook	295
	Honda waka	295
	Listen to the rhythm of the falling rain	296
	Onehunga Bay	297
	Waka 42	298
	Waka 46	299
	Waka 99	300
	Rāwiri/David	301
	Arohanui	303
CHRIS TAMAIPAREA	Another poem about trees	303
TRACEY TAWHIAO	Listen to me scream	304
	Blessed is blood	305
	Māori girl	306
	A lawyer and a builder	308
APIRANA TAYLOR	The womb	309
	Poem for a misplaced bushman	310
	Feelings and memories of a kuia	311
	Takin' words to the muso	313
	Poem for a princess	315

APIRANA TAYLOR (continued)	Six million	315
	Haka	316
	Te ihi	317
	Fishbone	318
NGAHUIA TE AWEKOTUKU	Pukeroa	319
	Moon poem	320
	For LMS 145, a bone flute at the British Museum	322
	For 6742, a hei tiki at the British Museum	322
	For one trophy of the Waikato war, now in an unnamed museum	323
ALICE TE PUNGA SOMERVILLE	mad ave	324
	Daddy's little girl	329
	First draft of a waiata tangi	329
NORMAN TE WHATA	This street	331
MAHINĀRANGI TOCKER	My eyes close to see you	333
	Privilege	334
HONE TUWHARE	O Africa	336
	No ordinary sun	336
	Hotere	337
	To a Maori figure cast in bronze outside the Chief Post Office, Auckland	338
	Kitten	340
	On a theme by Hone Taiapa	341
	Haiku (1)	342
	Salvaged	342
	Rain	343
	Heemi	344
	The New Zealand land march on Wellington, Hepetema 14–Oketopa 17, 1975	346
	Rain-maker's song for Whina	347
	We, who live in darkness	348
	Bird of prayer	349
	The old place	349
	Old man chanting in the dark	350

HONE TUWHARE (continued)	Pupurangi	351
	On becoming an icon (!)	353
TRACY WATSON	Kōauau (NZ Māori flute)	354
	Kōpū (Venus)	354
REINA WHAITIRI	Lincoln Hall – Hawai'i	355
	Ka tangi	357
	One times three	359
HAARE WILLIAMS	Koroua	360
	Bellbird and flax flower	362
	Patches hide no scars	363
	Kūmara	364
	Koha	365
VERNICE WINEERA	Song from Kapiti	366
	Wellington, circa 1950	368
	At Laieloa	369
	Hokule'a	370
	The farm-boy rides a Yamaha	371
	Boy in a sleeping bag	372
	Tāniko	373
BRIAR WOOD	Rotomahana	374
	Rangiputa	375
	Kūmara hōu	376
	Whenua uenuku	378
REWA WORLEY	The separation	379
Select Glossary		382
Acknowledgements		402

Ka rere te maramara
Ka rere ki te pūtake
Koia i piri ai
Koia i tata ai
E tūpā whaiā

INTRODUCTION

Whakapapa is the fulcrum around which Māori construct iwi histories. It is also the source from which we draw inspiration. Everyone and everything, including poetry, has whakapapa, and the kaupapa of *Puna Wai Kōrero* is to explore the one hundred and twenty or so years of poetry written in English by Māori. As far as we have discovered, the earliest poem published in English was written by Apirana Ngata; all subsequent Māori poets writing in English can trace their poetic whakapapa to Ngata's achievement.

Sir Apirana Ngata was a true visionary and his mauri lives on in the people and in his work. It was Ngata who collated hundreds of annotated songs in te reo rangatira, culminating in the pre-eminent anthology *Ngā Mōteatea*. This is the most important collection of Māori-language song poems ever published. Its four volumes were completed after his death by noted scholars, translators and linguists, including Pei Te Hurinui Jones, Tamati Muturangi Reedy and Hirini Moko Mead. Ngata continues to be a guiding light for Māori so we accordingly begin this anthology with his poem 'A scene from the past'.

For Māori, contact with Pākehā and their literary forms provided an exciting opportunity to express their experiences in new ways. The traditional forms of oral poetry remained – such as waiata ringaringa, waiata tangi, waiata aroha, oriori, karakia, haka and whaikōrero – but writing words down in a new language and using different forms created new genres. Māori quickly and enthusiastically began experimenting with composing, writing and creating, and the work collected here in *Puna Wai Kōrero* is but a fraction of what has been produced over the years. It soon became clear that there was a limit to what we could fit in this book, though we regret that we had to be so selective. Further anthologising – of song lyrics, for example, and slam poetry – will be needed to show the variety of work being produced and to research its whakapapa.

Puna Wai Kōrero is a tribute to Hone Tuwhare, whom we acknowledge as Aotearoa's poet laureate. He is certainly worthy of that title in the Māori world and he stands alongside those considered to be the best New Zealand poets. Since the early 1960s Tuwhare's poetry has been enjoyed by generations of readers and his work has been translated into many languages. The numerous references to

Tuwhare in this collection demonstrate the high regard in which he is held and, although he will be ever missed, his mana lives on in the large body of work he leaves. His son Robert has generously given permission to publish the poems included here. We extend our thanks to him. Some of Hone's poems selected for inclusion are the personal favourites of the editors, while others will be recognised as iconic representatives of his work. Ngā mihi ki a koe, e Hone.

Our matua Selwyn Murupaenga kindly allowed us to use the title *Puna Wai Kōrero* for this anthology. Murupaenga was a pioneer, one of the first Māori to be involved in radio, film-making and television in Aotearoa. He produced a long-running (1971–96) weekly National Radio programme entitled *Te Puna Wai Korero*. The word 'puna' refers to a wellspring, while 'wai' means both water and memory. 'Kōrero' refers to talk, stories, the mana kupu of a highly charged language as well as that in everyday use. The title of Hone Tuwhare's 1993 collection, *Deep River Talk*, also expresses some of the essence of what *Puna Wai Kōrero* can mean.

In most previous anthologies of New Zealand poetry, Māori poets, while there, have been given only cursory acknowledgement. One purpose of this anthology is to bring together the many Māori poets who have contributed to the literary landscape of Aotearoa in one anthology, with Māori editors – the major criteria for inclusion in *Puna Wai Kōrero* was declaring tribal affilation/s. The political and social commentaries in the poems present a unique perspective on Aotearoa and the wider world, from the early days of contact to the present. While poets such as Hone Tuwhare, Robert Sullivan, Rangi Faith and Arapera Blank are established poets, others have not yet had the recognition they deserve. With *Puna Wai Kōrero* we wanted to provide a space for as many poets as possible of Māori descent.

The pioneering work of Witi Ihimaera, D. S. Long, Irihapeti Ramsden and Haare Williams set a benchmark with the publication of anthologies of Māori writing, *Into the World of Light* (1982) and the multi-volume *Te Ao Mārama* (1992–96). These important anthologies introduced New Zealand to a broad but little-known and little-understood Māori world and gave voice to the many writers who would not have otherwise been heard. In the introduction to the first of these books the absence of Māori literary anthologies is noted, even though Māori writing is described as 'the pou tokomanawa of New Zealand literature'. Writers such as Patricia Grace, Witi Ihimaera, Keri Hulme and J. C. Sturm are now well known for their fiction but Māori playwrights, lyricists and script writers still need to be anthologised.

We would like to acknowledge the work of Huia Publishers, who have been publishing annual collections of short fiction by Māori writers. They recently published

Huia Histories of Māori: Ngā Tāhuhu Kōrero (2012), a collection of essays by Māori scholars, edited by Danny Keenan. The Māori literary journal *Ora Nui* has published two issues since 2012, and other indigenous Pacific anthologies featuring Māori writers include *Mana*, and the award-winning *Whetu Moana* (2003) and *Mauri Ola* (2010) co-edited by Albert Wendt and the editors of this volume.

For this anthology we have attempted to find as many poets with a Māori whakapapa as possible. There must certainly be poets we would have selected had we been aware of them. Some others we have not been able to contact for permission to use their work. In both cases we regret their absence. While there is a wide range of voices and perspectives in the poetry, there are generally elements which are identifiable as Māori. Sometimes the Māori connection is obvious while at others it is more obscure, more subtle, or perhaps not there at all. There may be direct references to traditional songs in te reo or to well-known personalities, or allusions to other poems or poets. Many poets refer to Māori who have spent their lives promoting and supporting Māori rights and their respect is clearly expressed. The many references to local legends and incidents may not be recognised by all, but for those connected to them by tradition or through memory, there is great pleasure in the reading. Although the Glossary includes brief explanations of some historical events, comprehensive coverage is impossible here. We hope that future students and scholars will find it a worthwhile and exciting research project to explore the many references to times, places, events, situations.

In selecting poetry for the anthology we wanted to ask questions of the poets and their work. What identifies Māori poetry? or a Māori poet? What compels us to identify as Māori even though our links may be tenuous, or slight, or forgotten, even hidden? It may be painful to remember who we are or where we have come from, but frequently there is a sense of what it is to be proudly Māori. It is often the exploration of whakapapa which effects a connection. With aroha and manaakitanga, we support the work of writers who have asserted their Māori identity through their whakapapa.

The poetry in *Puna Wai Kōrero* comes out of the countryside, from the towns and cities, and from many countries around the world. The Māori diaspora is spread across the globe but wherever we find ourselves we continue to identify as Māori (mostly) and remain connected to Aotearoa – after all, this is the one and only place on earth where we can claim a tūrangawaewae. The voices are many and diverse: confident, angry, passionate, respectful, proud, despairing and full of hope, expressing the full scope of what it is to be human, and especially, to be Māori.

Much to our delight, artists not widely known for writing poetry offered us work: Witi Ihimaera, Paula Morris, Ngahuia Te Awekotuku, for example. Both Ihimaera and Te Awekotuku have previously been anthologised in poetry collections but it is a privilege to be allowed to include their work here. It is gratifying to have poetry written especially for *Puna Wai Kōrero*: by Paula Morris, Briar Wood, Jacq Carter and Amber Esau, for example. We are also fortunate to have poetry from long-established poets such as J. C. Sturm, Trixie Te Arama Menzies, Keri Hulme, Apirana Taylor, Roma Pōtiki, Hinemoana Baker, and Phil Kawana. We note that Hawai'i-based poet Vernice Wineera, who continues to write, was the first Māori woman to publish a collection of poems, *Mahanga: Pacific Poems*, in 1978.

For consistency and in keeping with contemporary editorial practices in the use of te reo, we have chosen to use macrons rather than double vowels for te reo words in most poems, even if they were not used in the original publication. We do not provide footnotes unless a poet has specifically requested it, or the note is necessary for clarification. Where it has been possible to establish the date of composition (in italics) or first publication (in roman), this is provided at the foot of the poem. The Glossary at the end contains translations of terms and any essential information about the poems. The biographies give iwi affiliations and provide brief information about the poet.

We believe the range of poetry presented here is varied enough to offer something of interest for everyone, although this is not the sole purpose of *Puna Wai Kōrero*. Having read the collection through from beginning to end many times, we realise there is a narrative thread which connects the many iwi, hapū and whānau of Aotearoa. Through language and ideas, through stories and shared experiences, we discover and rediscover what it is to be Māori. *Te kōrero te kai a te rangatira* – and may we continue to be well fed.

APIRANA NGATA

Apirana Ngata (1874–1950) of Ngāti Porou was the first Māori to complete a New Zealand university education, gaining an MA and a law degree. In 1927 Ngata was granted a knighthood for his immense contribution to Māori cultural and economic revival in the first half of the twentieth century. He instigated Māori land reforms and health and hygiene programmes. Among his many achievements were his serial publications of waiata in the *Journal of the Polynesian Society*, later and posthumously published as *Ngā Mōteatea* by his protégé, Pei Te Hurinui Jones. His intelligence, tact, persistence, charm and political skill brought him considerable success in his many endeavours.

A scene from the past

A description of the Maori haka by Apirana T. Ngata.

(Prologue.)
We reck not that the day has past;
That Death and Time, the cruel Fates,
Have torn us from the scenes we loved,
And brought us to this unknown world.
In mem'ry ling'ring, all too hazy,
Blurred, uncertain, still they charm us.
Ah, we love them! Language doth but
Clothe in artifice our passion,
Doth but to the world proclaim
We are traitors to the past.

Traitors? when our hearts are beating,
Thrilling stirred by recollections?
Present, Future? Them we know not;
For us no memories they hold.
Traitors? when our ears are ringing,
Filled with echoes from the dead?
Deaf to all, these chords alone
Make heavenly music, penetrating
Souls by strangeness long since deadened,
Now in sympathy vibrating.

Traitors? Nay, we scorn the name!
Bigots, blind fanatic worshippers,
Idolaters serving things of clay,
Call us, and that name were dear!

On life's rough stream you launched us forth;
You thought to buoy us, gave us hope.
Your sturdy oak, our flaxen bark,
Your iron-clad, our humble reed,
Made sorry company, and you glided,
Well equipped, the whilst we trembled.
Ah, no! your hope but kills all hope;
You crush the life you wish to save.
Nay, rather leave us with the past;
In mem'ry let us wander back
Amid the scenes we loved of yore.
There let us roam, untrammelled, free,
For mem'ry, like that herb, embalms,
Preserves, endears our recollections.

(The marae and hui.)
One dear scene in my mind's eye is floating,
Martial, warlike, yet so graceful;
Stag'd in meads that heard no bleating,
Save of savage babes at play.

There the old pa stands to-day,
Where the mountain, clad in koukas,
Bends with gentle slope and fondly
Show'rs kisses on the stream.
Rippling, laughing, winding, moaning,
Hies she on to join the ocean,
Emblem of a race that's speeding
Sadly onwards to oblivion.

Day is breaking on that pa,
All within is bustle, stir.
'Tis the hour of dedication,
Te Kawanga, solemn consecration,
When our whare in its beauty
Tukutuku, pukana e korirari!
Duly to the gods in Heaven
With our war-dance must be given.

  (The assembly of the tribes.)
All day long, from far and near,
The crowds pour in to see and hear.
Amid this group are chieftains bold,
Rewi, Taonui – names of old.
Yonder Kahungunu, mere in hand,
Frowning marshals forth his band –
Te Arawa, Tainui me Te Whakatohea
Whakaata, Taupare, Tuwhakairiora.

A noble sight th' intruding band.
But grander yet unfolds itself,
Yonder, massed, one sea of forms,
Maids with warriors alternating.
In the van are maidens lovely,
Dressed in mats of finest fibre,
Cheeks with takou gaily hued,
Plumed with quills of rarest huia.
Beyond – but no; no more is seen,
Though hundreds lie to shout 'Haere mai!'
The maids must first display their graces,
Then we'll gaze on warriors' faces.

  (Maidens' welcome.)
Softly and gently, and chanting most sweetly,
Uplift they their welcome, 'Haere mai! Haere mai!'
With knees bent gracefully, with slow step and gesture,

As soft as the panther; yet queenly and stately.
Hark! now it is changing, in chorus they're joining;
It swells and it rings, it bursts forth triumphant.
In voice and in gesture; in body and limb,
Their welcome is spoken, 'Naumai! naumai!'
How nimbly they foot it, how supple their bodies;
Ye nymphs and ye naiads, beware of your laurels!
These children untutored, by Nature endowed,
May charm yet Apollo, the god of all graces.

   (Chant while withdrawing.)
Kihei aku mihi i pau atu, e hine!
Rokohanga koe ka pikauria e!
But now, behold, the nymphs subside,
The rhythmic motion's ceased, and lo!
The ranks give way, the van files off,
Unfolding terrors to our view.
Rows of warriors, dusky, war-like,
Line the earth and make it bristle;
All recumbent, silent, speechless,
Seeming in lethargic sleep.

   (The men's welcome.)
Aotearoa's sons, ye warriors stern!
Awake! awake! they come! they come!
'Welcome, ye strangers; Naumai! Naumai!'
Respond ye to the call so feebly,
Though your war-paint glows so fiercely!
'Welcome ye strangers! Haere mai! haere mai!'
Ha! ye sluggards, raise your voices,
Up and stamp and tread like Maoris!
'Tis the haka powhiri, war-dance,
Fierce and warlike, savage, martial!

(The whakaara.)
Ko te iwi Maori e ngunguru nei! Au, au, au e ha!
Ko te iwi Maori e ngunguru nei! Au, au, au e ha!
Ko nga iwi katoa ra, tau tangata e taoho ai koe,
Taoho!

Ha! your blood is coursing now!
Ha! your spirit's roused at last!
Ha! the welcome rings out clear!
Powhiritia atu! Haere mai! Haere mai!

Heads erect and bodies stately,
Proud, imperious, yet be graceful;
Arms and limbs in rhythm moving,
Mars, Apollo, are reviewing.

(The grand powhiri.)
Tena i whiua!
With motion majestic, their arms now wide sweeping;
Now circles describing, then to heav'n up-lifted,
Their bodies set firmly, yet limbs in mid-air!
Tena i takahia!
With knee joints set loose;
With frenzy in gesture, with eye-brows contracting,
With eyes glowing fiercely, with bounding and leaping!
But, mark, mild Apollo, the War-god is soothing.

'Powhiritia atu!' 'Haere mai! Haere mai!'
Ha! warriors are leaping; the ranks they are surging;
The War-god has conquered; the war-cry is raised!
'Tis sounding, 'tis swelling, 'tis roaring, 'tis thund'ring!
Ha! Frenzy, thou workest; 'tis blood now they smell.
'The battle! the battle! our taiahas and meres!'
They shout as they leap; a madness has seized them.
'Tako ki to kai rangatira! Tako!'

(*1892*; 1908)

HIRIA ANDERSON

Hiria Anderson (Ngāti Maniapoto) lives with her whānau in what was once her grandparents' home in Ōtorohanga and has established a small studio there. She attended Queen Victoria School: 'Hone Tuwhare visited our English classes as a guest and was most influential.' In the mid-1990s she was involved in Ngā Puna Waihanga o Tainui – Māori Artists and Writers – and formally trained in visual art under the tutelage of James F. Ormsby. Visual arts and creative writing are a big part of her life. She is currently undertaking an MFA. She is also dyslexic.

Forked tongue

You stared me in the face
even looked me in the eye
without a flinch of your furrowed brow
not a wrinkle in your upturned, thin-lipped mouth
with flailing hands you uttered:
'And even though we govern the waterways
it won't stop you praying to "your" god of the sea'
and you expected me to smile, and then you said:
'We will be better caretakers because we have money'
and you expected me to feel better, and then you said:
'It's not just "us" that pollute the water, it's all of us'
and you expected me to agree with this, and then you said:
'You "can" eat the shellfish, after we clean the sewerage up'
and you expected my child to eat, and then you said:
'We will all benefit from this sale, they need our sand'
and you expected me to believe this!
I will never believe this!

(2007)

Mate kite

It wasn't up to me who I'd see
they'd just be there doing their own thing
as if I wasn't there . . . like I'm the ghost or sumthin.

But I noticed them; they would tumble like leaves
down from the trees and swirl all around me
and I would cradle them in my arms
like memories.

Who lent their eyes to me?
The threads that they have woven said
We had it comin, you and I.
Next time I hope they bring pizza.

(2006)

TE AWHINA ARAHANGA

Te Awhina Arahanga descends from Ngāti Tūwharetoa, Te Āti Haunui a Pāpārangi, Ngāti Hauiti ki Rata, Rapuwai, Waitaha, Ngāti Mamoe, Ngāi Tahu and a sprinkling of Scottish and English whakapapa. She is a writer, researcher and social historian. Te Awhina has been resident at the Michael King Writers' Centre, has won the Huia short story competition, has contributed short stories to Radio New Zealand, and has been published in various poetry anthologies and journals.

Evening high

Don't tell the world
specially about oneself
that sweet tender
devotion
is not obtainable

when you've
tasted
mellow
bitter
sweet
unrequited love

(2011)

HINEMOANA BAKER

Hinemoana Baker (Ngāti Raukawa, Ngāti Toa Rangatira, Te Ātiawa, Ngāi Tahu, Germany, England) was born in Christchurch and raised in Whakatāne and Nelson. She is a poet, recording artist, singer-songwriter, occasional broadcaster and tutor of creative writing. Her first collection of poetry, *mātuhi | needle* (VUP, 2004), and her second, *kōiwi kōiwi* (VUP, 2010), draw on aspects of her mixed Māori and Pākehā heritage. Her third, *waha | mouth*, will be published during her 2014 term as writer in residence at the International Institute of Modern Letters, Victoria University, Wellington.

Te tangi a te rito

Bones, in this place the soles
of my feet are not null; how
must I walk? My throat
has not woven the call. My throat

has not spoken the harakeke. The north
you say, is thick with it.
Open-mouthed for the host but not
so silenced in the throat. In this kitchen

violence placed its thumbs on the bud
of the call. In this garden violence
pinched us back.

The softness drops
from your forehead, shame
darkens my mouth to a
museum, to a purple
gallery of pūhā and pāua and the sounds
of these things
that keep a family well-fed
and its friends
at your table in the singing
summer.

(1996)

Urupā

the dead
the dead
the dead

up to their eyeballs
watching over
and over us

dancing, falling
over like tōtara
the small leak

in the canoe or
the big rent in the hull
they lie in us

(2004)

Liver

I hang out the washing
at night.

Each peg squeaks
into place.

You, in the kitchen light,
warming my back.

§

I'm worrying again
about your liver

as if it helps.
I feel around

on you – which side
is it? How big?

§

You have nightmares
and kick me in your sleep.

Sometimes
I kick you back.

(2010)

Matariki, e

you have gone home

you made me feel
I had discovered fire

you have left the room

you made me feel
I had invented the wheel

in the end
room   we gather
round you

you made me feel
the sun wheeled in me
the moon on my tongue

(2010)

My life part II: I think you're on your own with that one, bro

My father's curling kidney. A funeral a month.
The mackerel sky and a steam train.
Red dust from the 1920s.
Blue fountain pen trailing up and off the page.
Matilda's metatarsals, Banjo's jaw.
And still and still. Slowest jump ever.

I make the joke about how I taught her everything she knows.
Until one of us got chilblains
and the dachsund ruined it. Or the dalmatian.

Everyone but me in aprons. Butter glazing my fingers.
Welsh rarebit lumpy with flour; crumbling fudge.

We all say *it wasn't a shark it was your kidney*. Peace lifts
the photograph off the wall. They weren't just sisters
they were two white horses. The sun glanced off the windscreen
I swerved and you swore. My scarf pink, my mother's

blue, bone tipping above the surface of noon. She sweats
and still, and still, she sleeps while they
bandage her. What to do with fabric and skin.
Your ankles are weeping pus. Your
eyelids. Keep kneading

and still and still. Butter glazes.
He died on the operating table, nineteen years old.
Watched his girlfriend crying over him and came back.

Fuck that priest and his last rites.
The bed was the one you held me down on
instead I bled out. Or a wētā.

And still and still, screech-giggling, a sour smell in my armpits,
hoards of them following me up the footpath.
The black and silver radio, dial like a safe.
Tongue-burn, clouds of steam, crowds waving
identical flags. The crows are children

who have had something taken from them,
something edible. *What are you . . . thirty-two? Thirty-three?*
Wood tells the truth. Outside the room I shook and
shuddered while the Zimbabweans laughed at me.
There will never be a gap in this State Highway 1
traffic that someone will not willingly close before you can join in.

The wind makes a sound through eight different chimes.
It's not the fault of the game, says Peace. I draw the ferns
in a chart alongside mucus and masturbation.
I put down the books and say a prayer for concentration.
That place online where you can listen

to thousands of crickets slowed down and
they sound like the Mormon Tabernacle Choir.
Yes, and a Lakota soprano sings with them in Italian.

(2013)

ROIMATA BAKER

He uri nō Te Ātiawa, Ngāti Raukawa, Ngāti Toarangatira me Ngāi Tahu. 'I have grown up around many great storytellers: my parents, my aunts and uncles and of course my grandfather, who in his old age recalled a world I could only ever imagine. He was a proud man who would remind us that we descended from great navigators, inventors and thinkers. I wrote this poem at age seventeen, within a year of his passing, in remembrance of an upright man whose influence has stayed with me throughout my life.'

Koro

It was good to hear your
voice again,
Koro.

I was listening to the
Māori radio station,
when your voice came over.
They played a tape of you,
talking about your
younger days.

It was like sitting once again
in the lounge, on Mātene Street,
listening to your hardcase stories.

I never realised how much
I missed you.
And how I missed the way you
clicked your tongue when you were
in awe of something, or your
cups of tea and bread.
And believe it or not I miss
that walking stick, too.

Well, your snotty-nosed
know-it-all mokopuna is still
the same.
She hopes to see you again some time.
Maybe you could tell her another
one of your stories.

It was good to hear your
voice again,
Koro.

(1994)

HILARY BAXTER

Hilary Baxter, of Taranaki, Whakatōhea, was born in 1949 to James K. Baxter and J. C. Sturm. She had several poems published in university magazines and her collection of poetry, *The Other Side of Dawn*, was published in 1987. Although a long-time resident of Darwin, Australia, she eventually returned to Aotearoa and died in Paekākāriki in 2013.

Reminiscence

I remember as a child
my father would carry me
high up on
his shoulders or head
I would suffocate
in the red knitted jumpsuit
and father wearing
his old gabardine coat

He would gallop through
the Karori bush
with me precariously above
across the paths banks
lost streams
made of wet brown leaves

Then coming up
the gravel drive
onto the old road
no more would I feel
as though my throne of trees
looked down on the world

that lay there waiting for me to grow

(1987)

I am going back . . .

I am going back to the land
I am going back to the marae
and I will relive Jerusalem
before I die

(1987)

October 1972

My joy is a tribal joy
my loneliness is strong loneliness
and my sorrow
is pathways of flowers
leading to the river
where the taniwha moves

and the moreporks called
for a barefoot father
my father
disciple of the Māori Christ

I hear an old man singing
and there is sunlight in his hair

(1987)

ARAPERA HINEIRA BLANK

Arapera Hineira Blank (1932–2002) was a descendant of the tribes of Ngāti Porou, Ngāti Kahungunu, Rongowhakaata and Te Aitanga a Māhaki. She was born in Rangitukia on the East Coast of the North Island, was a teacher and poet, and one of a small group of Māori writers in English during the 1950s. In 1959 she was awarded a special Katherine Mansfield Memorial Award for her essay 'Ko taku kūmara hei wai-ū mō tama'. She said of herself: 'I enjoy words that sparkle, whether they be Māori, my mother tongue, or English.'

Expression of an inward self with a linocut

I build something up,
complicated and complex,
I hope,
but alas!
nothing so deep emerges.
Only simple lines –
hacked out of a piece
of worn-out lino –
that curve and dip
to a traditional line
almost moronic
in their upward
outward bend to the left
to the right
what the hell!

Why should I lie
to myself?
I am what I am
carved out of a long line
of heavy-footed deep-rooted
simplicity
wanting to love well
eat well die with the thought of
kūmara vine stretched out
reproducing an image –

many images of itself,
its hopes
drenched in warmth
with roots forever seeking
the sun.

(1986)

Dreamtime

When you feel
heaviness of spirit
belly tighten
deep hurt under your heart,
reach out for someone,
no one comes,
turn inwards.

Fall into gentle breathing,
listen to the music
of silence,
lie still, float, on
velvet black,
till your body
is bathed in calm,
slowly unfold your
pain-easing dream.

Imagine you came
into this world
in a cloud of
red-orange-gossamer
silk, shimmering up
with the dawn, along,
down to a dew-damp earth,

that warmed with you,
filled her people
song-rich with hope
for spiritual peace,
now,
tomorrow, and tomorrow.

'The sun rises,
the sun sets,
the sun rises.

He rā ka whiti
he rā ka tō
he rā ka whiti.'

(1986)

After watching father re-uniting with sons in prison

For the whānau

He waited to be admitted
sweating, emotion hurting
like groping kūmara
in a waterless land,
wondering would they tell him
Piss off you bastard after
his silence and their descent
to a nightmare world.

They came, defiant-nonchalant
gazing, grimfaced, dignity
unruffled, masking pain,
knife-deep on recognition.

He searched for something
creating a soft-fall
into a dreamtime world
pain-eased in loving again.

Ka kōrero mai tōna ngākau,
waiho rā, taria te wā
ka hoki mai te wairua!
Tell them what eats your soul,
wait for the healing.
We each have a time
for weaving delicate threads
into a breathing world.

(1986)

Auē, taukuri ē!

My head tells me to write,
my heart does not,
wrinkles, the sting of sweat rash,
tell me to move
before I grow too old,
and lose that gift
that comes with dazzling green
and fines to a summer glow.

But, eight hours, and eight lines,
and then no more.
Out of my reach the magic
hovers, sometimes
disappears, and I am
left with nothing
but this kēhua straddling,
blotting out the fervent song.

(1986)

What can I?

Say to you who bore me,
fed me on mother's milk,
washed and caressed my flesh,
hugged me when I ached
for no reason at all,
when I yelled or screamed?

What can I
say to you who listened for my
heartbeat to make sure that
I lived, breathed, and one day
gave you pleasure with
a little smile, a
contented nod of my head?

And do you remember?
Now that I am grown too big
for you to nurse at your breast,
too big for you to scold or
give advice to,
that once you wept for my life,
prayed for me that I grow up
to remember you with love?

For I do,
that I owe you so much
for years of sweating in the kitchen,
on heavy feet too tired to
remember even, that once,
you were young, full of
excitement to be young and alive
to every note of the throated
bird that sang of an endless summer.

And I know
that I cannot take unto myself all your aches and pains
soothe your tired limbs
for you are too proud
now to want me to
put your feet up on a soft cushion,
hold your head when it aches.

And sometimes I have
this desire to do unto others,
all that you have done for me.
And whenever someone does
something like unto you
to me,
I want to
give them the whole world
until my feet feel the aches
that you felt,
my body labour as yours did,
and my heart be forever
open unto all.

And I hope
that it's not just a dream.

(1986)

Rangitukia, soul place

From Hikurangi the Waiapu
carves wide grey lines to turbulent seas
asserting mana – vibrant sounds that
echo on the wind.

Eroding hills succumb to progress,
muted bush in hollows lies, with
bones of whānau undisturbed,
mānuka, pūriri, giving way
to sunburnt grasses, creaking pine trees
now the home of shrieking magpies
swooping down on the unwary
echo on the wind.

Kūmara gropes its way between
kiwifruit and creeping grapevine,
women weeding, rhythmic earth songs
echo on the wind.

Three miles south of Te Uranga
a battered one-way bridge still stands,
monument to frequent bashings
by way-out drivers soaked in booze
at way-out cost in the Tiki pub
'Bloody hell I must be pissed!'
splintering wood and scrunching metal
echo on the wind.

Down the road to Te Uranga
Paopaoku, Taumatapuihi
once the pā of shouting whānau
echo on the wind.

Lima homestead round a corner
where our Aunt once ruled her family
Uncle Tom her careful husband
descendant of the Portuguese,
fed his sheep on worn-out grass
straight across the Waiapu
on the slopes of Pohautea,
fattening on sheer wind.

Past Auntie Huinga's, Te Uranga
Te marae o te whānau
Hinepare, tuwhera mai
ki tō iwi marara nei!
Soul place of the gathering kin
for funerals, weddings, celebrations,
waiata, whaikōrero
echo on the wind.

Across the road from the marae
Tapere-nui-a-Whātonga
where all of us kids went to school
echo on the wind . . .

Once upon a time my granpa
dumped me wriggling over the fence
too whakamā to go to school
with raggy pants and scabby bum
and all those kids yelling at me
Ya-ya-ya got a scabby bum
holes in your bloomers ya-ya-ya
Ka mau te wehi!

Teachers seeming all too clever
ruling with rod and ridicule
at my relations' morning talks
about shooting pigeons every Sunday

shamed into a mouth-dry silence
when a voice booms out, Don't you know
stupid child it's against the law!
Ka mau te wehi!

Untold dodging morning school
so they would not have to read
coming in too late for lessons
mumbling the worn-out dumb excuse
My father said go up the bush
Sir I was looking, looking for . . .
'A lost elephant I've no doubt!'
Ka mau te wehi!

You can't fool me I've heard them all
this village is a crying disgrace!
He filled his chest with heated air
'No wonder you're unteachable!
There's weeding kūmara, shearing sheep
chasing pigs or bobby calves for
God knows what since everyone's poor!'
Ka mau te wehi!

Water melons apples ripening
expert thieves in pine trees scheming
Turanga and his famous notice
pasted on the shop-front window
'Persons caught in my pea-orchard
will be persecuted by me.'
Children yelling, 'Piss-poor spelling!'
farting on the wind.

No matter what one's sex or age
as long as one could walk upright
everyone learned to milk a cow
before one learned to read or write

warming feet on winter mornings
on green hot shet from cows' backsides
knee-deep mud and raupā feet
seldom bought gumboots

Mostly in the cowsheds yelling
others in the pine trees singing
Miritene Miritene
he like a Hēni Pūtia
his horsee, poro te waero
pukutere skinny behind
fathers elsewhere occupied
Ka mau te wehi!

Home-made bread in the *Gisborne Herald*
pork-fat mixed with golden syrup
kānga waru pudding with clotted cream
grandma saying, Ka mau te wehi!
You don't appreciate how hard we work,
I can't understand this moumou kai

And my mother saying, Don't waste a thing
just eat up and shut up, had enough!

What's important to me now
is changing seasons different songs
winter and my raupā feet
autumn corn and pūhā rich
spring and green and hope renewed.

From Hikurangi the Waiapu
binds many whānau to the sea,
on the other side her sister stream
the Waikaka renews my song
above her Ō-Hine-Waiapu
another soul place binding bones

Hawaiki-nui-ki-Aotearoa
Rangitukia-Te Uranga.

We are inheritors
of interwoven dreams
whose pāua-shimmering music ever
echoes on the wind.

(1986)

MARINO BLANK

Marino Blank is a descendant of Ngāti Porou and Ngāti Kahungunu. Her mother Arapera was Māori, her father Swiss German. She was born in Taumarunui, spending her early childhood in Panguru in the Hokianga harbour. 'My mother was a poet, my father a photographer. I was bought up in a tradition that valued prose and creativity.' She currently works for Auckland Council in the parks department, and is completing a landscape architecture qualification at Unitec, a quest begun twenty years ago.

Childhood

I remember the ache of
kūmara by full moon.

I remember ghoulish
stories in the dark
and fear like a haunting
and a thrill
kept me listening
listening to tones
and then in the
dead of night
my light still on
I dreamt of sweeter
things.

I remember stories
of pounamu
and knowing its cool
and eerie touch.

Standing alone
we are entwined
like the roots of
the kūmara vine
strong and confused.

(2005)

Minstrel

You are a song-bringer
a minstrel who exhorts the soul
to look skyward
I am given once again the desire
to fly and reach for those
unknown territories where the fearless wander.

You are a warrior
who instils in his people
the desire to battle.

I turn my head.

The sun rises
the sun sets
the sun rises.

How do I explain you?
A magic-bringer
a peace-maker
a lover of the afflicted!

You are
the lover who created
beauty
a thousand pieces of broken glass
mend to become
a lattice
a filigree
which others may once again adore.

(1992)

What to wear to a gynaecology examination

nothing

blue halter-neck top
green loose-fitting satin pants
enough to breathe
red sandals
easy to kick off

and a spare of underwear
wrapped up in a plastic bag

(2007)

PEARL DE VERE BOYED

Pearl de Vere Boyed was born in 1933 of Ngāpuhi, Ngāti Hine, Ngāti Te Ata and Ngāti Kahungunu iwi. In 1988 she published a collection of poems entitled *Piki Mai, Kake Mai* (Moana Press). In her work she attempts to reconcile Māori and Pākehā ways while still expressing a sense of Māori identity.

The changed land

Four years old
was a really good time to know the world –
riding high on my father's shoulders,
seeing it all through his blue eyes
and memories of long distanced Choptank
flowing into the Chesapeake.
A good time to walk those three miles
to the family gardens at Mangaiti –
talking to the bearded old men who lived
suctioned to the mangrove trees
rocking securely to the songs of the harbour's breath –
green silver grey wisps, counting the tides
in and out, up over the mudflats
and into the seclusions of the creek beds,
washing around salty roadside swamps,
lipping the rushes and scampering crabs;
whispering soft kisses to the pōhutukawas
that bent in greeting and echoing the kiss
away up the valleys and across hills
where the song was nothing but safety –
unconditional in its constancy.
A good time for mind following the wild geese
winging with purpose to the open sea –
flashing white flyers calling their secrets,
honking the change of season to the patient
long-legged kōtuku guarding the exposed channel
where he caught his midday meals.

It was a good time to know the old lady
with the moko, sitting on her apple box,
a thousand and one stories in her eyes, brown,
clear, secretive and always travelling,
accepting things gone and remembered,
telling it all to a small child who sat
cross-legged at her feet, sharing the privacy
of a long life and bones long since laid to rest.

Four years old was a good time to know only one world.

The war years were not good times to know the world –
divided into Us and Them, Him or Me –
weighed down with patriotic urgency,
standing before the flag, praying
for the destruction of the enemy
each school morning, torn between love and hate –
the only escape withdrawal into a dream world;
all walking with death, buried and living
or just rotting where they lay; war frenzy,
clutching the land and children, hills, harbour,
mind and eye – sleeping and waking, taking its toll –
tolling the bell nightly at nine, all the way from London.
I am Big Ben, I tell the time!
Not a good time to know a crucified world.

After the war, the men came home disenchanted
with their patriotism and asking why; the half-men,
dismembered and bitter, were pitied and feted,
and the whole-men got farms and prospered
while the poor people bought red poppies
one day a year and remembered suitable thanks –
waiting for things to come right . . . for growth
and progress; but when it came, it came seeping in behind
closed doors where the jackals had come to Caucus
in their council chambers, on boards and committees,

sitting in council seats, growing in filial fatness,
decreeing in their prosperity
Who would be Done
and Who wouldn't, Who should lose, Who gain . . .

Not a good time to know the world.

(1988)

Moonrise in January

She was
a long time approaching
but when she came
she came very quickly
spilling
her whole body
over the hill
in a rush:
a giant yolk
of moons within each other
centred with
the embryo
of yet another month
of tides
coming and going . . .
her path across the bay
drew the shapes
of sleeping tents
tied down against a stiff breeze

and in the
blinking of an eye
she had shot away
to hang suspended
four inches

above the hill's horizon
gazing
at the beauty of her work
across the peninsula . . .

and three white geese
talked quietly in their sleep.

(1988)

Freedom of choice

He left home that morning
as usual and caught the bus,
not exactly shining faced
but no unwilling snail either;
pretty bright kid, reading at three,
school at four but only because
it was a country school and
his father the Head. I said as he left:
'Good luck with the paper today!'

U.E. Prelim maths –
knew he could handle it, no problem,
bright kid. Had to fight like hell
to take Māori language – had to
do it by correspondence –
work on his own in the library,
as long as the seventh formers
weren't needing all the cubicles.
Started learning myself then,
to keep one step ahead of him.
He made School C in it,
but shed some lonely tears along the way.
You don't know what it's like

working on your own,
he once slapped at me.

That U.E. maths day stands
pretty clear in my mind
Friday, and the sun shone insanely
for that time of year.
I spent those three hours concentrating
on keeping him spiritually
encouraged, reassured; and sighed
with relief when time was up.

Come ten to four he drifted in
from the bus eating an apple.
'Good paper?' I asked.
'Didn't sit it,' he said. 'I sat on the steps
in the sun. I was not mentally prepared!
And I've had my last day at school.'
It was his sixteenth birthday.

(1988)

Still clearing the land

Who do you think you are anyway, eh?
You, who still wants to take all the Māori has;
you, who wants the whaikōrero, the aroha, the mana:
what for, eh?
Haven't you taken enough yet?
Don't you know yourself yet?
You White! You cheat!
Where's your Māori wife now, eh?
You sleep with all those Pākehā women –
where's your Māori wife?
Not good enough now, eh?

Too fat after thirty years?
Too old?
She nothing left for you to take –
that it?
You got too much greed for one lifetime, eh!
Still clearing the land, eh!
You White.
I tell you what, White Man!
You clear the land on top; you bury us;
but soon, your rape destroy the skin of Papatūānuku –
and underneath, her belly full of Māori, eh!
What then, White Man?

(1993)

BUB BRIDGER

Bub Bridger (1924–2009) was a poet and short story writer, who often performed her own work and drew inspiration from her Māori, Irish and English ancestry. Her writing was widely anthologised and she published several book-length collections of poetry, including *Up Here on the Hill* (Mallinson Rendel, 1989) and *Wild Daisies: The Best of Bub Bridger* (Mallinson Rendel, 2005). Her writing is known for its comic energy and its idiosyncratic fantasies. She was a well-known performer who acted on stage, and she also wrote for television and broadcast radio.

Summer's coming

I've been hibernating since June
curled up
sluggish with cold
stiff in all my bones
with self-pity
wrapped round like a blanket
but now it's November
and the sun
licks the land warm again

So I've had my hair cut
and put on my red dress
my pseudo-silver earrings
bounce big as bangles
as I walk

Tomorrow
I'll go to town on my bike
to pay the gas bill
and all around the bays
with the promise
of things to come
the sea will be dancing
and the hills
spilling with daisies

(1995)

At the conference

Sydney University, August 1988

In the midst
of all the academic discourse
in language fearfully
intelligent and intimidating
there's a lady
knitting
sitting there listening
smiling
while her hands fly
in cobweb-fine cotton thread
she is knitting a cloth
for her dinner table
I take the risk

and disturb her concentration
'Excuse me,' I whisper
'how many stitches?'
Without
taking her eyes off
the presenter of a paper
that has me totally confused
she murmurs
'Two thousand.'

She has made my day!

In a lecture room
stacked
with literati from all over
the world
and not missing a word
she is knitting
two thousand stitches
into a dinner cloth

(*1988*; 1995)

Enigma

I can't understand
people
who don't like dogs
make prisoners
of birds in
cages
keep the curtains
drawn
against the sun
and stay bleak

in marriages
where only anger
relieves
the boredom and only
bitterness
feeds the soul

(1995)

Johnny come dancing

to Long John Montgomery

1

On Douglas* Bridge
on Douglas Bridge
they were dancing! Dancing!
And he seventeen swinging home
through the twilight
a day's work done
and not a care in his head
stopping in wonder
What dancing! Dancing!
Their black curls bouncing
and their red shoes flashing
five little girls – dancing! Dancing!
With their dark eyes gleaming
and their green dresses shining
saying – Dance Johnny! Dance!
and we'll give you a shilling!
And he danced and he danced

---

* pronounced 'Dooglies'

and he danced till the dawning
then they were gone
with the grey of the morning
and Johnny limped home
clutching a shilling
and his mother cried out
and covered her head
Oh! Johnny my darling
you were not in your bed
and the fairies were out
on Douglas Bridge
Did you dance with them Johnny?
Did they give you a penny?
When he showed her the shilling
she kissed him goodbye
then she wrapped him a loaf
and a coat for the weather
and that was the last
they were ever together.

2

He wept and he cursed
and he called to his mother
but the five little girls
dragged him down to the river
then he begged and he pleaded
that they take back their shilling
but they shook their dark heads
– It's no good your crying
you danced for our shilling
now you'll dance till you're dying
you'll dance down the road
and you'll dance to the sea
and you'll dance till you reach

the last country
but it won't all be sorrow
though you'll always be lonely
and you'll weep when you hear
the wild north wind calling
then they jumped in the river
and when he looked over
there was only a swirl
and the sound of their laughter.

3

So he walked to Lough Foyle
and he met a sea captain
one man short
to sail for New Zealand
Where's that? asked Johnny
Is it far far away?
It's further than that
and we sail in the morning
I'll come then said Johnny
there's nothing to stop me
if I turn back now
the wee folk will get me
and I'll drown in the river
below Douglas Bridge
and I'll always be cold
and I'll never be resting
for the five little girls
will be dancing and leaping
and my dear dear mother
by the bridge there weeping.

4

So he sailed for New Zealand
on the outgoing tide
and it wasn't all pain
and it wasn't all grieving
just so long
as he kept on dancing
and the new land was almost
as green as Ireland
and he married a girl
with her black hair waving
and she led him a dance
and she sneered at his pining
for a two-roomed cottage
with a rammed earth floor
and nothing to keep
the wolf from the door
and she scoffed at his stories
of little girls dancing
with their black curls bouncing
and their red shoes flashing
but she stopped when she saw
his quick feet flying
for where had she ever
seen such dancing! Dancing!
with his long legs weaving
and his blue eyes sparkling.

5

So he danced through the years
through the love and the hating
through the birth of his children
and her final betrayal

and he danced to his death
one mild spring evening
and he called out her name
as he fell to the floor
and the five little girls
came through the door
and as he lay dying
he saw so clearly
they all had her face
and her black hair waving
with their dark eyes gleaming
and their green dresses shining
and the very last thing
that he ever saw
was her dancing . . . dancing . . .
. . . dancing.

(1995)

Ode to jokers

I find falling in love so easy
'cos there's thousands of beautiful guys
the world is alive with the darlings
of every colour and size
they're there in the streets to be ogled
on foot and riding in cars
on buses and trains and on aeroplanes
in shops. At the pictures. In bars.
And oh! at the beaches in summer!
All youth and shoulders and thighs . . .
I go down there and I sit and I stare
with big dark shades on my eyes
and no one would ever believe it
as my eyes dart about with sly stealth

they think I'm a lovely old lady –
that I'm there for the good of my health –
but I'm not . . . It's the jokers I covet
all that flesh on those beautiful bones
and the smiles and the teeth and the torsos!
And all those erogenous zones!

Right now I'm ready for action
I'm dying to fall one more time
in over my head and right into bed
with a toy boy just into his prime!
So come on you gorgeous young fullas
I'd like you to show me the way
with a boy about forty I could be quite naughty
so take me! And lead me astray . . .

I cannot of course swear to love you
to be faithful for e'er and a day
but I really am kind and will keep you in mind
if you prove that you know how to . . . play . . .
So just leave your telephone numbers
in a box you'll find as you go
and I'll give you all rings you lovely young things
and invite you all up for . . . you know . . .

(1995)

Wild daisies

If you love me
bring me flowers
wild daisies
clutched in your fist
like a torch
no orchids or roses

or carnations
no florist's bow
just daisies
steal them
risk your life for them
up the sharp hills
in the teeth of the wind
if you love me
bring me daisies
wild daisies
that I will cram
in a bright vase
and marvel at

(1995)

BEN BROWN

Ben Brown (Ngāti Paoa, Ngāti Mahuta) was born in Motueka in the South Island of New Zealand in 1962. He is a writer, poet and performer. Since 1992 he has published numerous children's books, short stories for children and adults, poetry and non-fiction. In 2006 he won Best Picture Book with the artist/illustrator Helen Taylor in the New Zealand Post Book Awards for Children and Young Adults. *Between the Kindling and the Blaze: Reflections on the Concept of Mana*, a collection containing poetry and short prose pieces, was published in 2013 by Anahera Press. Ben tours and performs regularly around the country. He lives and works in Lyttelton.

I am the Māori Jesus

A response to Baxter

i *AM* the Māori Jesus
And i don't like
mussels and parāoa
Give me fish 'n' chips
with tomato sauce

Fresh white bread
and loads of butter
Butter makes
this country great
So feed my whenua
to the cows
for all i care

My father Hōhepa
worked at Wattie's
where they made the sauce
at least until redundancy
Now mother Mere
works behind the bar
at the Metropol Hotel
and does some cleaning
in the mornings

And you
will know me
by my Kēnana hair and
my wrap-around sunnies
whose eyes
you cannot see
But trust me
they have seen
my other Father's light
and not
been blinded

So i can say
that i have met
the Devil personally
and been tempted
by his retinue
of sweet-mouthed whores

and silver salesmen
dripping promises
of Mammon
and extravagance

Yet underneath his
snakeskin smile
he wears a bland suit
of a nondescript shade
that fits him quite well
and he spends his days
conducting secretaries
who write infringement notices
demanding restitution

And i have been up to the temple
where i met the moneychangers
who offered me
a competitive rate of interest
and a little pink plastic pig
to put my shrapnel in
and fee rebates and a free holiday
in the Republic of Fiji to go with my
Visa card and my mortgage

But my other Father's house
has many mansions
and i don't pay no rent
so i don't need no mortgage
and anyway the bankers
turned out to be wankers
who didn't know their numbers
But all that imaginary money
went into somebody's pocket
Sure as Arabs own oil
and your arse points downhill

and Mom & Dad America
got foreclosure sales
and dead kids in the desert but
STILL THEY BELIEVE

Meanwhile there's a whale
needs saving
up near Kaikōura
but the bros got there
before DOC did
and they ate the bugger
back at the marae
like so many loaves and fishes
They made taonga whakairo
carved treasures
from his teeth and bones
So honouring the beast
and showing its
true worth

i shot up in a filthy flat
with a skinhead panel beater junky
who had his own name
tattooed on his dick
that you could only read
when he was hard
The implication being he was hard
when the needle bit the flesh
and spelled BARABBAS
i sold him
the last taste of his life
and saved his junky soul
in doing so

i lay down with
a wahine named Mary

Ah sweet Mary
So many Marys
and not enough time
to lie down with them all
And don't get Freudian on me now
though she does bear
some small resemblance
to my mother
given grace
And bless her anyway
Her willingness to suffer all
the rage of Men
Yet freely shed her tears
with love
upon my tired
feet

i walked the roads
i raised a deadman from
the street beneath a tree
where pigeons routinely
shat upon him
dead or alive
i shared his bottle afterwards
drank a cheap toast to his life
before he told me to
piss off
But before you go boy
give me back my bottle

It don't matter eh
Coz i got my brothers around me
My apostles twelve in all
or maybe thirteen i dunno
Been a while since i counted
but we're a righteous crew

Staunch as
Patched up
Yo-fuckin-yo-bro

i got Jake the muss
and Tū the freezing worker
and Billy T James
in a black shearer's singlet
i got Hone Tuwhare now
there's a man who likes his mussels
i got a Rastaman from up the coast
i got several of his brothers, hell
i got the horses they rode in on
i got a slick-suited lawyer
from the city
and i even got you Hēmi
Every crowd needs a doubter

So you won't catch me
walking on Wellington Harbour mate
Too bloody cold and windy eh
and too many bureaucrats pushing
compliance with occupational
safety and health regulations

Na not me man
i'm off up north with the bros
to the Hokianga
Choice dak eh
and a nice place
forever to leave from

Warmer too bro

(2010)

Chur bro

Hey Hone
Where'd y'get those lips
From up north somewhere eh
They lover's lips man
I hear you had the touch too eh bro

Mind you
All you wahanui fullas
Talk it up
Got the gift eh

Anyway
What brings you down
This way bro
Muttonbirds and oysters
Maybe
Cooler women
Greyer seas
Both more enigmatic

I like your hat too bro
ka pai te pōtae
Styley man
A hat says
A lot
About the head that
Wears it

Statue bro
Stink joke eh
But a mighty poem
Yeah that's you alright
Standing in the
Valley freezing your

Balls off
Brass monkey
Bronze brother
Unmoved by all that birdshit
Critics and seagulls eh bro

That's a neat trick too man
Turning the Pākehā's
English into a
Reo all your own

Chur bro

(2013)

Moko

Take a look at my face
Got the right shape
for the moko
Got the haughty jut
to the jaw
Got an appropriate nose
for the koru bro

I got borstal stars
and a crooked cross
But I never been inside eh
They just bullshit schoolboy tats
Idiot stickers cost me nothing
but a inky needle and
some discomfort

Yeah but I wear my moko
on the inside bro

Old school chiselling
in pigment and blood
Cut with an albatross bone

This line is my father's line
This line is my mother's
Here is a mountain
A river
A suburb
Here is the chanting karakia
of a young man bleeding
beneath the blade
Tat-tat-tat-tat
Tat-tat-tat-tat

Here is a road in the footsteps of a warrior
Here is a path in the broken feet of a slave

(2010)

TANIA HINEHOU BUTCHER

Tania Hinehou Butcher, of Te Arawa, Ngāti Raukawa and Tainui descent, writes fiction and poetry. She studied at the University of Auckland and Auckland University of Technology, then completed her Masters thesis at Massey University on New Zealand's approach to terrorism. She is now a secondary school teacher of English, history, religious studies and social studies. Her collection *Smudged Red on Cheek* was published by Totem Press in 2003.

Māori Bay

On occasions, you can see the real
face of Taiepa,
the profile reveals a hawk mind
overbearing and uncompromising.

When the Bedouin sea,
stone-flicking and juvenile,
submits unwittingly, I will
wet my fingers and press the seed
into soft ground.

Once did I see the child
form above his head,
taking shape before my eyes
in the womb of sky,

she heaved, she blistered.
Then thrust him into the open,
and she slid, slid back
into mist.

(1996)

In memory of: Hone Tuwhare

They have taken you from the swamp, in words
that slide to page your grand-parented chiselled walls.

The cold kleptomaniacs
with envious eyes of plums, pelican-bagged, done.

Raging river-stones hiss and sigh
as I step between them.

I have lined your verse in crisp cotton.
Down to sea level there is something between us.

You are here, the silent giant clothed in your best.
I see your black trailing cloak, it's humming a mournful tune.

At the head, old dears deliver their stately welcome and retire.
The punctuated sea is tailored for the scene.

The potato bulbed, plausible winter flowers are yellow with love
while madam death is waiting in the wings.

(2008)

Seaweed chaplet

She removed
the weed chaplet and flung
hair over the side like rope.

The monster surfaced and
with hooks for arms
fought and stunned her.

Saving herself
she clawed the hair,
that indigo navel string
rubbing on the bow.
Each held an end in this tug-of-war.

Close to a no-win situation,
in an effort to distract
the marbly eyes, she spun a yarn
of bloodlines.

She took the slack and leaning over
flicked hair
as a whip
and threw the chaplet
of seaweed its way.

(2003)

Muriwai

On this hungry coastline
bearded by monkey apple trees
I sleep naked with the door ajar,
a book in my hand and open.

I answer the phone with eyes shut.
What are you doing?
I don't answer
but should have.

The world tugs me
and I stretch to a transparent veil.
I dream on wet sand like a tight black sheet.

Tangaroa holds me as he would a cello.
My breath covers him like a shroud.
I want to stop the sun – while
I die in his arms
on the crest of the Taiepa.

(2003)

JACQ CARTER

Jacqueline Carter is of Ngāti Awa, Ngāi Te Rangi, English and Irish descent. Her poems have been published in a number of anthologies, including *Ora Nui Special Edition: A Collection of Māori and Aboriginal Literature* (2013), *Ora Nui: Māori Literary Journal* (2012), *Mauri Ola* (2010) and *Whetu Moana* (2003). One of her poems, 'Matariki Turns', provided the lyrics for a choral composition, commissioned by the Hamilton Civic Choir and composed by Janet Jennings in 2011. She is a mother of two and lives in Auckland, where she works at Sacred Heart College.

If I am the river and the river is me

Composed for 'The River Talks', a call to action to support the rejuvenation of the Ōmaru River in Glen Innes, Auckland.

If I am the river and the river is me
then for years I haven't flown so easily
in fact I sit and am sedimentary
and the paru has stolen all my clarity

If I am the river and the river is me
then few of us actually know my history
Ōmaru could mean absolutely anything
making me just a dirty stream

If I am the river and the river is me
most of my people have forgotten me
and they and those who live nearby
throw rubbish into my blinded eyes

If I am the river and the river is me
my purpose has been taken from me
it is not safe to drink from me
nor fish or wash or swim in me

If I am the river and the river is me
what future do I see for me?
Pollutants and chemicals still spilling into me
or somehow yet the cleansing of me?

If I am the river and the river is me
I hope that today you do more than remember me
and our words and dances and our songs
will see action right these many wrongs

If I am the river and the river is me
I pray my health will be restored to me
so I can again be a source of life
to all of those who seek my side . . .

(2013)

Our tūpuna remain

Nothing like a lone-standing nīkau
in the middle of some paddock
owned by some Pākehā
to make you feel mamae

Surrounded by maunga
who serve to remind you
that once that whole paddock
had that same sense of tapu

It's a bit like that urupā
in the middle of that reserve
that used to be a papakāinga
till some Pākehā had it burned

So consider yourselves warned:

it'll take more

than
a change of name

a chopping down of trees
a burning down of whare

to make us forget

our tūpuna remain.

(1998)

E noho rā

Let my body
bear the traces
of your passage
over me

like the land
of our ancestors
bears the tracks
of their feet.

Let my face
bear the lines
of our passage
through time

the layers
of our knowing
etched like thin
blue lines.

Let my heart
bear the rhythm
of the passage
of my blood

as it swells
with the call
a karanga
to my love...

E noho rā, Tongariro
E noho rā, Te Taupō-nui-a-Tia
E noho rā, Tūwharetoa

Me tū tahi ahau
hai mānuka

Me tū tahi ahau
hai mānuka.

To the statue of Wairaka at the mouth of Ōhinemataroa

Girl
they made you a bit skinny didn't they?

I mean

If I didn't know it was a statue of you
I might've thought you were a lamp-post or beacon
for people who can't navigate in the dark or something...

And I bet if I were to get right up close to you
I'd find they've sculpted you
the way those first ones would've painted you
which is more like a Roman than a tupuna Māori!

But do you hear the people at the marae named after you
and across the whole country
referring to you?

And not that bad to have a place named after you!

And of course the people often quote you . . .
(and you were centuries before any feminism e kui!)

But then some of us say
it wasn't you
that it was Muriwai
your Aunty
who was older than you

but kai te pai
we all have our truths
if not whole,
nothing but
or absolute.

(1999)

Comparatively speaking, there is no struggle

When people like you tell me

things aren't as bad here
as they are elsewhere

I wish you had been there

in the Waikato
or amongst my own people

the century before last
and every day after that

standing on land
that is no longer yours
fishing from waters
that no longer run pure

or at every hui
on every marae
that activates the words
mana Māori motuhake

which is every
marae in the country.

You seem to think things
are better off here
because you don't see us dying
or visibly fighting

as if it all happened
in yesteryears.

I tend to think

that one of the worst effects of
colonisation

is when people no longer fight
because they don't see a need
and think that

comparatively speaking
everything's all right.

So how many Māori
have you convinced today
that really us 'Mahrees'
should consider ourselves lucky
that things could have been worse
as they are with the 'Abos'?

(*1997*; 2003)

Me aro koe ki te hā o Hineahuone!

If Hinetītama
can become Hine-nui-te-pō

crushing

the next man who tried to interfere with her
between her thighs

then I too can deal to any man
that would enter me without my permission.

If our tūpuna wāhine
can have the courage and the vision

to leave their homelands
in search of new homes

then I too can leave any place
that does not nourish and support me.

If that great ancestress Wairaka
can summon the strength of any man

and drag that great ancestral waka
from the sea with her own bare hands

then I shall not allow myself
let alone anyone else
to think of me as less
than his or her equal.

This is what we mean
when we speak of mana wāhine

it is the strength that is within us
by virtue of our descent from Hineahuone

which is why
when you meet a woman
you really ought to hongi

to pay heed
to the strength
that is women.

(1998)

SAMUEL CRUICKSHANK

Samuel Cruickshank is 'a Māori-Scots kid who was conceived in Christchurch, gestated in Tonga and eventually surfaced in Labasa, Fiji'. He later spent time in Hollywood, California.

Pākiri: midnight sea

Where the orange moon
is silently strong

rising like a fiery tonsil
from throat of sea.

Here, in this place
    of beauty,
where the midnight
    landscape
holds her breath,
and gasps with want of
    words.

Here, in this place, I rest
and sit on cedar-decked stage
hugging my knees
which hold my throat.

As my breath leaves my
chest, and rises with the
lungs of the moon.

(2003)

HARRY DANSEY

Harry Delamere Barter Dansey (1920–79), Te Arawa, Ngāti Tūwharetoa, was born in Auckland and educated in Rotorua. He served in the Middle East and Italy in World War II, entering journalism on his return. He became a specialist writer on Māori affairs and in 1974 was awarded the MBE for his services to journalism. He was also a cartoonist, playwright, broadcaster and two-term Auckland city councillor. In 1975 he was appointed Race Relations Conciliator, a position he held until shortly before his death in 1979. His published works include *How the Maoris came to Aotearoa* (Reed, 1947), *Cartoons by Dansey* (1958), *The New Zealand Maori in Colour* (Reed, 1963), *Maori Custom Today* (New Zealand Newspapers, 1971), and the play *Te Raukura* (Longman Paul, 1974).

The old place

This is the place where the old people
lived. They caught the birds, stored
them in their own rich fat, grubbed
fern root, loved, mated, buried
their dead in the rocks and crannies
and on the high cold hill.

Here came Uenuku, broke the tapu
of the chief's spring, left his

deed in a proverb. Here the
old man hauled a tōtara, with
his own hands hewed a ridge-pole
fifty feet from the sound red heart.

There by the alien pines his house
stood, silver-grey in its dotage,
and his church there where the
six-foot fern sways brown and dusty;
all vanished in the scrub fires
in the years when no one cared.

So I park the landrover, climb
the slope, push aside the broom,
hope for a sign from the past
from the old dead people,
but there is no more comfort here
in the fierce bright silence
than the rasping tūī finds in
black bark and the hard pine needles.

(1964)

SHELLY DAVIES

Shelly Davies (Ngāti Wai, Ngāti Porou) thinks poetry is the best kind of medicine and consequently self-medicates on a regular basis. She has published short stories and poetry for over twenty years and even sometimes admits to the occasional academic paper. She has edited volumes of *Waiataata* and *Toroa-te-Nukuroa* through Te Wānanga o Aotearoa. She is currently terrorising the corporate world with technical and business writing training through her company, Waiora Design Ltd, and having a ball doing it.

four haiku for chris

had I known
I would have held you
more tightly

the water took you
green-fisted el niño waves
pulling you under

we buried you
overlooking the sea
beautiful man

our son has your smile
your pain and your anger too
I hold him tightly

(14 February 2011)

HENARE DEWES

Henare Dewes (1943–85), Ngāti Porou, was born at Waipiro Bay on the East Coast. He was published in a number of publications, including *Rongo*, *Te Maori*, *Te Ao Hou* and the *NZ Women's Weekly*. His poetry addresses concerns about Māori identity in a time of urban migration.

Tihei mauriora!

Strange thing happened today
applied for a flat in Remuera
got knocked back
cause I'm a Māori,
funny that!
Hell! I can't even speak the lingo
don't even know my māoritanga
whatever that is.
Once I spoke Māori
but the teacher strapped me
and made me learn Pākehā so hard
and respect Pākehā so hard
and be like a Pākehā so hard,
I'm real good at it now
got papers to prove it too
yet I still couldn't get this flat
cause I'm a Māori
funny that!
I should've bowled that landlord
but I'd have gone Pāremoremo
bugger that!
that's where lots've Māoris go.
Funny that!
I'd go back to my marae
if I knew where it was
and prove, I'm not
an Uncle Tom.
Auē!

I wish those Pākehās
would make their minds up
about who I belong to
that's the worst of being half 'n' half,
the Pākehā half is always
getting the Māori half in trouble
funny that!
In my next reincarnation
I'm coming back
as a full blooded Māori,
that'll scare the tūtae
out of all those
Pākehā statisticians.
I'm going to Ponsonby tomorrow
gonna get another flat,
this time,
I'm gonna be a Samoan
Tihei mauriora!
whatever that means.

(c. 1982)

Te ao hou

My people cry out
but the baskets of food are empty
and the promises that filled them,
nurture the thistles
of abandoned courtyards.
Behind glass panes
the tekoteko stares helplessly
while the manaia
bows his head in shame,
and the shopkeeper keeps on smiling.

I see confusion
in eyes that avoid mine
and sense anger
in the clenched fists upon their backs.

E tū rā!
Hold tight your māoritanga
lest your calabash overflow
with the greed of today,
and the death of yesterday
is a meaningless wave of tomorrow.

(1975)

KIM EGGLESTON

Kim Eggleston, born 1960 in Picton, is affiliated to Ngāi Tahu (Ngāti Huirapa) through her mother's people at Arowhenua. She published several books of poetry on the West Coast in the 1980s, and appeared in magazines and anthologies around that time. She has spent much of the past decade at sea, or living on land in hot places doing various jobs from public-sector librarian to teaching English in Hanoi. She currently lives in Darwin.

On the beach

Humming with visions of fever, dust trickling
through the thatch. You know chess? asks the Italian man
who came yesterday. He peels a plate of fruit. Buffalo doze
in the sun roped to boats on the sand.
I stir lemon juice into my tea

inured with heat, preserved in sheens of salt.
The sea glitters like nylon. Old people wade in the shallows
with baskets and wide straw hats. A two-stroke motor
spluttering. Ma brings him a bottle of Coke

tucks my hair up from my neck. Molto bene he says.
The girls are dusting talculm powder
from a large pink jar on the shelf
over their freshly washed skin.

I've been here for weeks I think. Living without mirrors
or walls, the papers he bought on the taxi-boat
already three days old.

Rarely strangers appear, like the flare of a match
in a lantern, to sit on the kitchen bench.
Call for a bowl of chilli and rice. Slice a mango
with a thin smooth-handled knife, then reach over suddenly
to push the white rook into check.

The girls shake out their hair.
The beach is empty now, a deserted flapping tide. The world
is a snare of light, flung into a careless sky.

(2008)

Before the rains

The loud cry of a tiny gecko
on the faded plaster wall, drifts
of mosquito coils. The back
veranda closed with sweat

Desultory conversation, the scrape
of plastic chairs, and from a cold
corner at the bottom of the continent,
your old hunting mate sprawled upon the floor

A man could perish in this heat, things could slide
from his control
like a deal gone wrong in the dining room
of a yum cha restaurant

A woman whose father was born in the desert
tossing coins in the dust on the side of the street.
He's beginning to blur at the edges
to slip from the grasp of his damp skin

only the thump of the ceiling fan
sounds like a chopper coming at dawn
with a strop. It makes him cling to the hope
that help is near at hand.

(2012)

AMBER ESAU

Amber Esau is a New Zealand-born Samoan/Māori/Irish poet studying under Robert Sullivan in the creative writing programme at Manukau Institute of Technology. She is from the village of Manase in Savai'i, Samoa, on her father's side and of Ngāpuhi and Kāi Tahu descent as well as Galway Irish descent on her mother's. She has been published in the journals *Ora Nui*, *Blackmail Press*, *ika*, *Hawaii Review* and *Landfall*.

Numiamatumua

for my great-grandmother

Life crushed with waves into new lands
flickering tongues of fragrant nights
our kids these days flower
                        into colonial hands

In each cold winter where
I remember palms so full
heat stuck on skin in beads
sweating pearls
black moon pearls
pāua   cannot decide
which hue it takes

Feet cushioned like coconuts
dropped   high up   onto sand
I remember the land
a guilty poison coursing the streets

tap tap white bone on brown flesh
tatau
carried from Fiji
I have no twin
to lighten the weight

Ignorance
I don't know the *fa'aniusila*
there's no teaching an aged bird
new chirps
I'll bite through a turtle shell
then unload
into the ocean
salt water and blood
diluting

dilating eyes
tiny suns
that catch
my smile
and lay it over yours

They said
Deaths reach
struggles
to this new place
Forever a body removed
                              there's better healthcare with us
but earth can bury
a heart

and I've seen
blood stretched to a rubberband

these kids flower
                into colonial hands

age has broken me down
yet I listen
to translate
the old songs
of our land.

(2012)

Crushes

You held out your
hands
spread fingers
to ready the catch
feet planted
as cool wind and cheers
hovered over you
one of the defenders
had caught up
and walled me

from a shot
but I saw Pita   pre game
                     his hand
                     in yours
& aitu grow
like black mould

(2012)

Pray to be wrong

I ran
into the
night
stars carved
out
of ancestors
glitter
and guide
I ran
through
the
pulse
of night
that thrums
down
empty streets
at night
I ran
wind licked
skin
eyes
slow to make out
the contours
of shadow

& ran
her fale
punctured
the dark
forest of
houses
lights danced
and curved

(2012)

Tongue

The lounge is flagged
by grey photographs
waving

dark eyes
and dark delights
afro-ed like
spun coconut rind

A mini faleoʻo hut like the ones
I saw back in the islands middle-fingers
from the wall unit.

You didn't tell me you
were Samoan
but I hardly listen

to friends
to family
to the ashed carcass
of an umu pit

and I could be
wrong
I assumed you were Tongan.

We've been dating
for a few weeks
you've been waiting
for a few weeks

tonight

we'll breathe
in the daisies plucked
petals and watch
the juice squirt
into wine

I'm hungry
I'm thirsty
I'm tired

you dress me in your eyes
and roll me around
as I make excuse/excuse

Dad never taught me
how to be Samoan

to take the tongue and
cut it open

to watch as bloodwater verbalised.

What's that photo of?
I point at one behind you.

You look at your phone
before the frame.

Your grandfather
was a part of the Mau you say
a picture of him
with his lavalava.

I ask what Mau means
and you tell me.

I thought it meant
broken.

Some things don't break
you promise.

(2012)

Horoi

    We enter like hands
    open out
      to cleanse
    before the gate
    water snaps
    its fingers
    along our side
    Mum tells us
    to wind up the windows
    as we mould ourselves
    into the lay of rocks
      crunching
    with
    crisp coercion

summer immersion
leaving behind
the city
& green is new
to me
cows grinding
into grass
mountains
the shrivelled kina roe
on the horizon
water
sizzles
as
we
submerge
dip out
of worries
that follow
the stream
swim out of my hair
dip in
to wai whenua
learn
the ways
blossom
my Samoan father
would say
going up to great
grandpa's old house
young
refreshed
water
but now
there's a bridge.

(2012)

RANGI FAITH

Rangi Faith (1949–) was born in Timaru, and is of Kāi Tahu and Ngāti Kahungunu descent through Teone Paina and Paranihia of Moeraki. He is a retired primary school teacher and is presently living and writing in Rangiora. His publications include *Unfinished Crossword* (Hazard, 1990), *Dangerous Landscapes*, an anthology of New Zealand poetry (Longman Paul, 1994), *Rivers Without Eels* (Huia, 2001) and *Conversation with a Moahunter* (Steele Roberts, 2005). A new book of poetry, *Spoonbill 101*, is due for release in 2014.

Spring star

My dog howls
at the sea booming
over the
windthrown pines;
he is not alone.
Pūkekos scream
in the spring
darkness;
it is the time
of the star
across the moon,
it is time
for the sighting
of new mountains.

(1982)

Official opening

When we were called to assemble
at the gates and the metal plaque
by the woman under the umbrella,
the rain was coming down in buckets,
& the man with the carved stick
made it plain and clear in his karakia
that the gods were extremely happy –

that the land was soaking it up;

years ago it was the only bush for miles
and that's always saddened me

they came up the Bridle Track and they saw it,
or you took out your notebook and you drew
a row of menacing mountains nothing like
the ones you knew at home
& God knows what was beyond – you didn't have a clue

there was an unbelievably wide and flat land in front
stretching forever north and south in the heat,
and there were thickets, copses in the distance
against the low hills – one here, one there –

they were few and far between even then
& wouldn't take much milling

well that was then –
today's few words
are for planting young trees in a well-kept earth
with three freshwater springs nearby –

plenty to keep up the goodwill

here the roots would go back down to the past –
a search for a time
when it was all tū kākāriki –
where the trees stood tall, & they stood green,
and they made you feel good

that's what I like about beginnings

(1993)

Losing our mana

Time was when a foot
would slip on one
under the river bank
as you stepped into
the black water,

now they say there
hasn't been an eel
caught
for the last three tangi

and the brothers
down the river
come out during the night
& cut the nets –

they have to do that,
there is no kai
in the river,
we are losing our mana.

(2005)

The stones stand

for each of us
there will be words
in the trees
and on the hillsides

& the stones stand

for each of us
a singing

of songs
and a falling of earth

& the stones stand

and at the gate,
water falling
from the air

& the stones stand

(2005)

The cage

Cave burial at Lake Hauroko, Southland

Draped & cared & sung for,
she is ferried by canoe, cheek, shoulder,
placed in the cave & cradled for guests –
her face to the wind & light of the lake:

her cave is sounded,
her island is graced –
cave, land, water entrusted
so that this land becomes
a watershed of peace –
will rain on lake & river,
and take the magic
through steel, bolt & bar
to the sea, unending.

(1998)

Catch & release, catch & release

> *Persist, v.i. Continue firmly or obstinately*
> *(in opinion, course, doing) . . .*

the blackback gull,
he hamuhamu māia, the bold scavenger,
is feeding again:

in the graceful, repetitive choreography
of catch & release, catch & release,
it will rise
from the hard sand
into the air,
carrying a shell
in an airborne vice
       to
       a certain height
       and then
       let go

the white light
spiralling down the air
to the beach
       where
       on satisfactory impact
       a designer beak
with probe, wedge & sidecutters,

scalpel & chopsticks
       will
       operate
to get the meat within.

With that done
the bird will fly down the beach.
Flying? Now that's something else.

(2001)

A measured tread

Kaiapoi Pā, June 2000

After one hundred & seventy years,
this is how the past can be:

no southerly or nor'west
to turn the flames from
a smoking canvas,

no cry
in the still air:

it is a careful stepping across,
where the stories have been
smoothed over;

or a measured tread
from post to post
along an ill-defined track

where the sketches
have yellowed

& become brittle with
remembrance;

a fading record –
image upon image –
of a story best left untold.

(2001)

Karakia to a silent island

How do I greet you, Motutapu?
How do I call across the darkness,
fish your still waters?

On what ears
do these words fall
& who is left to speak
for the tāngata whenua,
for the ghosts on the beach?

How do I greet you, Motutapu?
How do I feel your pain,
your battlewounds?
Where man has fed on man,
how do I celebrate whānau?

As my canoe glides
through your silence –
only this –
kia ora ki a koe,
kia ora, kia ora, kia ora.

(1985)

MIRIA GEORGE

Miria George (Ngāti Kearoa, Ngāti Tuara, Te Arawa; Te Tawera, Ngāti Awa; Ngāti Tinomana, Rarotonga, Cook Islands; Ngāti Rongo-mā-tāne, Atiu, Cook Islands) was born in Rotorua and schooled in Aotearoa New Zealand, the Cook Islands and Costa Rica. Miria is a poet, a writer for theatre, radio and television and an award-winning playwright. Miria's work has toured New Zealand, Australia, Hawai'i, Canada and the United Kingdom. Her stage plays include *And What Remains*, *Urban Hymns* and *Sunset Road*.

Still

I left Winter
where? I cannot remember

an immortal blue
suspended, endless

overhead.
Empty, beneath

my dim, pale face,
an audience for the sea.

(2002)

MAREWA GLOVER

Marewa Glover (Ngāpuhi) writes mainly scientific journal articles, as her academic career as director of the University of Auckland's Centre for Tobacco Control Research continues to eat up creative and writing energy. Poetry still escapes from quiet moments. Marewa has been a Huia short story competition finalist (1999, 2003) and has produced two collections of poetry, *Mooncall* (1990) and *Hui* (2000). She has had poems published in numerous collections both locally and overseas. In 2013 she co-edited *Ara Mai he Tetekura – Visioning our Futures*, a book on new and emerging pathways of Māori academic leadership.

Pounamu

no matter where
you bury me
no matter where
I fall
I will find my way
to water
I will find my way
home

(2001)

Ngāwhā

The kuia wait 'til the showers
      are all but done
and younger ones
      have gone to bed
They prepare the bath
      cooling it
with fresh cold water
The temperature
      slowly drops
though it would still
      burn the uninitiated

They turn the lights off
        and arrange the doors
allowing slivers of light
        to soften the dark
They shed their clothes
        quickly
politely not looking
        at each other's bodies
They sink in to the still
        near boiling water
glistening folds of skin
        bulky roundness
sits atop and below the surface
        just visible
They laugh, gossiping
        about recent births and tangi

(1997)

The shame of Tāneroa

Jack is a young Māori boy of seven.
He lives in the child cancer unit in Hamilton.
He's a happy child despite his condition
'cause his mother full of aroha
visits him often.

One day the social worker Wendy
overheard the mother talking with her son
She was saying, 'You'll be home soon Tāne,
we'll all be together again,
don't you worry Tān.'

Wendy thought, that was strange
the mother called him Tān

so she called her aside and asked
'What is his name?'

The mother replied
'Tāneroa is his name, Tāneroa.'
Wendy looked at the chart
at the foot of the bed and said
'But here it says his name is Jack.'
The mother shook her head
'No. What happened is that
when Tāne was admitted
they couldn't say his name
so they called him Jack.'

Wendy was furious
'This is outrageous' she said
'We'll just have to change it back.'

This happened in 1990
in New Zealand
the 150th year of the signing of
the Treaty of Waitangi
a year of celebrations.
This happened in a country
that prides itself
on its race relations.

(1991)

Waitangi II

veterans of the movement speak
repeating year after year the struggle
newly aware sit quietly expressing their support
by being there listening, agreeing
there is no protest inside the tent

smoke spirals up filling the blue and white marquee
the poison so strong some of us have to leave
stand outside on the edge of protest
the kaupapa is singular and almighty
TINO RANGATIRATANGA

rangatiratanga sovereignty
the right to determine our own fate
protect our own
decide for ourselves

is it also
the right to smoke ourselves to death
shroud our children's lives in illness
bury our heritage with the elders who die early?

(2001)

Te rerenga kēhua (white flight)

The grass is brown but tough
it's not so warm now
visitors to the beach are gone
void of Pacific tunes
Howick teens trying to drink illegally
smoke synthetic drugs
it's a local domain again

peaceful
fitting the exorbitant prices of the
homes breathing sea air
Pākehā hang on like the kikuyu grass
dried out
thin and sparse
mainly Mandarin conversations
sweeten the ear
native harakeke-like
we watch the ebb and flow
the colours changing
still
like the pipi we lurk
determined to survive

(*2013*)

Māori women's hui

Sleeping in the wharenui
encased within my bag
surrounded by women
I remember that other time . . .
encased within my bag
sleeping within my mother
surrounded by woman

caressed by the hum of voices
women's stories
women's snores
soft noises
woven into dreams . . .
dreams woven into the past
the past all encompassing
in the poupou

    the tukutuku
    the kōwhaiwhai

    sleeping in the wharenui
    in the belly of our ancestors
    feeling safe
    like that other time
    before birth

    (1991)

BRIAR GRACE-SMITH

Briar Grace-Smith is of Ngāpuhi descent and is an award-winning writer of plays, screenplays, short fiction and television scripts. Her first screenplay, *The Strength of Water*, premiered at Rotterdam and Berlin Film Festivals in February 2009. *Fresh Meat*, a comedy horror, was selected for the Tribeca Film Festival in 2013. The short film *Nine of Hearts* was Briar's debut as a director and premiered in 2012. Her plays include *Nga Pou Wahine*, *When Sun and Moon Collide* and *Purapurawhetū*. *Paniora!* premiered at the New Zealand International Festival of the Arts in 2014. She presently works as a development executive for the New Zealand Film Commission and lives in Paekākāriki.

How I got my name

    When I was born my mum said there was a pōwhiri for me.
    That's how I got my name. Pōwhiri.
    It started in that moment of labour when women wish they'd had an
        abortion
    or made him wear triple condoms with spermicide.
    She lay there trapped under a bright light, her sweat gluing her to a
        plastic
    sheet, silently swearing, 'Fuck you. Fuck you. Fuck you,' to the smooth-
    faced doctor and my good-for-nothing old man who'd only been there
        for the
    conception. Yeah, just when she thought she was gonna die she heard it.

> A karanga. Sweet and smooth. Calling me out of her swollen puku and into
>
> Te Ao Mārama. I swam out in a river of dark blood.
>
> Mum was so happy she said, 'Kia ora,' and the smooth-faced doctor thought
>
> she was meaning him and he smiled a tight smile and said, 'You'll need some
>
> sutures.' But she was talking to the woman she felt beside her.
>
> Hine Kōrako. A rainbow, pale and glowing, who called to me and helped my mother let go.
>
> I was called Pōwhiri after that happy event.

ROWLEY HABIB (RORE HAPIPI)

Rowley Habib (Rore Hapipi), of Tūwharetoa, was born in 1935 in Ōruanui, north of Taupō. Habib wrote and published his first stories while a student at Ardmore Teachers' Training College. He has worked at numerous jobs (mainly manual) throughout New Zealand, though he is now retired and living again in his home town. He has published poems, stories, articles and plays in many magazines and anthologies, dating back to the mid-1950s. Among other awards, he was the Katherine Mansfield Menton Fellow for 1984. His most recent books are *The Raw Men: Selected Poems 1954–2004* (O-a-Tia, 2006) and *Avenging Angel: Cuba Street Serenade* (O-a-Tia, 2012).

Mother and sons

The soliloquy of a dying mother

When I am gone, they will be glad, my sons,
all glad. Yet after I am dead
could they forget this dying skeleton upon the bed?
Fearfully clinging to life; hating to live
yet fearing death. Could they forget
and only remember the warmth of my breath
years ago? Or when the voice did harshly ring,
could they remember the love that forgave this thing?

Then some day, perhaps, beneath the crude walls
of some mill, somewhere within a young man's mind may echo,
'Auē! Kua mate taku Māmā. She's dead.'
Or if this other, my eldest, be loosened for a minute
from the worries of the other woman, his wife,
then perhaps within his mind may echo also,
'Auē! Kua mate taku Māmā. She's dead now.'
Or in the late evening of a dying day
on that last stretch of road home from the mill
perhaps even my youngest may think,
'Auē! Auē! Kua mate taku Māmā. She's dead. O she's dead now.'

(1955)

Tame Iti (behind the tattooed face)

I remember when we first met. That time at Hēmi's tangi.
'Tēnā koe' I said. 'Tēnā koe' you replied.
You drew your short, stocky frame up to its full height
when we embraced; bear-hugged in the way Hēmi had made popular.
(The pressing of noses wasn't in vogue then. Nor was
the full tattooing of the face.) Holding each other for a long time
in silent acknowledgement of the sad occasion. But also, I think,
in recognition of a kindred spirit and an unspoken sorrow
that went back deeper than the occasion.

And after, when we drew apart, holding the other at arm's-length
while we searched each other's eyes for some confirmation
of this, I found myself looking into the softest, warmest,
most sensitive eyes I have ever looked into.

I had, of course, heard of you, from when you were arrested
on Parliament Grounds, that time.
Much water has flowed under the bridge since, e hoa.
Our lives gone their separate ways. And, if mine, in the meantime,
has travelled the more conventional road to suburban sedateness,

yours has become the recognisable face of the feared activist,
with its ferocious adornments since acquired.

So it was with some apprehension that, on spotting each other
across the grounds at Eva's recently, we approached to greet;
to acknowledge recognition of each other. Wondering
what I would now see in the eyes half hidden behind the savage
mask. If the aroha I recalled would now be replaced
by an indifferent rage, even hatred!

'Tēnā koe e hoa' you said. (The voice, at least, was that,
that I recalled. The distinctive, husky, warm timbre.)
'Tēnā koe Tame' I replied, as we leaned in towards each other,
eyes closed, to offer our noses and foreheads in that intimate way
that kindred spirits acknowledge one another. (The pressing
of noses in the hongi being in vogue now.) Aware of the
emanations of that proximate famous tattooed face.

As it turned out, my fear was unfounded. For as we drew apart,
holding the other at arm's length, while we searched
each other's eyes for further confirmation of what we felt
all those years ago, I found myself again, looking in to
the softest, warmest, most sensitive eyes I have ever looked in to.

(Taupō, October 1997)

Ōrākau

Again the storming of the palisade.
Again the repulse.
Again the storming.
And yet again the repulse. Wave upon wave.
Throughout a day and a night and another day.

And now the numbers of the defenders lessen.
And now their ammunition runs pitifully low.

They weaken from lack of rest and food.
And sleep is a thing of the past.

Again the women and children in battle.
Again the use of sticks for bullets.
And still the invaders come.
Their numbers seem limitless.
For every man who falls two more move up to take his place.
They seem indestructible. The spirit of the defenders fails.

Yet through the ordeal, the sinking morale
these words uttered: 'E hoa!
Tēnei te kupu o te Māori.
Ka whawhai tonu mātou, ake, ake, ake.'
('Friend! This is the word of the Māori.
We will fight on for ever and ever and ever.')

(1963)

Composed on a summer's evening

Have you ever stood and listened to the bees working amongst the wild
    flowers
and wondered at the way their tone changed as they flitted from flower
    to flower
their drone high pitched then suddenly changing low,
caught in a pocket-vacuum of air. Or brought in on a sudden change of
    wind?

And have you listened to the thrush, working in the bushes
close to the ground. Finding its way through the thick undergrowth
noisily fussing, to where its young lay?
Or listened to the last rhapsody of the sparrows
as they gather in the trees to chat, noisy and restless, before the night
    falls?

And have you heard the blackbird's frightened cry
as it starts up from a hedge and wings away swiftly into the distance.
Or listened while a lone starling sings. Its song
clear and languid, spearing into the still night falling?

And have you heard the hush in the trees
brought by a sudden rise of wind. That just as suddenly dies?
Leaving you stilled inside and listening. And full of wonderment.
Trying to grasp something that eludes, just out of reach.
While somewhere a bird sings that, to you, is unknown.

And all the while the warm scents of evening lay heavy on the air
and the peace that comes with the falling darkness is deep-rooted within
    you.

(*Dunedin, 1961*)

Early morning meeting

For Keri Hulme

Not as I would have it, that first meeting of ours.
(That part of me left over from another time.
Romance! At my age!) I don't know quite what I'd
expected. A rapport, perhaps? Felt across a
distance of the platform? Us coming together?
A feeling, undeniable, but never said,
of you woman, me man? Consummated at some
later date in sex? Undeniable. But never said?
And me a married man!

    You know, we must have passed within feet. For
    I was waiting when your train arrived, stupidly
    hoping you'd recognise me. Even if I not you.
    I blush now at my ego.

Instead! a confrontation; hesitant,
. . . Can this be really her? In your look read,
. . . What the bloody-hells going on, anyway!
No magic here, even at that magic hour.
A gladness, yes, to finally meet. But nothing else.

Nothing to look at. Stocky in denims.
More man than woman. More Pākehā than Māori.
Frizzy hair cropped short. Devoid of makeup.
Face chapped from exposure to the weather.
. . . G'day! you said. (When we finally knew
who we were.) And wrung my hand.

> I do not know what impression you had
> of me. Formed in your mind during those couple
> of years in which we'd corresponded. And
> whether I disappointed?

You were quick to remove your sunglasses.
(I thought it was because they represented
the symbol of the famous. But your blood-shot eyes
told me why you wore them.) No attempt to preen
yourself. Tell-tale sign. By then I was right back
down to earth. No bullshit here. Typical

West Coast honesty. No mere stories then,
those letters of fishing excursions; days
out in the open, white-baiting.

Disappointed, at first, you were not soft female,
the void left by my shattered dream
began to fill with the reality of the person before me.
In the end, I wondered how I could have thought
you'd be anything other than what you are.

(*Eastbourne, Wellington, 1972*)

AROHA HARRIS

Aroha Harris belongs to Te Rarawa and Ngāpuhi iwi. She lectures in history at the University of Auckland, is a founding member of Te Pouhere Kōrero, the national collective of Māori historians, and a member of the Waitangi Tribunal. Aroha has published on a range of topics in twentieth-century Māori history, including her book *Hīkoi: Forty Years of Māori Protest* (Huia, 2004), and has worked with Te Rarawa on negotiation and settlement of historical Treaty of Waitangi claims, among several other iwi research and development projects.

Kina

You came to me from friends
wet with the Hokianga and
smiling.

Now
fattened slice of orange moon
slip from teaspoon to tongue
in holiest communion.

Nau mai and āmine oh sweet
sweet reminder of
the delicacy of life.

(2003)

JOHN HOVELL

John Hovell (1937–), Ngāpuhi, Ngāti Porou ki Hauraki, Ngāti Raukatauri ki Huarere, was born in Whitianga and grew up at Harataunga or Kennedy Bay in the Coromandel. He graduated with a BA from the University of Auckland where he studied English literature, classical languages, ancient history and anthropology. Best known as an artist, he has taken part in the activities of the Māori Artists and Writers Society, Ngā Puna Waihanga, and has established a particular reputation as a kōwhaiwhai artist. His poetic activity took place largely in the early 1960s, at a time when many of the feature writers of *Te Ao Hou* went to Kennedy Bay to camp and write.

Pāua tide

I remember I remember
at the Pāua tide,
how we went down from the road
to the flax bound beach.
The women sat on the high white rocks
sat and talked together;
and over their knees their dresses stretched
dark and smooth in the empty air,
sat on the sun warmed rocks
watching the men.

Once or twice in the year
only, does this reluctant tide
uncover in this way
her last, secret fringe,
watches the capture of her store,
the feeling, wrenching, and bearing away;
in this single hour, least hidden
and seldom exposed;
men grab at her
making the most of their time.

Reach out your artful fingers
that trouble the edge of the rock,
like the anemone's soft threads

feeling, feeling. Can you find
the curved shape, the hiding place
of the humping prey that clings and waits
blue in the shade of the boulder?
Wedge the sharp knife. Twist the point.
Lift to the light and the sun
the rivelling mouth.

The imperceptible afternoon slid
off our backs, as we
worked the rocks between us;
and behind us the sea weeds closed,
the anemone put out her stamens,
the starfish uncurled, and the water
stilled again in a perfect pool.
Then suddenly the sea breathed in.
The women, rising, shook out their dresses,
and the men came together up the beach.

I remember I remember
how folds of talk and laughter
flagged down to the squatting bay.
Look back now, over your shoulder;
sometimes we sense the sea's keenness
reckoning each item of depredation.
Only, in the smile of the women is the threat
forgotten. And the wind
and stone and water sing
an idle warning in the ears,
to homeward company.

(1966)

KERI HULME

Keri Hulme, Kāi Tahu, Kāti Māmoe, is also of Nordic and Celtic heritage. She was born in 1947 and is a West Coaster by choice and an East Coaster through her mother – Moeraki, Te Waipounamu, is her tūrangawaewae. Keri has been a teller and writer of stories all her life and is a published novelist, short story writer and poet. In 1983 her internationally acclaimed novel *the bone people* was published and won the 1984 New Zealand Book Award for fiction and the 1985 Booker Prize. Keri continues to write and publish and her work is inspired by her love of the sea, her coastal octagonal home at Ōkarito, which she built herself, her family and the many cultures from which she draws inspiration. She writes: 'I think of myself as a Maori writer rather than Pakeha that's the strong and the vivid and the embracing, the good side of things. That's where I draw my strength from.'

Pā mai tō reo aroha

Seaweed floats in a brown tangled rack, a tack out from the rocks.
It falls and rises, breathing with the water.

On the beach, the apricot and gold gravel turns rusty orange at wave-edge.
There is a long streak of irondark sand where Matuatiki runs out to the sea.
There are shattered black rocks round all the arc of bay.

The cliffs are made of claystone, greenish and ochre, with odd intrusions of pink melted rocks. The thornbushes along the tops slant away from the sea. They are shaved and trimmed and wounded by the wind.

At each end of the kaik' bay the cliff goes down in humps to stand blunt-nosed against the sea. But the rocks creep further out, black arms, reefs. They are full of secret pools. The unblinking eyes of octopi at night.

Today, a cloud of midges weaves and
dances through the evening sun.
There are mysterious glassy tracks on the
sea.
Thin waves hush in, pause, slide away.
Moeraki, calm as untroubled sleep . . .

At night, the penguins bray under the
cribs,
Sometimes the old ghosts from
Kihipuku steal in, for warmth and
company.
The dog will prick his ears and growl,
the cat snarl a little, then both sigh
and stretch and settle again.
We eat and talk and read until the
lamps flicker. Then we go to sleep in
the narrow cupboard bunks, and the
sea has all our dreams.

Every morning the shags stretch their
necks and slip off Maukiekie. Every
evening they return in a wavering
line.
Sometimes we have seen the living
black wheels of caa'ing whales out in
the woman sea.
Once I found an earwig big as my
thumb in the cliffs, moulding her
body round her pale brood.

When the seaweed is thick onshore,
the kelp flies swarm in their
thousands, pattering like rain against
the lighted windows.

On another day, the sea smashes in
against twin-armed Tikoraki. The
blowhole booms.
The elephant-black rocks rumble back and
forward in a murderous herd.
The air is thick and salt and full of
roaring. Great waves, crests streaming
back in long white drifts, explode against
the little island. Maukiekie, kia
manawa-nui!
Yellow foam scums the beach. Rain drives
down, and Matuatiki swells, carving
curving braids in the sand.
Further south, out of the reach of the reef,
the rocks Tūtimakohu and Te Karipi stand
on tiptoe, each suffocating pillar dreading
high tide in this lash and swirl of storm-
driven sea.
I crouch against the claystone, like a child
huddling close to its mother.
I watch the waves wage their long war
against the land, the land her long
resistance.

(1993)

He hōhā

      Bones tuned, the body sings—

See me,
I am wide with swimmer's muscle, and a bulk and luggage I
    carry curdled on hips;
I am as fat-rich as a tītī-chick, ready for the far ocean flight.

See me,
I have skilled fingers with minimal scars, broad feet that
    caress beaches,
ears that catch the music of ghosts, eyes that see the
    landlight, a pristine womb
untouched, except by years of bleeding, a tame unsteady heart.

See me,
I am a swamp, a boozy drain with stinking breath, a sour
sweetened flesh;
I am riddled with kidneyrot, brainburn, torn gut, liverfat,
scaled with wrinkles,
day by day I am leached, even between smiles, of that
strange water, electricity.

See me,
I am my earth's child,

      and she, humming
      considers her cuts and scars, and debates our death.
      Mean the land's breast, hard her spine when turned against you;
      jade her heart.

Picture me a long way from here –
back bush, a rainbird calling,
the sea knocking shore.

It is cliché that once a month, the moon stalks through my body,
rendering me frail and still more susceptible to brain spin;
it is truth that cramp and clot and tender breast beset – but then
it is the tide of potency, another chance to walk through the
   crack between worlds.

What shall I do when I dry, when there is no more turning
   with the circling moon?
Ah suck tears from the wind, close the world's eye;
Papatūānuku still hums.

But picture me a long way from here.

   Waves tuned, the mind-deep sings –

   She forgot self in the city, in the flats full of dust and
      spiderkibbled flies;
   she forgot the sweetness of silence in the rush and roar
      of metal nights;
   no song fitted her until she discovered her kin, all
      swimmers in the heavy air of sea;

   she had lost the supple molten words, the rolling thunder,
   the night hush of her mother's tongue;
   she had lost the way home, the bright road, the trodden
      beach, the mewling gulls,
   the lean grey toe of land.
   In the lottery of dreams, she gained prize of a
      nightmare, a singular dark.

But picture her a long way from there,
growing quiet until she heard herself whispered by the sea on
   the blackest night,
and echoed in the birds of morning.

        Keening, crooning, the unturned spirit –

I am a map of Orion scattered in moles across this
    firmament of body;
I am the black hole, the den where katipō are busy spinning
    deadhavens,
and he won't go, the cuckoo child.
Jolted by the sudden thud and shatter, I have gone outside to find
the bird too ruffled, too quiet, the barred breast broken, an
    end of the far travelling.

Tūtara-kauika, you father of whales, you servant of Tangaroa,
your little rolling eye espies the far traveller – quick!
whistle to him, distract, send him back to the other island;
I don't mind ever-winter if summer's harbinger is so
    damaged, damaging.

He turned full to face me, with a cry to come home –
do you know the language of silence, can you read eyes?

When I think of my other bones, I bleed inside,
and he won't go, the cuckoo-child.

It is not born; it is not live; it is not dead;
it haunts all my singing, lingers greyly, hates and hurts and
    hopes impossible things.
And Papatūānuku is beginning her ngeri, her anger is growing,
thrumming in quakes and tsunami,

and he won't go, the cuckoo's child.

    O, picture me a long way from here;
      tune the bones, the body sings;
  quiet the mind, the spirit hums,
        and Papatūānuku trembles, sighs;
          till then among the blood and dark

    the shining cuckoo spreads his wings
    and flies this hōhā, this buzz and fright,
    this wave and sweat and flood,
     this life.

(1992)

Hōkioi

'Have you ever been windwhipped?
Had your belly kneaded by want?
So it is with me, friend,
so it is with me.

I am given lone islands
with deep kilts of kelp,
stray birds and tired ghosts
to shelter in my arms –
I am a slender skein of muscle and bone
to stand against fear on their behalf.

I smell bad times coming,
a sharp intake of death,
I am eating our way to safety
building fat rib walls against famine
saving that monthly flush of blood
for real wounds
collecting anyone else's breath
against
the rending
the ravening
the hellbent raving cry of war.

    The wind is rising, e hoa –
    may all the nightfliers be friendly'

(2003)

E ngā iwi o ngāi tahu

for Rowley Habib, who asked the question

Where are your bones?

> **My bones lie in the sea**

Where are your bones?

> **They lie in forgotten lands**
> **stolen, ploughed, and sealed**

Where are your bones?

> **On southern islands**
> **sawed by discovering winds**

Where are your bones?

> **Whisper:**
> **Moeraki: Pūrakanui: Arahura:**
> **Okarito: Murihiku: Rakiura . . .**

Where are your bones?

> **Lying heavy on my heart**

Where are your bones?

> **Dancing as songs and old words in my head**
> **deep in the timelessness of mind**

Where are your bones?

**Here in my gut
strong in my legs walking
knotting my fists
but**

Where are your bones?

**Aue!
My bones are flour,
ground to make an alien bread . . .**

Mihi. Greeting. Weeping hello.
And to me, standing out as though
I'm the cripple in a company of runners;
to me, pale and bluegrey-eyed,
skin like a ghost, eyes like stones;
to me, always the manuhiri when away from home –
the weeping rings louder than the greeting.

(1982)

Winesong 15

I will sing a lovesong
– do not hide your ears
it is time for heartsongs and it is time for tears –
lady, I am a lover
lady, I am a thief
and I need your heart, love
as I need wine and tide and beach –

I will sing a tidesong
to while away your fears
you will hear the sea sound, you will hear deep prayers
but lady, I am a loner
and truly, I am a thief
and I will keep your heart-love
within my bottle's reach

and take it out in moonlight
and finger it with awe
until mazed with night caresses
I'll praise the bottle more.

When I sing this winesong
you'd better stop your ears
it only brings you emptiness
and strange and hopeless cares –

(1992)

Ends and beginnings

Where do I come from?
I do not ask the why of myself
at dusk:
then I make kits of green flax
to hold the bleeding silverbelly eels
the way my tīpuna did:
a mussel-shell edge
is the tool of choice
when shaving strips,
mine is stained shiny.

Where do I come from?
I do not ask the why of myself
at dawn:
then I sieve black sand
as the miners did,
treading their ancient hopeful trails
garnet, titanium, iron and gold . . .
the grave brown face of my shovel
wears a cold steel grin.

Bred on the other side of the hill
by the woman-sea,
who can say where I come from?

(1982)

WITI IHIMAERA

Witi Ihimaera is a novelist, short story writer and occasional poet. His most recent fiction is the novel *The Parihaka Woman* (Vintage, 2011) and the short story collection *The Thrill of Falling* (Vintage, 2012). He won a Ngā Kupu Ora Māori Book Award (2013) for the movie tie-in publication *White Lies*. In 2014 he was a member of the jury for the Fifo Oceanic Documentary Film Awards and travelled to France for the launch for the French translation *La Femme Parihaka*. He lives in Auckland.

My heart beats strongly

On a Sunday morning when you are asleep
I look at you lying with me and my heart beats strongly
     . . . ka patupatu taku manawa . . .
How lucky I am that for the rest of my life
you are my wife and I am your man

You think I don't know you are looking at me
you pull me into your arms and my heart beats strongly
     . . . ka patupatu taku manawa . . .
How lucky I am that for the rest of my life
I am your wife and you are my man

    My love for you is like a cloak of many feathers
    that I throw around your shoulders
    Let me carve the koru of my aroha like a sweetheart on a tree
    my desire I tattoo like a moko so all may see you belong to me
    and then . . . let me plait and weave the flax of our desire
    into each other's heart and tighten the tukutuku
    so it will never break apart . . .

    Our heart beats strongly . . .
         . . . ka patupatu taku manawa . . .

(2012)

Our watch now

If New Zealand had been Aotearoa
    just imagine . . .

The Treaty would have been honoured in 1840
Māori would have retained their tino rangatiratanga
    and Pākehā would have kāwanatanga

Being kaitiaki,
we would have heard huia still singing today
    our seas would flourish with the thunder of sounding whales
    Matariki would usher in Aotearoa New Year

This is not to say we wouldn't have had wars between us
and through the years, that there wouldn't have been pain and lots
of anger and tears

But . . . just imagine . . .
. . . what might have been . . . what we could have seen . . . and
what it might mean . . .

The Representatives we send to the United Nations
would be . . . from Aotearoa . . .
    The Prime Minister would have a tā moko . . .
    and might even be a wahine ariki . . .

Being kaitiaki,
the huia would fill the air with
coruscating beauty and incandescent trilling
pods of tohorā would thrill our blood
with regular soundings along our shores
the tales all children would have learnt
would be about whale riders, mountain movers,
and mythical taniwha
  Māori Earth . . . not
  Middle Earth

It's our watch now
the time to make dreams come true
today is a good day to begin . . .

    Kia hora te marino
    kia whakapapa pounamu te moana
    kia tere te kārohirohi mua i tōu huarahi
    āianei, ā ake tonu atu

    May the calm be widespread
    no storms, but a glistening greenstone sea instead
    and may the shimmer of rainbow lit spray
    ever dance over our pathway.

(2012)

O numi tutelar

At the British Museum, London, 25 June 1998

        3 in the morning
the streets deserted   I had forgotten
only derelicts & prostitutes are abroad in the night
forsaken lovers locked out
        (and Māori attending dawn ceremonies)

    Make way, Britannia, Albion, Victoria Imperatrix,
    make way our pūtātara are braying to bring down
    your walls   The dawn is coming and with it
    Magi, gift bearers from the South

    Piki mai, kake mai, homai te wai ora
    ki ahau

        We have come
from the utmost ends of the earth   a tribe of travellers

with our own Queen, ministers & warrior escort
to the land of our Treaty partner where
our treasures have been plundered
    (and Roma & I halfway round the world
    to read in a stairwell)

Make way, oh Egypt, ancient Assyria, Greece, Rome
make way   our own Cleopatra comes amid you
Semiramis, Te Arikinui, Imperatrix of Aotearoa
Māori women, gift bearers from the South

Haramai te toki, hui e, haumi e, tāiki e

So here we are
climbing upward   the Museum opening unwilling
to the dawn, the kai karanga calling, the warriors
pulling us in & Maramena asks, 'How can our
culture so small survive in this treasure house
of many cultures?'
    (The answer is simple: Godzilla was wrong
    size does not matter)

Oh antiquities of Asia, make way, lions of Judah
bow down, Babylon, stela of Islam make way
give space, oh Nimrod, Horus, Mahomet
we are iwi Māori, gift bearers from the South

E taonga tū mai, tū mai, tū mai

And in the great hall
for the first time we see   the past before us
the treasures of our ancestors a Pharaonic ransom
of immense psychic power, indeed we live
with our past   the ghosts among us
    (How can I explain? We have always walked
    backwards into our future)

> *Oh, ancestors, stand forever! Stand for yesterday!*
> *Stand for today! Stand for tomorrow! Stand*
> *for always! Stand! Stand! Stand!*

Take heed, oh Gods of all other worlds, numi tutelar
we come chanting, we come singing, we come
proudly from Rangiātea, there our seed was sown
we come, still voyaging by star canoes
by aurora australis

We are from savage islands, far to the south
we move through your constellations
make way   and where there is one
oh Gods, there are a thousand

We are Magi, bearing gifts
and our dawn is coming

> *Ka ao, ka ao, ka awatea*

(2003)

Una storia semplice

> *Leaving London, 7 July 1998*

If I should die in a foreign land
        do not leave me there
place me upon the bright strand of sky & sea
        set my eyes southward
and, just as the sun goes down
        call Hine Te Ariki
        to come for me

(2003)

SAM JACKSON

Sam Jackson is of Ngāti Whātua, Ngāpuhi, Ngāti Wai, Ngāti Kahu, Te Roroa and European descent. Her greatest loves are her whānau, philosophy and rangatahi Māori (Māori youth) development. She wrote 'Being Māori' as part of the 'Dirty thirty' thirty-day creative writing challenge in 2013 and the poem is her exploration of the stereotypes, expectations and burdens which surround 'being Māori' in Aotearoa.

Being Māori

Being Māori is not all
targeted entry into medicine
government handouts
and pay checks
from the iwi

nor is it child abuse
alcoholic family members
and sexual violence
spanning generations
like they say on the TV.

Being Māori is
an expectation from others
that you are fluent in English (or you're dumb)
and Māori (or you're not a *real* Māori)
but no other language.
Because then you're **really** not a real Māori.

It's an expectation that you know the names and histories of
every tupuna who ever lived
from every iwi
ever.
And that you know every member of the whānau
whose last name
is kinda like yours.

It's being the native informant
inclusion by speaking on behalf of
every Māori who ever lived.
Being Māori is knowing how to throw a good rage
because everyone knows
that alcoholic hunters and gatherers
who can sing in tune
AND who know the words to every waiata ever written
throw
the
best
parties.

Being Māori is land marches
and whining
about a history that's long been dealt with.
It's money in the pokies,
poverty that can be fixed by a hard
day's work.

It's watching the people you love
campaign for 'New Zealand Day'
and 'one rule for all'.
But, 'It's all good,' they say
'cos you're not like the rest of them.'
It's being told to, 'Lighten up,
it's just a joke, bro.'

Being Māori is meeting someone for the first time in public
and not knowing whether to shake their hand
kiss them, or give them a hug
so you give a distant awkward wave.

Being Māori is all hui and no doey.
Whanaungatanga and food.
Death by diabetes.

Actually,
being Māori is finding the balance between
responsibility and obligation.
Desire and expectation.
Privilege and
burden

because whether you want it or not
your heritage is written in your eyes
told through your name
and linked to thousands of other lives.

It's loving your whānau
but being forced away from them for days at a time.
It's knowing the importance of being centred
but not having the time to take your shoes off long
enough to plant
your feet into the earth

because you work all day
hiding your education.
And stay up all night
completing the paperwork that's been given to you
hours before the deadline.

Being Māori is having access to a world
that not everyone wants to see.

'They're a born-again,' people say
without ever realising you never took the time
to
see
me.

PHIL KAWANA

Phil Kawana was born in Hāwera in 1965. Of Ngā Ruahinerangi, Ngāti Ruanui and Ngāti Kahungunu ki Wairarapa descent, his whakapapa also includes Scots and Irish. Originally known as a short story writer, acclaimed for his two collections *Dead Jazz Guys* (Huia, 1996) and *Attack of the Skunk People* (Huia, 1999), since 2002 he has focused on poetry, leading to his first solo collection *Devil in My Shoes* (AUP, 2005). His work has been widely anthologised, broadcast and taught around the world. He currently lives in Wellington, in poetically correct squalor.

Rūaumoko, my lovely

I will show you fear in a handful of dust
T. S. Eliot, 'The Waste Land'

Tuatahi: Tūmatauenga taunts Rūaumoko

i

Claw with broken nails
    the crescents caked
    in chocolate blood
tear the flesh of earth
    rent her skin
    there are no stars there
sleeping

seek the withheld dream
    that burrows deeper
    bitter and void
through its teeth
    and out its ass
    into the dark
interred

rage against the passage of days
and the forgetfulness of gods

cry with ragged voice
    the echoes dark
    and darker fall
shout down the sky
    break his bones
    feast on the marrow
weeping

grasp the crumbled truth
    that entombs you
    fast and still
its feral bite
    the final grace
    no souls live here
unheard

rage against the muted wind
and the tyrannies of dirt and men

ii

slumped, hope bleeding
through ulcered wounds
into a dawnless night
placenta sky, itself in amber

trapped

in that moment when you wonder
is this that very moment
when the fulness of my soul
will at last be cloaked in light

but no

stay, you less-than-man
submit, it is the will of those
whose will cannot be challenged
this is the order of things

destiny

if you will; we are children
of the parentless, and that alone
has made gods of us, whom
no filial bonds constrain

freedom

we have gained for ourselves
by force we have unbound ourselves
ripped from our mātua's arms
no choice but stand or die

but you

kick lamely at those palisades
shut tight to your approach
and know, step forward if you wish
and I shall pick you from my teeth

iii

in darkness you have grown
hearing nothing – so dead
to this life which flares
in my nostrils like a rage

so dead to this life
that death itself lures

like a lover, a promise
of obliviousness

so dead you have no setting
in which to place your life
just the ignorant darkness
the flatulence of rotting gods

what comforts lie in cold blood?
what warmth in breath
so bitter? those comforts you have
are mere shadows, and mock you

iv

And all the stars, one by one,
and the sun and the moon
shall rise and fall without you

And the tides, and the rivers
and all that they embrace
will not moisten your dry lips

And all the eyes, and all the hands,
and all that they describe
shall flourish, yet not know you

And every wind, and every storm
and every rumour that they chase
will not quicken to your name

Hang your head, and be forgotten

Tuarua: Rūaumoko stirs

i

It sounds like death, this rumbling
that riffles the dark about it
and behind it, like a wake

(fold the sky in passing
rip it loose and let it fall –
it means nothing to me here)

I hear you in my skin
no deeper, rail all you might
with all your might, no marks

but my own shall canvas my skin
there is more art in pain
than in the vanity of importance

the gods can rage amongst themselves
tear the heavens down at their pleasure

this darkness is as nothing
as nothing as that beyond
no prison, no wall, no guarded path

glory in your hour of sun
spread wide those reaping arms
broadcast your fecund seed, for naught

but decay awaits you
and what you escape, your moko
will bear, history has a way

of catching men and mavens
and when the world has passed
your end, you'll find your end is here

so rage against this earth-bound life
let your pride claw at the winds

even the stars orbit this womb
where death awaits us, gods and all

      as above, so below
      as above, so below

ii

Flutter, God-Eater, without rest
hollow bones trailing
withering beneath you
the scent of death at your back
undiminished

a sudden wind could rip those brittle wings
and all the proud colours
and all the bright song
are the puffery of a season
distilled

once those wings have lost their lift
to whom will you cry?
whose hand will be outstretched
to stop your fall?

the sky weeps for what you have done
the earth itself has turned its back
your appetite reveals your sin
your pride conceals your fate

the sun, in its course
has warmed you,
calmed those recurring fears
that assail both tyrants
and thieves

and now you are content
with the company of fools
their flapping mouth cackling
like thorns thrown
on a fire

iii

The last standing God
power and jealousy
at either hand

nothing grows in ash

(2012)

Songs for my children

1

On september fourth
baby moves out
my little girl no longer

letting go of the bicycle
was just a portion
of this; so much

I could have been
I could have done

so much more than this
yet this is what we have,
as september cracks open

like a walnut in a dying man's hand
what meat we find is all we have
when we ponder, was it worth it

seawater stings, but cleans those cuts, boy
your granddad said to me

the day the rocks cut through my shoes
as I rushed to fill the sugar sack
I lifted my eyes from that sack but once

and now I am that old man
I have watched the tide recede
so many times, too many times

wondering what will become of me
will those moko call upon me
call me back to where, through tears

koro and kuia, thought dead as daydreams
spoon syrup on fried bread

2

girl, you have more mana
than you have knowledge to perceive
but that will come

that will come

we are all the sum of what has been
and the memory of what shall follow

3

Well, bro,
it's begun now

life is improvised
rehearsal is the past
the daydream

believe
trust your heart
you'll find your way

I have more faith in you
than I have ever had

in mere gods

I hope to see you leap
from the tallest of ladders . . .

(2012)

Scenes from a council tenancy

The Coughing Man fractures the light
slivers through the wire-mesh window
rattling lungs and doorkeys
shopping bag of empties
each a broken capillary, from which
the disappointed blood
is breaking now
heading for the surface

This dying fall is just a trick of the hiding sun
the western hills rise damp, cold
a shadow slowly shedding a shadow
blank walls fester, backs to the turgid day
the trolley wires weave a gauze
across the debt-slave suburbs
inhale the meth and anxieties
secure the script deep in a pocket

There are junk food wrappers
and supermarket bags of chemicals
and rags, in the tagged
piss-smelling stairwell
pass with eyes down
you do not know whose eyes you meet
and whose you dare not, here
in this other kingdom

The walls are institutional beige
a 'relax, you'll be here a while' tone
that whispers in scurrying ears
polished vinyl floors
layers peeling from the doors
vents that have not worked in years
years like an IV, dripping, dropping,
diluted as it falls, its moment gone

In the corridors, electric lights
burn without rest

Between the concrete block palisades
a young Samoan boy, too small for school
too big for a bedsit when the sun shines
is singing church songs, TV themes
jingles and gibberish, just to hear
the notes leaping and chasing
each other like rainbow-skinned fish
up wall and window into Pacific blue sky

It is good when the sun can prise apart
the silhouettes of hill and home
dries the pitted footpaths and pristine tea-towels
that block out a section in the columns of lines
a platoon in whites, guarding the old ways
grey-eyed old people, whisky-skinned and tired
dragged across the courtyard by kitchen chairs
fleeing the chasing shadows

There are always shadows here; they pass
like the tickle of cannabis still hanging
by the elevator doors, a lift
from the dank ooze of the refuse room
over which the whole building squats
the chute farts and the bins clatter

with symphonic glee, atonic
an echo in the dark you can smell

And behind the curtained windows
up higher where glimpses
of a farther life can still be had
the oligarchy of architecture and geography
has eased its planting pinch, but still
the prints remain, the vista from inside
designed from the outside and only looking in
the people laid out like push pins

In the corridors, electric lights
burn without rest

(2012)

Granville requiem

'The death of Mr C–, whose body lay in his flat for more than a year before it was discovered, caused an outcry over the duty of care provided by the city council to its tenants. But the council kept quiet about Mr W–'s death in similar circumstances. Mr W–, 68, had lived for many years in flat 45 of the dilapidated council-owned Granville Flats.' – Dominion Post, *23 February 2012*

We are the silt
we are the rusty stain
rinsed off
washed away
too insignificant for remembrance

voiceless, faceless
we are the broken

numbered in files
encompassed by plain manila folders

units of income
we are the less-than

the addicts, the drinkers
the broken-English refugees
the 'mental health consumers' –
the schizoid and the paranoid,
the traumatised and the depressed

we are the faces you turn away from

we are sought out only by the dealers
of cannabis and counterfeit goods
the clothing trucks, the money-lenders
and the sellers of cable TV subscription

we are not men
we are loss against profit
we are Wellington's secret

His name, for the record, was Wiremu
like my father, and of a similar age
we lived on the same floor

if I ever greeted him
it was only a smile in passing
if that

eight months he lay dead
unnoticed, ignored
(can the dead be lonely?)

I knew nothing until the police
knocked on my door
canvassing the tenants
piecing together Wiremu's passing

we remain entombed

meanwhile the council
and the tenancy managers
make reassuring statements with their teeth

while they sit on their hands

they have refined the theology of public speaking
answer the questions they wish were asked
deflect the questions with
inconvenient answers

they, too are human
with mortgages to pay
to be professional
means to remain employed

and that, after all, is all that matters

If a man shuts his ears to the cry of the poor, he too will cry out and not be answered.

we are the rebellious
the recidivists, the bad news
the eroders of profit
the creators of bad press
      so say the bureaucrats who watch us die

we are the drop-outs
the ne'er-do-anythings
the drain on the economy
the blight on the statistics
      so say the politicians who cannot gain by us

we are the despised
the forgotten
the spat out ends
the unclean cattle of the digital age
      so say the economists who cannot factor us

what we are
is the imprint of your aspirations
the offcut from your cloth
one day we just might
      rise up

and kill you all in your beds

(*25 February 2012*)

Urupā

We face the mountain.
The headstones are pale imitations
   of the sleeping maunga.
It is waiting, biding its time.
The land around us was seized
   and sold years ago;
the cord was cut, and we were set adrift
   into a strange new world.
We were born, we live,
   and we shall die.
I hope when the wait's over,
   when I follow Taranaki into sleep,
that there will be someone left
   to maintain the fence
   that keeps the sheep from my grave.

(2005)

HINEWIRANGI KOHU

Hinewirangi Kohu is an artist, poet and activist. Her areas of expertise include traditional Māori parenting and healing; Māori flute-making; and indigenous poetry and drama. She has been active on behalf of Māori women and their families as director and international representative for the Māori Women's Centre in Hamilton since its inception in 1984, and as founding member of the national women's group Te Kakano o te Whanau (1984), and has been involved in health centres and housing resource management. Her published works include *Broken Chant* (1983), *The Turning Face* (1984), *Screaming Moko* (1986) and *Kanohi ki te Kanohi* (1990).

Fried bread

Pākehā/White Woman:
subverting images in my head.
I want to be Pākehā.
I want to be a white woman.
It'd be painless – no ache,
just hardness – as spick as
stainless steel.

I hide my Māori ugliness
–   overdose on Judith Arden
    perfume,
      separate myself from my kind
–   deny Māoridom,

hating our whare's dirt floor,
kutu's stigma,
hating fried bread sandwiches
which harden with golden syrup,
swapping fried bread lunches
for dainty club sandwiches
and drink in a plastic bottle,
hating slurred Māori speech patterns,
trying desperately to speak like a Pākehā.

God, I want to be white – a Pākehā.
I will,
I will be,
I will be the best

brown skinned, black haired,
brown eyed Pākehā there is!

(1986)

Barriers

Kai ora

Hinewirangi speaking

Who?

Hinewirangi

What?

Hinewirangi

Can you spell that?

I reckon I can
can you?

No,
will you spell it please?

H I N E W I R A N G I

oh, yes,

High knee we rah gee

no

Hinewirangi

will High knee do?

No,
call me Rose.

(1986)

In ritual

In ritual
to Hinemoana – sea goddess
washing my hair
lifting my head skyward
– something grows on
my chin.
What strange fish clings?

In ritual
to Papatūānuku – earth mother
covering my nakedness
brown korowai,
my eyes cast upwards
– something grows on my lips.
What earth still clings?

In ritual
to Hinemanu – bird woman
filling my ears, whispering sounds
of kiwi, kōkako, tūī,

something flies upon my chin.
What frond's design is this?

In ritual
moko
you grow
– I feel your emergence
breaking the skin.
What anger is this I feel?

(1986)

Expectations

Māori women
young, strong,
you call to our menfolk
to get their act together.

Young Māori women
in a vision
I have seen
that our men cannot.
Their models come
from ngā tāne atua,
when they meet,
they clash, whawhai.

    – titiro

Tāne Mahuta fought with his brothers
to separate our parents,
Tāwhirimātea challenged all gods
because of the separation.
Tūmatauenga, war god,

Māui Tikitiki
fought for power he did not have.
Warriors are born in every male
to fight each other;
all wars were created by men
for power.

We have
nurturing, loving models;
every element that is earth
is female
they work together to maintain
for us a place to be born.
We have that power.

Young Māori woman
search your soul and know
what our kuia knew.

(1993)

Weep not for me

       Weep not for me
I go beyond the veil

       weep not for me
tears are not for me
       death is quiet
death is gentle

       weep not for me
my friends
       in life I shared
I danced

        cried
                laughed
fell to the earth with you
        now it is my time
to go
        we will meet again
so
        weep not for me

(1990)

PAULA KORA

Paula Kora, Ngāpuhi, was Dux of Whau Valley Primary and later educated at Whangarei Girls' High. As a child she wrote stories and poems and would recite these to the extended whānau. At high school she developed a love of poetry and was most excited by the simple free verse of e. e. cummings. During the 1990s she taught a poetry writing course at Pāremoremo Prison. She and husband Robin were regular readers at 'Poetry Live', held at the Shakespeare Hotel in Auckland. Paula continues to write poetry with a view to publishing her own work.

Te aute tē whawhea

It was in that dreamtime
no longer night and not yet dawn
the seas still and the winds
waiting to be born
from the lips of Heavenly Gods

It was in that dreamtime
I felt her hands touch my hair
and her soft mouth's kiss
moist upon my troubled brow
With expert fingers
she massaged my head

with a tenderness
I can only describe as love
and I let the wash
of her flowing spirit
sluice over the nagging pains
in my body

TE AUTE TĒ WHAWHEA
she whispered to me
in that dreamtime
when it was no longer night
and not yet dawn.

(1992)

[It wasn't your smile]

It wasn't your smile that attracted me to you
it wasn't your sleek smooth body moving with animal grace
it wasn't your long musical fingers
nor was it the muscled design of your thighs
it wasn't the colour of your skin or the feisty texture of your hair
it wasn't the sagginess of your face
and it wasn't your Rangitoto lips

It was the reflection of deep black pools of death
in your eyes
it was the reflection of wet blue waves of sorrow
in your eyes
it was the reflection of dull grey ships of despair
in your eyes

And it was the reflection of crimsoned passion
in your eyes
it was the reflection of the purpled sceptre of nobility

in your eyes
it was the reflection of that ephemeral emerald of spirituality
in your eyes

that I saw so clearly in my own

O Blind Man, please look at me when I look at you
and listen carefully with your beautiful brown eyes

(1992)

ROBIN KORA

Robin Kora (1949–2007), of Muaūpoko descent, was educated at Te Aute College. He excelled as an American Field Scholar, teacher, television presenter and actor, but his greatest love was for the written word. He wrote poetry over many decades and his work has appeared in several publications. He enjoyed appearing as guest poet at live events in Auckland and Melbourne. Robin valued poetry as a means of expression that demanded to be read out loud. Robin passed away in September 2007.

Suffrage

I recognise the woman in me.
And I welcome her with open arms,
arms that then enfold.

My chest is man,
succoured within from way back
by nipples I would look ridiculous without.
My loins I inherit from my past,
my primordial past,
from a tupuna who visibly possessed
the lure of both . . . man and woman.
And when I was called

in the fall of the standing coin
my manhood dropped
and I became the giver of life,
no more important than the receiver,
no less worthy than the mother.
When she felt the child move
my hands shook with anticipation.
When the sweat swamped her face
my lips sponged the waters,
my comfort wiped her brow . . .
or, at least, attempted to.
And, in the agony of birth,
in the lock between the rise and fall
the rushing of the forces
while the battle raged
with the giver and taker of life,
it was my woman's heart
that pumped with the empathy
and steady glow of support.
Mine eyes, my weary eyes,
paced the mountains and the valleys
of that wahine toa.
I saw the Maker stamp his mark
on the tortured face of passage,
I drowned in the desperate need of air
and gasped at the forced hurl of first breath . . .
I shared
in the peace and tranquillity of thanksgiving
and marvelled at the little things of life.

And what is left is my crown
combed to the side acknowledged
as my tender-gender half.
The side that would kiss his son on the lips
for as long as he will allow.
It is the balance of me

passed in living memory through my grandmother,
my channel, my stillness, my tukutuku
before and after the war.

I thus accept, as woman,
the power to vote
the power to veto,
and on this day
I cast my vote with the woman . . .
inside every body.

(1985)

Been fishing, Billy?

You brought your rod home
but you left your tackle-box there
open
for everyone to see
to sort through the hooks, the sinkers and the bait.

The bait!
You knew what would happen didn't you.
I can see you smiling now, you bugger,
the ultimate one-liner
(without the chuckle to prompt the laugh)
saved for the last. Nice one!
But not all of us are laughing
and that's funny too.
You should see them,
some of those who said they were close to you
smacked arses all of them
crying all the way to the camera.
Funny when one knows the empty truth
or at least a part of it.

Your highlighted media funeral
is antique classic tangi.
There was an understanding
there's always been that understanding
not lost to you from antiquity:
the whenua is planted
the head penetrates
the tree grows tall
the branches reach out.
And if the roots
God Willing
are still there
they pull you back to the whenua.

Just as the fish migrate, even more than you did, Billy
they have to go home;
a riddle to most
practised by some
the ritual Dance of Death.

When it calls
at any time, at any place
all worries cease
all joys overwhelmed
we turn and feel the path provided
pulling us back, pulling us back . . . aaaa

tōia mai, te waka
ki te urunga, te waka
ki te moenga, te waka
ki te takotoranga i takoto ai, te waka.

Nothing will stop it
one way or another we return.

If the flesh survives it dances
the fleshing dance of urgency;
nothing else matters
not beast, not mountain
nor waterfall or talk, nor tears;
the rhythm goes on, is strong
powerful, mighty, irresistible . . .

the words are meaningless,
the rhythm IS.

At the waterfall . . .
the rods bend
the whakapapa are cast.

It's an honour to be sought
at the waterfall
to fly against the current
to fight the forces calling in the foreplay
to feel a fingered hook
fancy the prey and move aside
only to be played for, outmanoeuvred by another
claiming, by the mouth,
deeper more profound beginnings.
The longer it runs, the harder the play
the more honoured the strike.

In that moment of truth
a drop of water (better in the rain)
becomes the pathway lit with splendour:
the tree cascading oceans
the branches joined as one
the leaves filtering emeralds;
when life sings with death
life fuels life
and death becomes death once more.

For an instant it's complete
breath in that grain of sand
light at the end of darkness
faith in the unknown;
returning ki te Kaha Rawa what we knew we understood
and returning too what we thought we never knew.

Ki te Pō, ki te Pō . . .
Ki te Ao Mārama.

Tihei mauriora!

(1991)

Tāne's zoo

There's only a stump left now,
a huge blood-red stump
ringed ten times my span.
But that mighty pulse of Tāne's child
used to pump outside our window.

Silent waxeyes and everywhere sparrows
would feed under its sheltering arms;
thoughtful thrushes and shimmering starlings
all found solace – and pushy mynahs too
when I wasn't vigilant.
Rosellas added their dash of colour and brief clamour
and two beautiful kererū perched there and slept
on their way to and from the bush.
It was simply bliss
being the ones shut gladly in our windowed cage
watching the visitors enjoy the peace and elevated silence.
I didn't even feel the urge to spit
or piss on them as they passed through.

Yes, it *was* bliss . . . just being able to absorb their presence:
they honoured our home,
they felt safe enough to return.

But they'll sleep there no more;
their sanctuary is gone . . . Tāwhirimātea was angry that week
and blew his brother's child away.
Now those kererū will grace another shoulder
and occupants of another glass cage
will adore them . . .
and be fed by them.

(1992)

Visit the sins

What drives a man
to slay his own flesh and blood?

I know . . .
because I came close to it myself.

I nearly went further
than just putting a hole
in my beautiful, pink, Angora jersey.

Remember the man who jumped off
the harbour bridge
the Nippon Clip-on
the coat-hanger
with his children a few years ago?

It was about that time.

Must have been something in the air
like Poverty
or a need for parachutes
certainly a need, now, to make light of it
to float it away
to float it away
to do what *that* father couldn't do then.

The process was the same ... slow, and painful
deliberate and painful,
painful and thoughtful.
Painful
because I knew exactly what I was doing
where I was going
where I had come from
and why.

I had come from my father
and my mother's father
and my grandfather's mother
and I visited the sins of the 3rd generation
the 4th generation
the 5th
the 6th
and ...

and this is where you went wrong, old man,
you did it.
I couldn't do it ...
I couldn't do it ...
I couldn't.

I
couldn't take my seed with me
as I felt
at first

was my right
my birthright
my wrong
my anguish
my vanguish.

. . . I feel for you . . .
because a part of me agrees
it was your right,
they were your seed after all . . .
I still . . .

It's just that . . .

every time I look at the bridge
the coat-hanger
the hole in my beautiful, pink Angora jersey
touches the waterline

and I judge from that
that I didn't have to fall
as far
as you.

(1992)

DORA ROIMATA LANGSBURY

Ko Pukekura te peke; ko Āraiteuru te tai; ko Uruao te waka. Ko Kāi Tahu, ko Kāti Māmoe rāua ko Waitaha te iwi; ko Ōtākou te marae; ko Karetai te whānau tipuna; ko Kuao Edmond Langsbury tōku pāpā; ko Dora Roimata Langsbury ahau. Dora Roimata Langsbury's poems and short stories have been published in a number of Te Wānanga o Aotearoa publications. In 2013 the Christchurch City Council created a fence wrap of her poem 'My father's footsteps' as part of the reopening celebrations, welcoming residents back into the Ōtautahi CBD. It was 60 metres long and extended half a city block in Colombo Street.

My father's footsteps

I can see you up ahead of me
I am following
in your footsteps

no matter how fast I walk
I cannot catch up

your footsteps are bigger than mine
but they were warm
and safe to step in

you turn around
and smile encouragingly
then return to your journey

thank you for your footsteps
when I can no longer see you
they will always be here
pointing me in the right direction

(27 June 2009)

The night they knocked the doors down (26/02/2011)

I was terrified
I felt like I lived in a war zone
it was dark
no electricity in our homes
I gathered with my neighbours
to protect our doors

They had come from afar
to help search for the missing people
but it was dark
the sound of the neighbouring doors
being pounded open
was more frightening
than the earthquake had been

(2011)

MARAMA LAURENSON

Marama Laurenson is of Tūhourangi, Tūwharetoa, Te Āti Haunui a Pāpārangi, Ngāi Tahu, Ngāti Hinewaka and Ngāi Tumapuhia i Rangi ancestry. She is trained in historical research, government policy and strategic advice and has been working in local government for nine years as a strategic adviser in culture and heritage. Marama has commenced a history project about her ancestry in Scotland and County Durham and remains engaged with hapū relationships personally and professionally, as well as working full time.

Tahu Brown Parata – ol' rolly eyes

I remember you, ol' rolly eyes
one flipped up, the other down
in a tall still frame of man

Your kids left the toast plate empty
with practised speed
under my useless hand
I looked at you, ol' rolly eyes
. . . one flipped up, the other down

On a grey Puke morning
Mavis in petticoat got up weary
you in a singlet splashed your face
at the wash house concrete tub
wiry hair jerked
as you turned, said, what!
Ol' rolly eyes, one up, the other down

A winter Roxburgh day
raisins a treat in meat paste jars
sent to a room without adults
we heard the rumble of talk and laughter
and pictured ol' rolly eyes
one up and one down

Ōtemātātā, summer bleached
Euclid monsters hauling the dirt
you drove into piles and dumped again
each day home
to Lindsay's gasps and waving hands
through cot rails
at your first footstep

Otago heat
ripening apricots not to be eaten
except as treasure in jars
put there by women
as you pitted and sliced

Patsy bulging with Tapi's child
brought hankies for my birthday
Ian a shilling pared from a half-moon wallet
David two china ducks
. . . things to look at in the car, and fiddle with
as the sight of your rolly eyes
lolled in my mind remembering, family

Later you shared the veil
of battle and bash on the other side of the world
your mates said you rode courier
up and down the convoy
a target, never shot

Leave in Cairo
bazaar sounds a knife stabbed alien robes
the walk off Crete with your boots on
dropped rifle, and bottle
walking on a march
and you . . . a boy

Sometimes your eyes didn't roll
eyelids drooped in stillness
to stop our knowing

We're here with you now
in the same room
and know what it was
for you
to live

Closed forever, ol' rolly eyes
I'll remember you
one up, one down.

(2003)

Hana Te Hemara – Muru Raupatu

i

No more your face
to smile
life
without you

No more your voice
to speak and sing
a blessing to weary
woman, dull soul
without you

No more you stand
to wave and point
a past whose grief we weep
without you

No more your balm
to comfort brutal hurt
in violent love's deceit
without you

So you lay
in stillness
the path where you began
your ending now
Muru Raupatu

ii

Today the earth was put
and rain now comes
to drench the ground
without my tears, there

darkness comes between
your life, this life
a violent knife that cuts
in flashes of glimmer
and steel a lightening edge

Unready and ragged
for life without you
my friend

A clamour of mourning
as droves of voyeurs geeked their fill
arse turning rude protesting
petals fell

To the tender stretch of blood
embracing kinship
left
without you

Your frailty
land
Muru Raupatu

(2003)

KATERINA MATAIRA

Katerina Mataira, Ngāti Porou, was born in Tokomaru Bay in 1932. Educated at St Joseph's Maori Girls' College, she became a teacher and was at the forefront of the revival and teaching of te reo Māori. In 1985 she helped establish the total immersion kura kaupapa Māori at Hoani Waititi Marae. In 1996 she was made an Honorary Doctor of the University of Waikato. She was awarded the Companion of the New Zealand Order of Merit in 1998 and in 2011 was made Dame Companion of the New Zealand Order of Merit. She is the author of three novels in te reo Māori. Katerina Mataira died in 2011 but will be lovingly remembered as a Māori-language proponent, educator, intellectual, artist and writer.

Restoring the ancestral house

Old walls creak
amid mason-bee hum
through cracked timbers
sun splinters ricochet from
the one good eye
of the tekoteko
supine upon the floor

And I . . .
ladder perched
hand poised tentatively
to trace aged scrolls
of clays blue-black and white and kōkōwai
adornments on the ribs of
the ancestral house
let the master craftsman return
from the loosened tukutuku panel
to guide the untutored hand

The shadows move
and the house is full
grey mounds humped upon the whāriki
sleeping
a child slurps upon his mother's nipple

in the corner
muffled lover shufflings
and the old men snoring

But only spiders
people the house
they
and the marauding mason-bee
are the spinners of tales
and the long night singing
no child
no lovers
and the old men stare
faded photographs
morose in their warped frames
drunk against the wall

And I . . .
ladder shaking
and shiny acrylic
and cement for the dry rot
in the tekoteko's back.

(1996)

ABIGAIL McCLUTCHIE

Ki te taha o tōku pāpā Wiremu James McClutchie, ko Ngāti Porou te iwi. Ko Te Rarawa te iwi ki te taha o tōku whaea. Ko Abigail McClutchie ahau. Growing up in Manurewa, Abigail McClutchie had an awareness of the inequities around her. It wasn't until she got to the University of Auckland that she began to understand the process of colonisation and the impact it has had to disempower, disengage, and dishearten people. Abigail currently works at the University Business School as the He Tuākana Coordinator and is interested in Māori and Pacific development around education, engagement, empowerment, and economy.

Go to the mountains

Go to the mountains
so that you may be cleansed
by the winds of Tāwhirimātea,
and be free.

Go to the sea
so that you may feel the peace
of Hinemoana's song,
and be inspired.

Go to the ngahere
so that you may be revitalised
by the energy of Tāne Mahuta,
and be transformed.

Go to the inner source
so that you may listen to the power,
of your inner essence,
and be enlightened.

for I am the Godforce within you.
TE AO MĀRAMA.

(2003)

LARISSA McMILLAN

Larissa McMillan (Te Rarawa) was raised in Whāngārei but currently resides in Wellington, where she works as a writer and an art director in the film industry. She also writes journalistic articles, artistic resources and scripts for film. She won 'best short script' via Huia Publishers in 2011 and has had poetry published in *Ora Nui*. Her writing influences are varied and wide, from Victor Hugo to Sam Hunt. 'It is the unnoticed moments that I find the most fulfilling.'

Idle

He is idle again, not for the first time on this bleak Sunday of wet and compact skies. An attempt at drawing inspiration from the view results in concrete nothingness. Several monitors stare back equally as uninspired, black oubliettes of information challenging him to pry. A bottle of Syrah, swimming in his memory from the night before, turns away in contempt.

An eye slips over, down and down, tracing familiar beige and brown. A spark is birthed, running across his brow, dancing down his arm and over hands that reach. Tuwhare delivers him inspiration and the man is moved
                              to write.

(*January 2013*)

Hotere

The bulb in this, old
second hand lamp,
flickers,
and dims,
yellow.

Cutting down the Lower Hutt highway,
Kate gives the news,
'Hotere's dead.'

That light,
has flickered,
and dimmed.

No more corrugated crosses,
no more red, white and black.
Lacquered panels, coloured circles,
but that's all right with me, Jack.

Dazed, angry and brave,
he burnt the track behind him,
paving the way,
for all of them.

But now,
my old lamp,
burns, yellow,
and
dims.

(February 2013)

TRIXIE TE ARAMA MENZIES

Trixie Te Arama Menzies was born in Wellington in 1936 and lives in Auckland with her husband Barry Menzies. She is of Tainui and Scottish descent. She has taught at secondary schools, at the University of Auckland and has been a kaiāwhina at kōhanga reo. Her four poetry collections are *Uenuku* (Waiata Koa, 1986), *Papakainga* (Waiata Koa, 1988), *Rerenga* (Waiata Koa, 1992) and *In the Presence of My Foes* (Waiata Koa, 2000). She is a founding member of Waiata Koa, a Māori women's artists and writers collective that was formed at the time of the *Karanga* exhibition in 1986.

Kōauau

To Richard Nunns

The smell of kānga pirau fills the dining hall
carried by waves of warmth from the piped heating
pork bone and watercress smells drift over too
voluptuous ancestors watch over everything
in the kōauau workshop bonedust chokes you
they are grinding dry bones, dust beckons dust,
ashes, our own vile bodies in the end

Yet children welcome us and play, intent,
messengers of sweet notes in their bone music
echoing clear the spirit voices sing
Go find your other bones! they call, from somewhere,
the Lady will flaunt her signals, should she want you
meantime, don't disappoint the ringawera –
the fires are lit, the creek has drenched the corn

(*Tūrangawaewae, June 1986*; 1988)

Climber

I tread a steep and lonely track
huge crevasses gape on either side
they open up further as I watch them
it's a mountain pass
narrow, only room to go single file
I can stop and rest, and have companionship
but must advance alone.
If I were to turn back it would be no good
there is only false comfort back there
there is no growth, it is stifling and dangerous
if I can negotiate this pathway
without falling into those abysses either side
perhaps there will be grass and shade, a sight of the sea
but meantime I must watch my step
there is an awkward bit coming up
even alpine mosses don't grow here
there are hand and footholds in the rock, but almost impossible to see,
the track twists upwards
I must force my ageing body on.

(1986)

Ki āku tipuna Māori

Where are my people of the tōnuitanga
I have shared the love-hate politicking of the family –
once there was a whānau but we are separated –
ka raungaiti au.

Once there was a black-eyed woman who was my ancestress,
she lurked behind the innocent eyes of my babies,
in the sweaty beds of love she was the one I sought but did not know it.
I never heard her name, this forgotten woman

she was my blood my bone my pulse my smell my breath
when I first danced with death she was my chaperone
later to be unmasked as procuress.

Sometimes I sense her in a patch of garden,
a place where crops grow by themselves unplanted
or a certain stretch of coast touched by a warm late season.

Worms gnaw her bones as one day they will gnaw at mine
when I find where she lies, there would I lie contented.

(1986)

Manuhiri

The poet is the guest of the podium
the bird is the tree's guest when it alights to sing
the river is the guest of the sea
as it pours its sweet waters into that salty flood
whose hospitality is returned when the tides rush up the river mouth
(20 miles up the Wanganui, they say, the water is still brackish)

the gull visits the wavetip as it pauses, screeching before the storm.
Listen to those baby manaia in their rocking nest
calling hoarsely, *ake, ake, ake* out of their pink and naked throats,
through their beaky carved lips
the darlings. Aroha ki ngā rangatahi e.

The man is a guest in the body of his woman
too late to cry rape at the time of the golden wedding
surrounded by congratulations and grandchildren.
The rapist has long since mutated into the househusband
he shares the chores now, would even change nappies.
Long years he has tilled the soil and with good husbandry
grown lamb, wool, cream and kiwifruit.

Her virgin beauty has slipped away, is now a guest in the memory
is the unseen party at the banquet
gives power to the knife that cuts the cake
and in time will reclaim the couple and all the guests, calling them home.

(1986)

Māui steals time

To Stephen Hawking

Misshapen in a wheelchair, keyboard happy
plucking the fiery fingernails of time
wracked by his premature disease which cradles
this curious man as he is drawn towards
the sharp-toothed entrance to the waiting womb
he spells the legends out to his proud brothers
uncertain and grave tidings relative
to the pebbled eternities he calculates

He baits the hook with his own blood and throws
the long flax line far out to sea, stretching
it out like starlight, teasing back; what fish
will rise between the palpable equations?
Time's club will beat and slow the rapid suns
Will Māui raid the database of God?

(1992)

Uenuku

Out from the unencompassed past you stand
beaming your radiance on us, Rainbow-named
Stranger to time yet owning those your kin
who flank you, softer spirals to your spines,

their fingers locked inside their rounded forms.
Who was the bold one turned yours round, up, free?
Body reaching out from embedding wood
sends the bands arcing in defiant waves;
Visible spectrum spans a watery sky,
combs out its ghostly locks by mirrored light,
watches the gathering masses from on high

Uniquely formed, inscrutable response –
rejecting questions that enquire too close.
But to all those protected by that power
such secret knowledge may we feast on there
that we too may float free and walk the air.

(1986)

Watercress

We sensed the place from fifty yards
as we passed the white upstanding trees,
then walked along the railway, on the sleepers,
or holding hands to balance on the lines.
Charcoal rock intruded under our feet,
gorse interfered on the side.
We knew the storm was coming, by the wind and the oddly yellow light
but we thrust through the gorse to the fence
tearing up young pūhā shoots as we went
to go with the watercress we hoped to find.
You said, dreamily, this doesn't look like watercress
    country
but we spotted the barrow, a small swelling
as if the earth was trying to hide something under
    her coat
I was embarrassed at intruding on something
    private

I felt I should walk away
Burnt gorse and mānuka, and a cabbage tree
With the first peal of thunder we were knee-deep
   in mud and watercress
We filled our kit, letting the rain soak us
searching the mound for bogs, penetrating the
   earth's secret places
feeling in each patch of mud for food.

(1986)

Ocean of tongues

So many busy tongues, they are like an ocean
washing me this way and that, like a piece of seaweed –
Do your worst! I deny nothing
Whatever you can think up to say about me
I admit in advance –
I do not intend to argue
I am tossed about, clinging to bits of wreckage from my canoe
hoping to rebuild it out of the broken ends
Would you think it justice if I drown?
Do not come to my rescue, the steering paddle has rotted
I would rather take my chance in the sea than be pierced by rot –
Rather, see to the paddle!
I will climb aboard the approaching ship that offers protection –
Meantime I remember my powerful ancestors and keep swimming

(1988)

KELLY ANA MOREY

Kelly Ana Morey (Ngāti Kurī, Te Rarawa, Te Aupōuri) is an award-winning writer, journalist and oral historian. She was one of the inaugural recipients of the Janet Frame Award (2006), won the Best First Book of Fiction with *Bloom* at the Montana New Zealand Book Awards in 2004, and held the Michael King Maori Writer's Residency in 2014. She has written four novels and three non-fiction titles, and tries to write a poem a year, not always successfully. She is a writer/photographer and copy-editor for *Show Circuit*, an equestrian magazine, and is currently writing a novel about Phar Lap, which will be published at the end of 2015.

Ture te haki

. . . you fly your flags of history quietly
for now
battle pendants hidden in wooden boxes
in blackened rooms
rotting and fading into dust under
well intentioned eyes
that wonder at your beauty and your stories and
your size
no land beneath the wool and cotton
and silk
the star of David, the cross of Mikaere and the
wounded heart
bleeding
no way for you to come home
you sit and wait for darkness to go quickly
for light to fall on your ruined threads
the flags are quiet
for now . . .

(1999)

Ordinary clothes

Sometimes I never want to wake.
Leave me in my ordinary clothes.

Pull me from sleep and push me down everyday garden paths.
Steer me into scented traps laid for the blind.
Smother me in a bed made of feathers and dark fern.
Then cast me adrift in a dishwater sea
with only coral and kraken for company.
But please
        please leave me in my ordinary clothes.

Wind me through your fingers until I'm abraded and worn.
Imprison me in a room that never sees the sun.
Perhaps throw me out of a moving car into the night
With no way home, without light or map or sign.
Or abandon me in a river in a brown paper sack.
With a weight around my neck, so I can't come back.
But please
        please leave me in my ordinary clothes.

You could break me in half or swallow me whole.
Hold me so hard I simply can't breathe.
Crushing me beneath your ocean of greed.
Wrap me in tendrils made of roses and thorns.
Carve your name into my skin with hammer and claw.
Recount all my failings, the scars, my flaws.
But please
        please leave me in my ordinary clothes.

But in the end you will lead me,
then lose me in a forest of tall trees.

Bury me tenderly in a shallow grave please.
But leave me
        leave me
        leave me
        in my ordinary clothes.

(2012)

Sticky ending

Because these are the days
when unkindness hasn't been invented yet
we are bare boned and snow blinded
And although it's far too early in the season
to burn bridges or build memorials
I do anyway.

Stripped of peel and pith
all that is left
is the juicy bruise
of a badly worded apology
and the sticky weep of blood oranges on a white plate.

Like there's a short answer and a long answer
to every question.
The memory of winter fruit
and wood smoke
both promised a messy ending.

(2012)

Mother's Day

It was the smallest of occurrences, my mother's death.

Don't bury me next to your father, she rasped.
And I laughed, turned the page of a year-old Woman's Weekly
No bloody fear!
Then she started to die from her toes and up
disconnecting.
Her broken breaths.
Each further away from living than the last.

If I had known everything,
how it would all unravel, these faded tatters of her lost history.
I would have told her
to run and run and run, for her life while she still could
never once looking behind her.
Not even to say goodbye.

So we took her home to Stratford.
And put her in the ground between two strangers.

(2011)

PAULA MORRIS

Paula Morris (Ngāti Wai, Ngāti Whātua) was born in Auckland in 1965, and has spent much of her adult life in the United Kingdom and the United States. She is the author of the story collections *Forbidden Cities* (Penguin, 2008); the editor of the *Penguin Book of Contemporary New Zealand Short Stories* (2009); and the author of seven novels, including *Queen of Beauty* (Penguin, 2002), *Hibiscus Coast* (Penguin, 2005) and *Rangatira* (Penguin, 2011), fiction winner at the New Zealand Post 2012 Book Awards and Ngā Kupu Ora Māori Book Awards. In 2013 she published her first book for children, *Hene and the Burning Harbour*.

English grandmother

You arrive on a boat, your suitcase ripe
with soap and chocolate. It's 1970. You're
not sure what you can buy here, how
civilised we'll be.

For me, there's a beautiful doll with auburn hair.
She is so foreign and surprising that I call her
Alison, a name I barely know and don't really like.
At Christmas you give us a swing-set.

There you sit, on a hard-backed dining room chair
– never the floor, like our real grandmother, the one
who calls us her mokopuna. You think that sitting
down to read the newspaper is lazy.

My sister is English and yours, but we're strangers
to you, my brother and I. You don't smile much.
I'm an odd little brown girl. I don't talk much.
He refuses to kiss you.

Now, I think, we could love each other. Like you,
I douse my food with black pepper, and festoon
the house at Christmas. I like to stand up
to eat my breakfast, to read the newspaper.

After a year you go back to England, disappointed,
relieved. We get a new dining table – round and
white – with chairs that swing. Don't swing,
says my mother. She is still your daughter.

(2013)

Pontefract

An icy wind at this high point. The
castle has crumbled away. We need
signs and pictures to make sense of it.

The tower where Richard was held, where
they starved him to death, is pale blue sky
and stony stubs. All the walls are gone.

In place of trees, chimneys sprout across
the plain, the ground below honycombed
with long-closed mines and sooty tunnels.

Next week there will be an accident
down there – a truck and a van of girls,
a hen party, strewn across the road.

Two cold months Richard spent here, waning
in the dusk of his room, not thinking
it possible that the tower could fall.

(2013)

Where

Where are you from, I ask the waiter.
He is from Brazil, Poland, Florence.
Sometimes he is from Mexico, and I
say: so is my nephew's fiancée.

In Auckland the taxi driver who lives in
Henderson is from Afghanistan. There are
forty of them there, he says. They love it, though
they have to make their own bread.

In New York the taxi driver is from Pakistan.
He asks me where I'm from, and wants to
talk cricket. His dream, he says, is to live
with his brother in Bradford.

In Auckland the dentist is from Brazil. In
Sheffield the café owner is from Auckland.
In London our waiter is from Glasgow.
In Glasgow our waiter is from Melbourne, like

my doctor in Iowa City, the nose specialist,
who leans over me on the operating table.
Where are you from, he asks me.
I tell him Auckland. Good on ya, he says.

Sometimes in Auckland the taxi driver is
from Auckland. He is not from anywhere
but there. My dream, I tell him,
is to bring back the trams.

(2013)

JUSTINE MURRAY

Justine Murray was born and raised in Rotorua. With parents originally from Tauranga Moana, she is Ngāi Te Rangi on her father's side and Ngāti Ranginui through her mother. 'I have always loved creative writing and poetry. When I was eight years old, my classmates and I wrote a picture book that was so popular with other classes that we adapted it to a play. That's my earliest memory of the power of story.' Married to Regan Murray, she is currently based in Wellington where she works as a producer in radio.

Staunch

I saw them gathering just before nine
a tidal wave of blackness as they congregated
en masse
amongst the crap grey sky huddled
an All Black team only small
and grey, and old
and willing, the weather
didn't faze them

Buckets of rain hailed from
one empty sky
as they sat and waited
and waited
11.30 came

They spoke and sat and sang
and spoke and sat and sang
and spoke and sat and sang
until the sun faded down from the
empty sky

Staunch as they sang
staunchy as they sat
staunch as they waited and waited
and slept

(2012)

To dream

To conclude is to decide
a dream that I have
it doesn't shine, but it waves
in its truest form

a kaleidoscope in a sense
of wonderment
as it dances
down the windy path

of Waiōuru, in an army
parachute spinning over
Desert Road
it reminds me of you

To become intertwined
like a lake and all in it
who slumber?
This is my true dream of you

(2012)

DEIRDRE NEHUA

Ko Huruiki me Taranaki ngā maunga; ko Ngāti Hau me Ngāti Rehua ngā hapū; ko Ngāti Wai me Ngāpuhi me Ngāti Ruanui ngā iwi; ko Deirdre Nehua ahau. Deirdre Nehua is a proud Māori nationalist, a writer, poet, traditional healer and member of the World Council of Indigenous Elders. 'I was fortunate to have had my grandmother Ani Kaaro Nehua Strongman instil in me her love of the written word', she says, 'and to have the beauty of my home, the Whangaruru Harbour, where rests my heart, to nurture that love.' Deirdre Nehua reads and shares her poetry with indigenous peoples all over the world. This poem was written a few months after her husband Syd Jackson died.

The abyss

I remember
when my heart would leap
at the thought of you
when the sound of your voice
the nearness of you
set my heart pulsing to a quarter moon
tumbling from mountain tops
where it caught the rhythm of yours
now as I lurch thru life
my heart pulses with pain
and I fall into the abyss
again and again
but you're not there
to catch me

(*January 2008*)

MOANA NEPIA

Moana Nepia (Ngāti Porou, Ruawaipū, Te Aitanga a Hauiti, Rongowhakaata) had an international career as a dancer and choreographer before retraining as a visual artist. He is now assistant professor at the University of Hawai'i in the Center for Pacific Islands Studies, helping to develop courses with a focus on arts and performance in the Pacific. The poems here were written as part of a creative, practice-led thesis entitled *Te Kore: Exploring the Māori Concept of Void*, for which he was awarded a PhD from AUT University in 2013. Recent writing includes work in *Ora Nui* in 2012 and in *Of Other Thoughts: Non-Traditional Ways to the Doctorate: A Guidebook for Candidates and Supervisors*, edited by Tina Engels-Schwarzpaul and Michael Peters, in 2013.

Ka tangi te ruru

Ka tangi te ruru
alone in the night . . .
rising, circling . . .
echoes reply . . .

fall to river,
stone and shore.

Koutuku north,
through floating mists,
ki Whetūmatarau . . .
my grief-laden tears

fall to river,
stone and shore.

Grasp these weary bones
and carry me home.

Let paddles sink deep,
into beating hearts . . .
direct,
swiftly,
to follow the tide.

Keep silver cliffs close,
so our faces be seen,
with incoming tide,
and warm rising sun.

At Kakepo rest,
canoes hauled high.

Let the traps be set,
and the rats be caught.

My people will feed you,
my mana restored.

(2012)

Kihikihi

Transparent messengers
feed dream-times
to store . . .
and walk about trails
to wander . . .
blind, burrowed, deep.

Memories layered,
spat upon silent root . . .
claw, crack and crevice . . .
emerge and release!

Under cover of night,
from coastline dawn . . .
Mai ngā pōhatu katoa . . .
Kua takahurihuri nei
Mai Kakepo ki te tihi
o Tawhiti nui . . .

Un-corseted waists
and shedding lungs . . .
heave in cacophonous roar.

Dance clapping knees
rise up
blood-flushed flight
Kei te wawā roa

>   *Ko wai tērā . . .*
>   *huri rā i ngā rori?*
>
>   *Ko te kihikihi . . .*
>   *haere ora i te ao e!*

(2012)

I held you

I held you in my arms
as you took your last breath.
And now you are gone.

Between us,
numb,
an empty stanza,
quiet pain.

Hope, memories flood

>   *E kore e mutu mai ngā wawata e*
>   *Me waiho i roto, te manawa e . . .*

And I am here
now to make of this,

just as you did,
from absence and loss,
and memories of other happier times
all sorts of wondrous,
imaginable, possibilities.

To create
is also sensing
you there,
then, and also here,
in that potential,
now . . .

> E kore e mutu, te aroha e,
> Ka pūmau tonu rā,
> I ngā wā katoa, ngā wā katoa . . .

. . . with words,

the spaces between them
and memories
enveloping, gathered, aligned,
shared,
part of me now
for a new awareness to emerge . . .

of momentary shifts,
tugs and pulls
upon body senses,
muscle and bone . . .
controlling,
positioning,
emotional forces,
hovering,
tilting, in-between

holding sway.

At some distance,
reflecting upon reflection,
he adds words from another source,

his other language
and their translations
... mokopuna, whānau ...
tender lines from Moetu's love songs
speak of a Kore
never ending,
commitment and eternity.

He presses these words
into his own expression of loss
and uncertainty
into the warmth and sway of his body
listening.

The video loops, fades through white,
washes over him,
recedes to find the line repeated twice
already
repeated again ...

> *E kore te aroha e taka e*
> *I waho i taku Manawa ...*

A familiar line,
similar pattern,
another song,
another page,
the same book,
but from another time,
and with another translation.

Tuini gathered meaning
through gathering others to perform,
repeating messages through song,
offering through repetition
within different songs,
and sometimes within the same song
as well,
subtle inflections
and turns of phrase . . .
turning one meaning into and onto
another for others to follow,
melodies, actions,
tunes to words . . .
sentiment, augment,
reflect, enhance.

Nothing Nothing gains in stature,
repeating, colour, meaning and depth.
Nothing, nothing, not always heard,
but painted absent, vivid with words.

The sheet remains,
an intransigent hush

with the devotion
of distant traffic humming
on Karangahape Road,
thought is transcribed, written . . .

and with the devotion and faith of
curiosity, a procession
of connecting steps emerges

Ara, course of action,
evolves un-scripted,
revealing form,

awakening thought,
between what has already been made,
what was always there,
travelled, placed,
whispered,
sung, touched
shouted and danced . . .

before

(*2012*)

MICHAEL O'LEARY

Michael O'Leary is a poet, novelist, publisher, performer and bookshop proprietor. His work in poetry, fiction and non-fiction, in both English and Māori, explores his dual heritage: Māori on his maternal side and Irish Catholic on his father's as well as his mother's. Born in Auckland in 1950, he was awarded a PhD from Victoria University Wellington in 2011. His Earl of Seacliff Art Workshop imprint has published some 150 books by New Zealand writers as well as writers from other countries. The compilation *25 Years of the Earl of Seacliff* (2009) documents his oeuvre. Michael O'Leary is a trustee for the Poetry Archive of New Zealand Aotearoa (PANZA). He now lives in Paekākāriki, north of Wellington.

He waiatanui kia Aroha

For Winsome Aroha

i

twilight falls
among the large stone buildings
grey monoliths – but undemanding
to the modern eye
as we walked towards the taxi
I stopped and wanted to kiss you

and you said maybe
- 	then we did kiss
holding our mouths together like beaks
- 	but sweet, ambiguous even
and I shuddered with emotion
- 	my whole being shook
- 	with the physical knowledge
- 	of our parting . . .

ii

      before we had met that evening
I had felt the fear and longing
of anticipation
– the uncertainty of what to feel
I sat in a café and drank slowly
a cool glass of orange
watching you
on the other side of the road
for a few moments
as you watched and waited
for signs of me
– then I drained
    the remaining liquid
      from the glass . . .

iii

I took your arm as we walked
to our meeting eating place
our time out to be together place
where time goes in split seconds
so that an hour seems a minute
- 	is gone too soon and forever

and out is what happens
    at the end of time . . .
    but those precious moments
we are there, in our time capsule,
make up for all our partings
    because I know what it's like
    to be without you . . .
All the years of wanting you
    have softened me up
    have made me sensitive
to the moments we are together
so that I treat each one
    like a treasure: taurite he taonga . . .

iv

you apologised for crying
(about your family) as we talked
– don't apologise to me, Winsome,
you have probably not given
    a show of emotion
(I was going to say weakness –
but I meant vulnerability)
    private or public, too often
but I have cried openly
for the want of you
for the fact that we must be apart
– so don't apologise to me . . .

v

    twilight brings
its gradual descent of the night
on Seacliff

        and the sea and
        the clouds touch
merge into one blue-grey hue . . .
as with the sky
and the land
the trees turn ever darkening
shades of green
the last remaining residue
        of crimson
is stretched, elongated
        diffuse across the horizon
        and these seen things
        are mirrored within
        as my thoughts of you
        are repeated over and over
        ever changing
        ever increasing with the days
        the same subtle blend as landscape
of colours and shapes
sometimes clearly defined
        sometimes barely discernible
        and sometimes
        the darkness is complete

vi

the incomplete nature of our beings
and the knowledge
        glimpsed at through you
of what we need
        to bridge that
                separation . . .

vii

the light beyond the horizon
  is te Marama
  who, when she shines
  touches the silent, sleeping
  soul of the earth
it is this unseen world
alive with the light
  of the unknown
where my love for you
  lies waiting –
beyond those tall trees
that rising darkness
and sensuous sundown
of strange, stark colours
te pō, te pō, te pō aroha
  the moonlight world
  of our understanding
  the Polynesian darkness
  of light . . .

viii

the other day
we met
  in a public way –
friends talking
a hongi
  and a kiss
from a girl
  who said you were too much for her
so much so
that she had to go
  (followed by dreadlocks, himself)

and the bond between us
couldn't help itself
as we embraced with a passion
and stood holding hands
– despite all that was around us

ix

the evil within me
which struggles for possession
of my mind and soul
in the ancient attempt
to bring me down
as it has done for generations
before and after me
–   is quelled
        by my responsibility to you

x

later I heard your telephone voice
full of the cares of domesticity
but still sweet
and coming from deep
within our history
so that despite the aloofness
and separateness
I sometimes feel
from your life
there is always a place
        at which we touch

xi

    the candlelight flickered
    and I was half in a dream
        – more like a feeling of missing
        you and not knowing you
    I stepped outside
    and there the moon was rising
    like the tip of a lightberg
    shining through the dense
    cloud cover
    and I thought
        this is how I know you
        distant
            with slowly
                evolving revelation . . .
    I am trying to think of you
    I am trying to imagine
        what you look like
        and all I can do
        is feel your absence
        like a mystery waiting to be solved
    I cannot be near you
    at our timeout of the month
    and the full moon is hiding behind the rain
    (the tears of Rangi, e Papa)
    the sky is filled with separation
    the horizon is the natural split
    between (the sea) the earth and the sky
        – but there is no split
        because there is
            no touching

xii

        a picture of you
        looks up, smiling
        and connects me
to the world of feelings
the deep questions of life and
love and eternity
which have had their evocation so often
        through you
you are my point
        of contact with life, yet
you are so distant and yet again
that distance is
        broken
as the fine fibre of love you weave around me
        tightens – it is
the dynamics of something set in motion
rather than necessarily an act of consciousness
–   the earth is sleeping
    dreams are walking around, entering
    each heart, each body –
each soul is enchanted either by dreams
or nightmares haunting the darkness
with ever greater darkness
        te ua, te ua, ngā roimata ahau
        te haunui o te wairua
        te ariki o te ao
and in the beginning was the word . . .

xiii

wrapped in a blanket
I sit and listen
to the wind blow

hard out along the coast
whipping up the water
scraping and shaping the land –
sending chunks of sure cliffs
crashing to the sea below . . .
cold wind was always
the worst to work in
sapping energy from my body
even before the first shovel-load
had been lifted from the earth
taurite ngā moehewa o Aroha . . .
but now the wind has dropped
perhaps it will wait –
then picking up my words
Te Hau will carry them
soaring southwards
over the dark hills
taking them gently
kia Aroha, down the valley
where they will reach you
as a whisper . . .

(1994)

Kia Aroha – rua

we sat silent at the foot
of the poet's statue
I had put my coat around you
to keep off the southern evening coldness
and, with my arm around your shoulder
we waited in the Octagon
for the time we would no longer be together

which came soon enough –
as your husband's car came to a stop
at the traffic lights
my arm moved instinctively away
and the seeds of the trees
which necessarily separate us
are again planted

but each time
we are apart we grow together
like an unseen river
beneath the surface of our lives
the aroha
is between us
as well as the distance

and that evening
we had laughed and danced, sung
and talked of death and darkness and light
the best thing was that we were happy
as we walked from the restaurant
to sit silent at the foot
of the poet's statue

(2003)

Hone Tuwhare: a personal memoir

E hoa, you have gone to the place beyond
that tug-of-war which was your life: that
struggle between North and South which
even continued after you were laid to rest.

But it was always like that with you: they
wanted you there while you were elsewhere.

Both of us, we were different kinds of poets,
Railway Workers first, comrades, drinkers

This koha o ngā kupu ki aroha is from
the centre: where the break in the rail
lies. And in the old days when we locked

our horns together in a hongi like bulls, we
who hear the magic whispers of sensual
kai-words, knowing it is ata-kahurangi in flight.

(*Paekākāriki, Waitangi Day, 2008*; 2008)

Bastion Point – Koha 22/5/88

Watching Koha last night
while people talked of pots and pans rattled
– it was like trying to understand
surrealism when all you feel is anger
the bland, semi-digested meal of television
feels heavy in the gut
– some things just won't break down

As those army trucks
rolled along the waterfront drive towards Ōrākei
the politics of Muldoonery (inherited from
the orange North of Ireland) was revealed
five hundred police surrounded
old men and women, children and dogs
young female and male warriors

All received the great Kiwi Koha
as the flightless bird blundered around
the ordinary bloke had struck a blow
for democracy – as with Rua, as with 1951

as with 1981 – this hapless nocturnal stuck
its beak out. When the first Great New Zealand
1 kg explodes we'll know the worm has turned

(2003)

For my father in prison, 1965

Doing time
        my father would have needed time to do this

To build a table
        made from matchsticks, our only family heirloom

Matchstick upon
        matchstick held together with some kind of glue

Just like the
        brick building which held him

Yes, that's it
        stone upon black stone which kept him captive

He entered through
        the heavily bolted steel door they held open

And when he emerged
        he had a matchstick table and was very quiet

Each matchstick
        represented a fragment of his life

Each fragment
        was there outside him, set in a glue and he was a shell

(1985)

Poem to your grandmother

i

digging up the ground
so that her life-long partner
could rest with her
      they found
her long long silver hair
      pride of her womanhood
had tangled round and round
the root of a breadfruit
          tree
in time, without a sound
woman and tree had merged
she had become nature
out of sight, underground

ii

but, as though to stake his claim
and make her not forget him – not
for something so simple as a breadfruit
          tree
her, her human love – I'll say husband
had died
      could only live one year without her, rather
and her breadfruit tree had to give her up

iii

a tree grows on a mound
of earth, under which he and she lie
in death as they had done in life,

together now without a sound
woman and man and tree have merged
have become nature hair and root and heart
out of sight, underground

(1984)

TRU PARAHA

Tru Paraha (Ngāti Hineāmaru, Ngāti Kahu o Torongare, Ngāpuhi) is an artist working within the fields of contemporary choreography, live art and performance. She has a Master's degree from the University of Auckland. She has worked extensively in Aotearoa and Europe, the United States, Asia and the Pacific as a dancer, choreographer and arts educator. Tru has featured as a guest writer at the Michael King Writers' Centre, Auckland Matariki Festival, Poetry Live, Kupu Rere, the Aotea Centre Festival and the Parnell Rose Festival. Her publications include commissioned performance texts, dance writing and analysis (*Theatreview, Yellingmouth, HINE-*), and poetry (*Blackmail Press, Intimate Kisses*).

Knowing entirely everything on Earth that is

To the poet Ai

Then, my argillite heart

struck by the mallet
split-halved apart
twin stone-adzes forming

with sacred names.
Out, from that
ragged canyon flew

eagles and a wild hawk;
dust storms;
leviathans; a butterfly

from some archaic
fortress.
Enslaved to my calling

I bartered with the gods
for a life, unutterably
sensual, revealed

my naked anarchy in
gold and vernal offerings,
feasted on solitude.

Knowing entirely
everything on Earth that is
I tend the questioning
seeds of a furrowed brow.

Allow me, to astonish
to astound
– first, as a woman,

then enter into my gorgeous
storehouse of bliss.
Ask me anything, *ask me*.

I am pure,
perfect, ignorance.
I know less than nothing.

(2010)

Northern territory of my bone-trail dream walking

i walk to the mountains, scale their various peaks, then settle awhile unmeasured

to glean out across sentinels and ocean-breaks.

Not for succour or my art, nor respite from the city where a hundred lovers war,

but to feel that mountain under me, it is enough, a mountain is unmovable

                                                            i am not its equal.

i walk to the waterfalls, trek the sleek taniwha where colossal wells descend

plunging the hunger and eager rage of water.

Not to bow to its credence, or seek absolution, not to purify my soul's wrecked institute;

but for the rare event of its voice i cannot comprehend. Water falls,

                                                  it is enough that i listen.

i walk to the caves (though it is forbidden) enter the uterine citadels to dwell

within those swollen arcs where glow-worms secrete.

And this is not a return to self, or archetypal ancestress, or a breed of religion,

but a pulsing through the dark for darkness sake. Caesarean night has no claim on me i am unborn.

i walk to the meeting houses, alongside stretch marked roads, gather deft handfuls

of waewae koukou, pūriri, to weave a grief garland.

Not for adornment, or custom, or for laying down at the heels of the dead,

but for each bone in my valley. The corners of the house can be seen,

                              the corners of the heart are hidden.

i walk to the gardens, vast cultivations of earthfruit in succulent yield, tread middens

and soil primed in the branch-burnings of rātā.

And i have not come here for tasting, or harvest, or to cram my hybrid seed into the wild

– just to witness the vividness of butterflies trembling over flower heads and foliage

                                      i cannot see beyond.

(2012)

Elegy

For Hone Tuwhare

Before dying,
commune with the mountain;
whirl like a dervish
remembering how.

Stars will grieve,
mating with flowers;
surrender, the red earth
as she opens.

After living,
prostrate by the river:
a thousand kisses
to a sunset sky.

Oceans will heave
salty with longing;
salute, the deep blue,
she tenderly yields.

While passing,
caress in the tree tops;
moan your delight
to a dawn song of bird.

Lovers will leave,
drunken with arrows;
forgive, the dark moon
she gently destroys.

(2008)

Core subjects

she was good at math
        but things didn't add up

                for instance the stats predicted she should've
              been in the lower rung academically
                  and at most getting C's instead of
                      A's or failing simple geometry

her one plus one would equal
one each.

she excelled at English
        yet, read between the lines

                technically I'd have expected some muddles
                      over *Green beans and Mash* (with a smart buddy)
                        not reading Yeats in playground huddles
                          and scanning through pages of poetry

that first year, hers was the
winning speech.

she had a brain for science
        still the data seem off

                when tests indicate a tendency to find
                      Western modes of thought and assessment very
                    complex for the Indigenous mind
                      let alone the demands of chemistry

know that she learnt what they
could not teach.

(2009)

In the belly of the paradox

universe rant
immaculate womb
         i die infinity
star particle reborn

beyond chorus of extinction distinctly resounding by forest lake swamp
         skin offering
beside furrowed bean pea beet potato courgette near Bastion pā bunkers
         to church palisade
behind middens broken glass backyard State-digs inside temple pot-hole
         terrestrial cave
atop mountain hiccupping vegetal thunder across continent romance
         tectonic hot plasma
over trail of ancestor revolutionary quest within border line territory
         hundred rank priestess
beneath province town village neighbourhood armour under sky bird
         leaf weaving
between pounamu doors of peace flag descendant around flower field
         shimmering colour scent hue
around blue planet atom incorrigible tomb between quantum existence
         tomorrows return
under current flow reign rip unorthodox tide beneath parameter
         endogenously made-in-NZ
within seagull bowels aftermath to a feasting over terraces bat cravings
         latent artillery
across silage sea shark wild ray piranha inside crater red scoria where
         cattle graze
behind skull valley croonings elusive insomnia near sub urban
         landscrape excavation trash
beside viaduct carbons ceremonial breathtank by adzes discovering lost
         new island

                    to a sleepwalker freedom oceanic wet dreaming

in the belly of the paradox

in the nerve-spine of the conundrum

    at the lip of the precipice

at the turn of the golden century continuum

to one divine origin progressively revealing by sperm whale beached in
    indelible sand
beside musket death warrior nursing moist seed near convoluted politics
    urban drift thesis
behind unveiled dawn maiden deadly inheritor inside dancing trenches
    such peach ripe wonder
atop skytower tongue piercing steel leviathan across kauri blood gum dug
    sweet wilderness
over land women lost art buried semen within tenuous griefs our flung far
    carrions
beneath placenta tree nourishing future prophecy under lore of
    continuance hope omnipotent
between lovers agape in deep flesh mystery round eye petalled children
    blinking dark unity

in the belly of the paradox

in the nerve-spine of the conundrum

    at the lip of the precipice

        watched
at the turn of the golden century continuum   once

        the sun
        the

```
                                                    moon
                                                    make
                                                    love
            make

                                                    fuck o
                                                    bled

                                                    celestial

                                                    orgasm
                                                    into
            clouds

            and then
                                                    me

            ?

            (2012)
```

EVELYN PATUAWA-NATHAN

Evelyn Patuawa-Nathan was born in 1933 and is of Ngāpuhi, Ngāti Torehina, Ngāti Hau and Ngāti Maniapoto. She is the author of a collection of poetry, *Opening Doors* (Mana, 1979). She is believed to be the third female Māori writer published, after Patricia Grace and Vernice Wineera. Evelyn lives in Sydney, where she has worked both as a teacher and as a tutor in women's prisons.

Summer in the Kaihu Valley

I return with summer to my village
the same poplars stretch and unfurl
taking care not to squander

a moment, just watching
the flow of the Kaihu
in her seaward quest.
Now summer prods, impatient
with a finger of ardent reason,
whispering new secrets
promising to retell things
forgotten by my jaded senses.
Fresh hues on a bushland canvas.
She holds aloft scarlet-tipped fingers
halting the hours
so I may know again
this hesitant valley of my birth.

(1979)

Old man and his dog

The old man
was expecting a visitor,
an important one.
He washed and shaved, carefully,
then put on a suit.
A government visitor.
He let the dog loose
before going to sit
on the verandah seat
where he observed the road
three hundred yards away.
He whispered to the dog
fondly in Māori,
gave him a bone
and patted him.
The dog responded, tail wagging
and nuzzled him back,

then took his bone
down near the road
and waited.
The old man dozed gently
on the verandah.
It appeared no thought
could animate his leathery face
immobile in its balaclava frame.
In time he was joined
by a grandchild
who shook him alert.
Briefly they spoke, heads together,
exchanging platitudes the way
the very young will
with the very old
where there is love and trust.

(1979)

Waikato lament

Green wandering fingers
of kikuyu
prying into an old kūmara pit
playing over limestone belly
and naked rock
have not quite covered,
cannot hide,
the faded emblems
of a land-lost people.

Blood-soaked, in time's
memory
spirits of Taupiri
raise keening voices

anthem of injustice
echoing down
through the night.

(1979)

Aboriginal on the last train home

For ten years
he found himself
the last passenger of the day.
He was alone on the dim-lit
railway platform, and then
alone on the train with his ten cent ticket
folded in his pocket.
He laughed like a madman
with a mad secret, slapped his thigh
and took a swig from his can of coke.
He was happy the government was spending
all that money just to get him home.
Another ten such years of travel
and they would have paid him a fair price
for New South Wales.
He rocked with silent mirth
all the way back to the mission.

(1979)

Opening doors

Before opening the doors
onto the street,
to the curious eyes of the world
I open myself,

to make adjustments suitable
to the needs
required by the weather.
A brolly, rainhat, galoshes
or a flower to outwit
my flagging psyche,
maybe a brandy to support the flower.
Then I choose with care
the outer self I shall wear today.

(1979)

PARE PAUL

Pare Paul was named after her great-grandmother, Pare – a name she is very proud of. Raised by her grandparents in Aotearoa's sheep-shearing capital, Te Kūiti, Pare started writing during her college years in the late 1980s. Her love for writing 'short, silly' stories came from a passion for telling them. She enrolled in a creative writing class at Manukau Institute of Technology in 2011, where she acquired some very useful skills which she now incorporates into her own teaching.

Game on Punk!

Little bottom on cushions,
positioned for a showdown

Round one – **Fight!**
Fingers tap furiously
unblinking eyes fixated
mortal battles beast
smashing each other's skull in.
The ninja warrior
draws his silver blade,
samurai slices up
through rungs of bone and marrow,

a head rolls off and freezes
steel capped boots
cranium crushed to fragments
blood gushes into a pool
fatality awarded
Yeeeah! – snaps the little bottom on the cushion.
Game on Punk!

Round two – **Fight!**
A beauty in white flesh,
round-house kick in dazzling heels,
scatter his teeth into a red milky way
her too quick whip
slices down through iron shields
slashing of limbs
slams his nose into his helmet
a deadly kiss placed on his lips
his powerless soul claimed
O fuck! – says little bottom on the cushion.
Game on Punk!

Final Round – **Fight!**
Red-eyed beast
glares at the beauty
his jagged claws curl
her too quick whip lashes his neck,
peeling flesh from his arm.
His eyes ablaze
he quivers revenge
reaches past her intestines
clenches her vertebrae
grips every bone
rips out her spine her pelvis tibulas and femurs
immerses them in a pool of sweltering acid
burning flesh pours from her sockets
her brain mashed over brick walls

and her body dissolves into a smouldering pit.
Owned by Red-eyed beast.
Ohh Yeeeah! says the little bottom on the cushion.
My game Punk Ass!

(2014)

On court

Saturdays on seven
the high wired gates open
voices hiss and squeal.

Shoes scuff
the black tarmac bustles
legs flurry and bout

tempers rise and fall
eyes stab each with icy glares
the whistls shrill

a woman pumps her fists
short skirts flutter and freeze
knees lock to a halt
girls turn red and cry.

Hot salted chips file out
red sauce on steak and cheese pies.

Violent cheers hush
leather pounces stop
Browns Rd traffic dies.

(2014)

KIRI PIAHANA-WONG

Kiri Piahana-Wong is a New Zealander of Ngāti Ranginui, Chinese and English ancestry. She has degrees in law and English literature from the University of Auckland and is the publisher at Anahera Press. Her work has appeared in many journals and anthologies, most recently in *150 Essential New Zealand Poems* (Godwit, 2014), *A Treasury of New Zealand Poetry for Children* (Random House, 2014), *Dear Heart: 150 New Zealand Love Poems* (Godwit, 2012), and *Mauri Ola: Contemporary Polynesian Poems in English* (AUP, 2010). She is also a performance poet, and MC at Poetry Live, New Zealand's longest-running live poetry venue. Her first poetry collection, *night swimming*, was released in 2013.

Hinerangi

Near the end of my
days, I knew.
Time moved through
me like the wind.

With every outbound tide
I felt my breath receding,
my life running from me
like the river feeding
the bay. And the
longing.
I was tired.
I longed to merge my voice
with the world-song, become
a single drop in the ocean,
be everywhere and nowhere.

My skin felt too small.
With each turn of the moon,
I felt more hollowed and
so grey.

I spent these last weeks
atop the cliff above the bay,

looking westwards. Three
moons waned, grew fat and
full, and thin again. The sun
set each evening in my eyes,
as I kept vigil. Anchoring
myself deep in the earth, I
felt my roots grow deep
and strong.

I died there.
My sons and the husbands of
my daughters came and gathered
up my body and carried me down,
one last time across the long black
stretch of bay.
I was laid to rest in the ground,
in te urupā.
My bones are still there, but I am
gone now. I went on my last journey,
to Te Rerenga Wairua, the cape of spirits.
They called me, and I came. I flew.
I danced. I left, and I began
the long return.

Perhaps you would like to hear
I met him again in Hawaiki,
the afterlife. I did not. The truth is,
I did not care. All that I had bled
for in the world of tears I put aside
here. I existed as spirit.
I slid outside the trap of time.
I was more than myself now. And
I was less. I let the world-song
swallow me.

(2013)

Tidelines

6am –

The sun rising behind me
The sea roaring at my feet
On the lip of the precipice

Everyone hunched in quiet
boxes, houses scattered to
the hills, precariously leaning
towards the sea, here we are
surrounded, ready to surrender
the day to the surf, dissolving
other imperatives into the
dust, into the black iron-laced
sand, tracing the time
against the rising breeze,
the tide ticking in, the river
in flood, swollen by rain

And still time passes
it washes away my footprints
Every day I make new marks
imprints on the beach
lines on the page

I walk and I string words in long lines in my head
I write and I skip words across the page like stones

I let them sink
I watch them slowly spiral down
through my mind
Down and down, until they reach the ocean
Deeper, into the abyss of collective dreaming

Until they are no longer my words
Just a passing thought you were having

Early one morning,
in your bed,
in your house,
in Piha,
waiting for the tide to come in.

(2011)

Four paintings

In the morning
the light touches the walls
like a painting
the morning sun falling in thin brushstrokes
her hair a dark tangle
his face blurred with sleep

Painting #1: How She Fell In Love With Him

In this painting, she is wearing
the red dress she likes to sleep in
and it has fallen to her waist

He is naked
his arm curves around her
his mouth pressing against her neck
in the place she most likes
him to kiss her

Painting #2: Their First Fight

In this painting, she is sitting
in the outside area of a bar
wearing a black lace dress.
The night is a solid block of
darkness behind her.

He is sitting next to her, wearing
a pale green shirt, his hair
dishevelled, his back slightly turned
to her, facing away.

Cars pour past in streaks of
bright light.

Painting #3: Whatever I Said, I Didn't Mean It

In this painting he is standing alone
on an empty beach.

The sky stretches away in a blaze of light.

Painting #4: The Reunion

In the last painting she is
standing looking down a road

She is wearing a purple and gold
dress and her hair has blown
back from her face.

It is early evening. Above her
the sky is golden, wide open
and empty.

(2012)

On the day you left me it was raining

On the day you left me it was raining.
People were out in the streets, drinking
and playing, wearing wigs and silly hats,
stealing road cones and vandalising other
people's cars. All the windscreen wipers
on every car in my street were sticking
straight up. France was going to play
Wales later that day.

On the afternoon you left me it was raining.
I lay on the bed bleeding you away in pieces
Asking you to please stay one minute longer
Asking you to please come back to me
On another day
In another year
At another time that might suit you better

There was a sparrow on the tree outside my
window, chirping, and the wind was blowing
pink petals all over the lawn. I saw Gretchen
outside, in the garden, singing to her beans.

I had talked to you every day I carried you so
close to me. I had imagined you would have
your father's green eyes, my dark hair, and
all our excessive creativity, but naturally
without our most reckless qualities that would
have made you a troublesome child to raise.
I even talked to you about inconsequential things
Would you eat your vegetables or prefer
McDonald's like your mother
I apologised to you for our non-stop diet of Happy
Meals mixed with caffeine and potato-top pies
I wondered would you like vegemite or marmite
Would you have an imaginary friend

But on this day
I lay curled up, holding the clotted bloody
remains of you, and saying –
Please come back
I am sorry that I ever said I didn't want you
That I wished for one second that you weren't there
Please come back to me

The ambulance came and for a while I passed
out, and when I woke up Kyla was there.
She bought me a book of angsty female
poetry, the biography of Slash (to remind me
why it's a bad idea to date musicians), a pink
blanket with hearts on it, an apple, a banana,
a trashy magazine, a packet of grainwaves, and
some gingernuts. It is always a good idea to call
a mother when you have an emergency.

After a very long time the day ended. The sun
went down. Eventually it rose again. There are
so many birds calling, early in the morning, and
the sun on my face felt like a benediction.
Much later in the day, I walked to the beach and
saw that the tide was coming in. I lay on the beach
and ran the gritty sand through my fingers, and
thought of all the ways in which something you
never wanted could leave the most gaping
emptiness when it leaves you, and I wish
I could say the sight of the sea filling up
the beach eased some of that emptiness, but
all it did was remind me that every day, the
tide comes in, only to go out again.

(2012)

BRIAN POTIKI

Brian Potiki was born in 1953 into the Kāi Tahu, Kāti Māmoe tribes, and lives near Rotorua. He has written, directed and acted in five history plays set in the South Island, and in 2009 finished *Maranga Mai: Radical Maori Theatre in the 1980s*, a book about the play *Maranga Mai*, a seminal work of Māori theatre from 1980 to 1981 that he directed, co-wrote and acted in. His book of poems and songs, *Aotearoa*, was published in 2003 (Steele Roberts) and a book of plays, *Te Waipounamu, Your Music Remembers Me*, in 2007 (Steele Roberts).

jill

there's one thing that keeps me
from the whare pōrangi –
the thought that one day
i might own a battered lime-green volvo
& three things that keep me
from my grave –
the grandchild who astounds me with her poetry
the feckless love of humanity i get
from a second glass of guinness
your love
like
rain
on
a
green
leaf

(2003)

hone

*i can feel you making holes
in the silence rain*
i can feel you making holes
in my brain, hone
in my brain

hēmi & ani are gone
jean, harry & ron –
but i won't wait until i'm gone to say
you're my old man, hone
you're my old man

i can hear you making holes
in the silence rain
i can feel you making holes in my brain, hone
in my brain

(2003)

down at bluff

inside the lean-to taxi office
i remember those same smells & sensations
from visits i made with my mother
to two-storeyed wooden buildings
in mt victoria wellington

i walk into the open lobby
of the seaview guesthouse &
there's sunlight on a busted-up
chair on the verandah

i sense my father & uncles round here
recall my aunt sybil's story –
the night she &
owen watched beer from upstairs
running down the walls

(2003)

dutch portrait

rembrandt picked up an old bum,
on the waterfront, amsterdam;
took him to his studio
where a fire was lit
& gave him wine,
dressed him
in the robes of a king
& painted him *crying*.
a corduroyed roadmender
with handlebar moustache
on the road to anywhere –
he hangs suspended
on a gallery wall
& in the guise of a king
weeps for roads
he'll never mend

(2010)

it's all about feel

in late january, a summer sea
viscous as milk
and the air too hot for birds,
bees & butterflies,
i went for a dive

in grey plastic sandals
& black rugby shorts,
a ten-litre white bucket
in one hand –
groping, searching, seeking,
finding hoary orange
& black-encrusted mussels

the kelp,
having clung to the rocks for months,
looked at me lazily –
my hand,
as if under a skirt,
seeming to catch it off-guard

(2010)

hiroki's song

i know i have four more days to live
as i dreamt the other night
i am to be hanged
tēnā koe te whiti

they will not try you these Pākehā
they break their promises
think of me
tēnā koe te whiti

a Pākehā came to defend me
on the day before the trial
there were no friends
tēnā koe te whiti

i asked the court when i could speak
they said after the lawyer has finished
i was not asked
tēnā koe te whiti

i waited for them to ask me
the judge put on his black cap
to pass sentence on me
tēnā koe te whiti

(1990)

ROMA PŌTIKI

Roma Pōtiki was born in Lower Hutt in 1958. Her tribal affiliations are to Te Rarawa, Te Aupōuri and Ngāti Rangitihi. She is a playwright and commentator on Māori theatre, and has been a theatre performer and director of a Māori theatre company. She is also a curator and visual artist and has work in the permanent collection of the Dowse Art Museum in Lower Hutt. Her poetry collections include *Stones in Her Mouth* (IWA, 1992), *Shaking the Tree* (Steele Roberts, 1998) and *Oriori* (Tandem Press, 1999), a collaboration with visual artist Robyn Kahukiwa.

Bound to

bound together in the darkness
our faces push out of the night
man and woman struggle with each other
sigh and breathe as one wrist locks another
and hip bones press
flat against the boards.

catching and getting caught.
Māui's net is thrown
and scoops us both in its rough binding.

lashed by old seas
the new fish gasp and twist onto the shore.

one thigh rolls
the other slumps
a summer crescent hitches itself into the sky.

no one is crying,
we both smile.

(1993)

Te kōkā, te whare tangata

You present yourself, each kete yours to discover.
You blink and stare, but I do not know what you see.
Threaded to me still
my child and all those who reach back in time.
Whakapapa joins us to Tāne-nui-a-rangi and the womanly,
first formed self.

Hinetītama, I think of you now,
whaea to our earthbound beginnings.
It was you who shattered sound,
let the karanga fly
as you called your child to break into the outer world.

Cloak me as I watch,
the crescent pin is firmly fastened
and I clasp close the most precious gift of any time.

> In my excitement and relief, I see you standing –
> a house for the living in each generation, a welcome in death.

> As your status changed, so too mine.
> We weave ourselves to many lives.

> The living house, warm-blooded verdant shelter,
> from your diffuse light we face the sun.

(2004)

A cloak and taiaha journey

Dark shapes sing in my head
on the way to the Cape
a cloak and taiaha journey,
dusty road
a narrow skimp of dry land
on the way to an airless dive
– leap to infinity.

I nearly fall asleep
and in the near dreaming
see the skinny arms and bodies
of old ones
etched, chiselled and curled
their unearthly features holding the tatau of land,
sky and water.

They do not speak in the language of sound
but directly to the ones seeing them.
The black whorls that carve their limbs
are strong in shape
and delicately meet on each ridge,
each peak and feature.
When they dance it is light and deep
their thudding hardly noticed till you realise
a pattern of breathing.

I do not remember being born
and these ones similarly placed
continue to raise skin,
blow soft stinging currents on hair.

If they had stones in their hands
you'd feel them on the back of your neck
before you fell.

They are here in waves
in melting, creosote washes
the speechless tūpuna stamping out messages –
old codes
drop by drop, oil on the tongue

seeds.

They are everywhere
in the hills and mounds of this place
the women and men, the others.

Though I see a few there are many,
sinking and rising they renew themselves –
communicate.

(1996)

The decision of the taniwha

You think people don't know what you do
you think you have fooled them
with every smile
every kia ora
every kiss and nod.

You have been twisting and worming for a long time.

I have watched you getting people
to agree to things they don't understand,
watched you getting a quick yes
when the truth should be a considered no,
put up with your clever bullying
which passes as 'being political'
with those who don't know enough yet –

but the sharp mirror, the stony flint,
the tuatara heart and the decision of the taniwha
are coming.

You have been calling all of these through:
      the people you scared
      the hurt of those wronged
      the energy used to contain the fear
      the unsettled wairua of those affected by your craft.

All the power that was taken
will come back tenfold,
all the power will come back
and in the howl of a cleansing wind
and the surge of powerful currents
you will be carried to meet your creation.

Everything you most fear is travelling to you
everything you most fear is travelling
everything you most fear
is here already.

Even though you will want to think murder
it is you who called the taniwha
and you who will have to work for release.

The rest will dance a slow dance
in the light of her scales,
drink enough blood
to gather strength for the real work.

(1996)

Toetoe turn

Moon cloaks
pale and incandescent
waving above the bedroom window.

Toetoe rains,
falls down
drifts of wheaten silver, just-born green & yellow
the occasional amber-touched shower
and the traditional golden stem,
thin and proud in the night.

I dream of old women marching,
they hold the toetoe, toetoe above them –
in a procession they walk the earth
up the hills
to the meeting places
the heaving rocks
where she&he she&she he&he might be found.

Usually it is dusk or dark or dawn.

I have not seen them move together in the day
yet.

Torches flame the nightly light,
some say even the surface of rivers and lakes can show
the path.
Stumbling forward, or sedate and vaguely safe within
the known group,
striking out or treading slowly,
we hear we smell we see and sense
where we will move.

Moonstone & feathers
pāua and crab

mussel and tuatua
pipi and pūpū and oyster.

Toetoe, flax-seed
pīngao and tī-kōuka

all these adorn the cloak
I wear.

My mother, my father
leaders of the monumental procession –
each in turn, the moon's rotation.

(1996)

Flight

We have flown halfway round the world
to stand among lions.

They face us
stone and chiselled granite
the grins of an empire
holding the keys to a house of treasures.

We have been lovingly fitted into
a small room
but a small room it is
and in this space the red kōkōwai spills
and flies its angled journey above our heads
as karakia move amongst old ones
from a time that grows closer as we visit the past.

Red kōkōwai and suddenly
the room fills with the movement of the sea,
forests and tūpuna sighing and whirling slowly above us.

I close my eyes –
no Jesus in the temple
no exchange of money.

A bird spills ochre from its loving beak.
A gift to encourage the many journeys
of return.

Speaking out

To all the smug men
who think that speaking the reo is going to save them
who think that language makes them one better than someone else
particularly women.

To all the men who think that just being born
and speaking our own language
is enough
I'm telling you it's not.

No, it's not enough,
though it may win you a job in the new corporation
it may mean that Pākehā ask your advice and pay you
it may mean that Māori women who are intimidated by your supposed
knowledge
bow and curtail
and perhaps even sleep with you and have your children.

Getting a tohu degree means something,
but it doesn't give you the right to make others feel less-than-you,
less than you in your new-found opulence
pounamu-coloured opulence, Apple Mac opulence
citing your 'boil-up' past or your oppression.

You don't impress me
though I admire hard work and persistence, intelligence and

the ability to get things done.
It doesn't impress me if it tells lies about women,
if it ignores children, if it is so rigid
that it forgets justice in the insecure worry
that we will 'lose everything'.

In the rush to retain tradition I've even heard some men
(and women)
say that
women don't do the haka. What nonsense.
We always did, we always will.

For the truth to be told about a culture all parties have to be
in on it.
Especially if you want it to survive in a useful form.
So,
don't use the language as a weapon against each other.
It's a taonga, one of many,
not a gold Rolex fixed in one position.
Who defines time anyway?

MARAEA RAKURAKU

Maraea Rakuraku is Ngāti Kahungunu ki Te Wairoa, Pahauwera and fiercely Tūhoe, as are many of her aunties. 'This poem is dedicated to Aunty Nancy Timoti, the truthsayer; Maria Heu Rangi, who taught me about which sugar bowl got used at Matahi; my fellow aunties Mere, Hari and Leanne; and to the fiercest auntie of them all, my mother Ameria Rakuraku.' Maraea's writing appears in the University of Hawai'i journal *Call and Response* 79, *Huia Collections* 4 and 6 and the online journal *Shenandoah*.

Aunties are Boss

It doesn't matter how many babies you have, how many times you marry
    or divorce, how skinny or fat you become, how many degrees hang on
    your wall, how flash your car or house is or how old you get,
Aunties are Boss

They always talk to you like you are 14,
everything they say is a directive, even when it isn't,
there's a bed over there,
have a kai and get a cup of tea

They ask you to clean the wharepaku and then they do it properly when
    you've finished,
they suggest you 'throw your eyeballs around the wharekai' when you
    ask, where's the tea towel?
You then watch as their eyeballs swivel in their head when you ask,
    'where do the dishes go?'

They send you to the shop to get tomato sauce and back again five
    minutes later to get toilet paper,
they sack you off the computer as soon as they walk in the door,
they tell you to stop eavesdropping and leave the room when they are
    talking to your mother,
Aunties are Boss

They squeeze lollies into your hand when the other kids aren't looking,
they tell you, your tāne is not good enough for you
not directly
they do this, by ignoring him
for years,
they tell you, your wahine is not good enough for you
not directly
they do this,
by loving your children,
Aunties are Boss

They will remind you how precious you are in a Facebook post and
    message in all the other Aunties,
when your parents separate, they pay for your music lessons, school
    stationery bill and uniforms,
they send texts to your mother daily reminding her why she is better off
    without him,
Aunties are Boss

Aunties will tell you not to talk to Koro, Nanny or your Mother like that
and to pick that lip off the floor
and if they ever hear you talk that way to them again
you'll have them to answer to,
they will tell you to stop using Koro or Nanny like they're an EFTPOS
    machine,
they will tell Koro and Nanny to stop acting like an EFTPOS machine,
Aunties are Boss

Aunties are Dragon slayers
ready to plunge swords into the hearts of monsters,
Aunties are Taniwha crouching in the river
prepared to throw you back to shore should you stray too far,
Aunties are Patupaiarehe
silently watching from afar, certain that you will become exactly who
    you are meant to be as has been divined from your parents, your
    parents' parents and your parents' parents' parents

Aunties
Aunties are Boss

(2013)

VAUGHAN RAPATAHANA

Vaughan Rapatahana (Te Ātiawa, Ngāti Te Whiti) was born in Pātea, raised in South Auckland and is a long-term resident of Hong Kong. He has a PhD from the University of Auckland and a Poupou Huia Te Reo qualification from Te Wānanga o Raukawa. Published widely internationally in a variety of genres from fiction to original philosophy, he was semi-finalist in the inaugural Proverse Prize for Literature and highly placed in the 2013 *erbacce* Poetry Prize. He was poetry editor of *Māori and Indigenous Review Journal* until 2011 and co-author of *Teaching Poetry* (User Friendly Resources, 2011), the first Māori–English teaching resource in Aotearoa.

Aotearoa blues, baby

'typical bloody Māori'

she snitched,

assuming
me
one
of her kind;

'you don't look like a Māori'

her brazen
shibboleth,
when
I protest . . .

[smug
 &
spiteful,
            bourgeois
               &
            blinkered.]

another
   of

       the
           ilk

= my own cousin, on the *pākehā* side =

pukes
        out

the familiar
dead
homily:

'Māori are lazy, they don't want to work'

                          (where?)

'and end up in jail anyway'

                        (you wonder
why? *e mōhio ana ahau!*)

she
should have
known
better,

her
nasty
sneeeeeers

fulcrum
of
some
OTHER
caustic
core rage.

she
didn't intuit
my
own
inner
tube,

swell
fulminating,

just
about
ready to rupture,

r e a c h   o u t

& strangle her
in irredentist fury . . .

but then

'that brown one'
                                       (taku hoa wahine)
would have been

tino
mokemoke –
                                            (maybe)

– with me
      just
scratching
tats
                                    up
in
                                     ∧
Pare

– where
I'm
supposed
to be.

got those damned Aotearoa blues, baby
slicing through my soul
keep a man way down under, baby
never can be whole

(2011)

JEAN RIKI

Jean Riki is a media producer based in Sydney, Australia. Her tribal affiliations are Te Arawa and Ngāpuhi with matrilineal claims to Irish and Scottish heritage. These poems were previously published in the *Ora Nui* anthology of Māori and Aboriginal writing that gained exposure at the 2013 Frankfurt Book Fair. An earlier poem, 'I've Never Been To Malibu', was published in the first *Ora Nui* journal in 2012. A short story called 'Te Wa Kainga' was published in an anthology of Australian writing, *Waiting In Space* (Pluto Press, 1999), and was taught in Australian and New Zealand universities.

A third migration

Atutahi's gift

Ngā waka e whitu	Tokomaru, Tākitimu,	*He puts the boys to sleep with*
e tau nei	Kurahaupō,	*boogie every night*
Hoea hoea rā	Aotea rā,	*and wakes 'em up the sameway*
Tainui, Te Arawa,	Ngā waka ēnei	*in the early bright*
Mātaatua	hoea rā,	*They clap their hands and*
Hoea hoea rā	E ō tātou tūpuna	*stamp their feet*
		because they know how he plays
		when someone gives him a beat
		He really breaks it up when he

> *plays reveille*
> *He's the boogie woogie bugle boy*
> *Of Company B!!*

My skin aches
for the ice-cool silk
of Awahou stream.

Do you know it?
Once known
you never forget.

28 December 1980
Second migration day.

Belongings shipped & sold
Mum's tear stains
not yet dried

I've a new blue dress
and a Lady Diana haircut.

In the photo taken that day
Mum looks tired
she didn't sleep last night
and won't properly again
for at least a year.

Dad holds her close,

bearer of
Atutahi's face and semblance
and the same intentions
of an adventurer.

§

E Koro
I have no photographs
no remembered embrace
no sage words of advice
no memory of the sound of your voice,

you were gone
a dozen years before
I was born.

Stories are silenced
for the sake of children
and in doing so
future journeys are seeded.

I'll unweave your mystery
and it stings because
there is nothing to hold,

existence in story and anecdote
exposed and unfolded
like precious origami.

Forgive my mythmaking,

required to move you
from the ephemeral
to the visceral.

§

Tamatekapua's charisma
and wife-thieving ways
make an inheritor of me
of the First Migration

the oar in water
the chant in air
the kūmara in earth
the first explorers,

the beginning begins.

§

When Atutahi woke in
the North African desert

(A Company B-Boy)

did he long to see
the Rotorua steam uncurl
from the roadside?

Did he long
for the acrid assault
on the nostrils
of sulphuric recollection?

Did he join
to see the sights?

Or to escape

as his son did
to a dry-hearted island?

§

In ole Sydney town
the harbour twinkles
like a harlot
made up for the dance.

Red white candy stripes
at the top of the hill,

a capitalist Santa Clausian
gateway to debauchery.

Down at The Block
tales of Black Power
and White Idiocy

back up against buskers
and council workers

sweep past the homeless
and the tertiary educated.

This town bred me
and I love her for it,

but I want a divorce!

Or at least a trial separation.

§

Seeds are sown
by my Koro

It's Atutahi's Gift
for a third migration.

§

The sands and smells and sounds
of the African desert
speak to me now
in riddles in dreams,

the Sphinx mouths a cryptic question –

of what are you made
my restless and
wandering child?

(2013)

Last stations

> *'Familiar things lull us.'*
> *– Jeanette Winterson*

Tarkovsky's art
shifts glaciers
undisturbed for millennia.

Ancient fires are lit
and Carthage blooms again.

§

The streetlights
irradiate muted shades
like Scandinavian tile
resting silently on
a brace-let-ed arm
slender and brown.

Across from him
at the café,

elle dit:
'Je ne comprends pas.'

Malheureux,
il ne comprend pas aussi.

'You will forget my skin.'

He wants to say this
to her, shake it in to her

the way she's adding sugar
to her unmilked tea.

'You. Said. You. Would. Leave. Her.'

She can't believe
the ple-thor-a of
clichés set in rows
like the diamonds in
the rings he
gave her at the
        Jindy getaway.

Et Maman.
Toujours, Maman.

A decade of
something resembling Nirvana
annhilated in a
tsunami-sentence that
falls from her mouth
like an A-bomb:

'Elle ne voulait rien dire pour nous.'

Solaris, mysterious
neither of them felt it go
when it did.

When it ends –

there is no
turning the switch
to 'off', no
trainguard announcing
last stations.

No newsreader reeling
off the latest fatality
in Afghanistan.

When it ends
it decided on
its own, you
had no say
in it, there's nothing
to be done, cos
it's all over
now, baby blue.

§

I don't talk
about 'it'.
Nothing to say
on it.

§

Amongst the talk
of counterfeit educations
and film deals
and who did who
with what and where,

in the modestly priced Thai on King
a declaration over diner-talk-and-squawk
and a robust South Australian red:

'Paris. Intellectually petrified!'

Paris!
Toujours, Paris.

Paris,
Je t'aime, je t'aime
though you treat me cool.

Elegance worn delicate
as espresso taken
in the Champs-Élysées morning light –

where sirens wail
like Miles did
when you loved me
day and night
when you made
everything all right.

Paris, je t'aime
je t'aime.

§

'She faked it the whole time!'

No referee to
blow the
fulltime whistle.

And I wondered why
you got that
look in your eye
just like when
we did it and
did it and
did it and
didn't give a fuck
what anyone said!

Not even our 'better halves'.

There was no half-time blown.

§

She never understood men
men never understood her, and
it was understood
that she was
to be understood.

Shadow-boxing recollection
bruises like a bare-knuckled
back-alley fight.

§

'You will forget my skin.'

He will recall
her touch
relieving him of the day
drawing his cries in the night,

then, after it was over
on the redeye, first thing
to home and its comforts
its wife and its children
its Beamer in the driveway
Its pool parties and teenage daughter Lolitas.

She could stab
mim with her fork
like Beatrice as Betty
in that arthouse film from France.

But the crowd in the café prevents her.

§

Adopted mother, your sins
I lay down now
Karenina-like
on cold Moscow steel.

§

Truganini –
a violation
twice over,

a keepsake
I pack with the Kleenex.

Twice over
the putting to the sword
of honour.

Flour baked into
a final feast.

Poisonous Medician violation.

Twice over
in the interests of
proprietal expansion
exploratory entitlement –

in the interests
of genocide.

§

If poesy be a kind
of archaeology

a violation twice over

then I, like
Truganini ask you
not to display
my sketches
here on this canvas
of love, sex, death
endings and goodbyes

without a crooked smile!

Do not cry or mourn me;

for I invent these farewells
in anticipation of a future that
will decipher the
simulacrum of reality
that we make
each day.

§

It's the usual fare!
The last hurrah!

§

Because when it ends
who sends
the form to
redirect the mail?

It's last stations!
For one!
For all!

§

Nietzsche's dancers
dance on,
dance on, dance on,
dance on,

Dionysian and immortal
in their own charming way.

(2013)

REIHANA ROBINSON

Reihana Robinson is a writer and artist and organic farmer living in the Coromandel. Her writing has been published in the United States and New Zealand in a number of journals including *Landfall, Cutthroat, Hawai'i Review, Trout, Melusine, JAAM, Takahē, Cezanne's Carrot* and *Blackmail Press*. Her poems have appeared as part of *AUP New Poets 3* (2008) and her first volume, *Auē Rona*, was published by Steele Roberts (2012). She has held artist residencies at the East-West Center, Honolulu, Hawai'i, and the Anderson Center, Red Wing, Minnesota. Artwork is held in collections in Europe, the USA and the Pacific. She was the inaugural recipient of the Te Atairangikāhu Award for Poetry.

Thinking of my father

It's a book on the Chippewa, the Land of the Red Lake Band
I'm reading and there the voice of my father speaks from the page

– What are you giving me for Father's Day?

It's the ripe voice of fragility swinging over the telephone wires.
Has he ever asked this of me?

It's the distance between he is talking about – he wants that taken away
A gift of subtraction.

It's in these images, three decades old, printed by the University of
Minnesota Press that I hear the voice of the father

I'm seven years old following his black gumboots
I'm watching the earth turn
under his spade and I'm placing the cut seed potato

It's the hot front seat of a new Vauxhall Velox and
I'm sitting in my white singlet and underpants between my fresh parents

We're riding a summer holiday on windy unsealed roads
Right and left

You say
– I want to be your right-hand man
and yes you are

only tonight I'm travelling light
my carapace of memory scored with such long love.

(*24 August 1995*)

Humility

With what we call hands
you create out of hard bone
shapes of such tenderness –

petite voyaging craft destined
never to set a toe-tip on water
never to feel the flush of waves
against prow

Never to swerve into a pellucid sea
bearing the weight of strangers from the forest

In your hand
bone becomes your lover
you pass not fluid
but from the still place –
your spirit
and

poof

there lies proof
on my bosom at rest
a small waka

You know the truth of this,
as the startled gaze of strangers
from the forest
bears the imprint of awe.

(2008)

Noa Noa makes breakfast for Caroline and me, or, The tea ceremony is introduced to Samoa

The Missionaries. Misguided as usual. Decide en masse
to convert the native women
who are perceived to be holding the purse strings.

So the women observe the missionaries
in their tea drinking. Which includes the refined use
of what is shaped like a jam spoon.
And is in fact a jam spoon.
Because pikelets must be eaten with the tea.

Never mind the wheat which must be imported
as taro isn't any good for baking pikelets.

So the witnessing begins.
Methodically by Methodists mostly
and it catches.
Only. Who has the teacup?
Who has the saucer?
Who has the precious leaves?

No one woman in the village has
all the utensils or all the ingredients.
Each prizes her own contribution.
And when the tea ceremony is announced
each woman brings her own offering.

And the cup of tea begins.

So when Caroline's daughter made the ritual 21
each of Caroline's friends gave her
gifts of tea. A cup. A spoon.

This long morning we sit in a colonial outpost
and sip our English Breakfast tea
and Noa Noa soon to be 21
pours tea for Caroline and me.

(1990)

How it all began

Such pitiful pleas –
her thirsty brats.

Husbandless, she
bends her will, grabs
a calabash, heads off
through the ngaio trees
and mamaku ferns.

Such pitiful pleas –
her thirsty brats.

She stumbles. Her curses echo
through forest and starlight.

Stuff you, moon,
boil your pea brain with pūhā.
Put your flat head into the cooking pot.

The one time I need you,
you hide.
Coward, cheat.

I am the sleeping moon,
an ashen cloud conceals my beams.

I am aroused, enchanted.
This is the wife I dream of.

Don't you know I am no ordinary moon?

Did I set the clouds to stall?

There's no light for Rona.

I slither around her, buffed and highly sexed.
She succumbs

wrapped in my sensations,
my reflected-light limbs –
we become lovers.

The story is that she pines for her lost infants.

That's a lie.

We fuse all night long when you are staring up at us.
But you can't see that far.
Just ask her –

Rona, are you happy?

Oh yes, my love
oh yes
come lie with me
take off your slippers.

Her brats grow, invent haka.
You know where that got them –

no land, no language.
Free entertainment every rugby match.

(2012)

God of ugly things

Hey you wētā come out,
come out of your log cave,
glissade down alpine scree,
jump from arboreal homes in kauri and kahikatea,
run from ruru, saddleback and kiwi,
hide from kākā and long-tailed cuckoo.

A tingle-tangle gathering of leaves

Your mate, the huhu, fragrant almond to the taste,
white puffball on the tongue.
Demonstrate your ardour, your stinking pile of love.
Eat up your buttercups, daisies, tussock.
Flee the Gordian worm.

A tingle-tangle gathering of leaves

Your wired nemesis now walks on two legs,
using propellers –
thwap thwap.

Alchemy in a tin shack's scullery,
your foxtrot turning to stumbles,
diurnal rhythms disrupted.

A tingle-tangle gathering of leaves

Nymphs reassembled without ballet shoes,
nymphs who can only tap dance –
painful arthritis jiggering their segments.

Come out, wētā,
give us a kiss, before you become
forgotten fauna.

(2006)

Pāua

Do you regret the original
agreement, the one where you get to
bleed in exchange for a half pearl?

Called by your sea companions
when your tyranny takes over
little god and *vacuum mouth*
behind your hard back.

Looted poachers
with sharp eyes, your shiny rock
home sucked clean.

It's that foot of yours,
gets you into trouble.
Hide your foot.
Bank your shell.

(2011)

Ninety Mile Beach

Waves as small as envelopes crest –
a peel, a flap.

Tanned boys pant, are patient, watching. The long
sea lip is barely grinning.

Horse riders natter in the local lingo,
hard sand slip-slop.

Full and round he lights the white sands
whiter as night clasps the broad beach.

Fishermen and girls slip hulls over gentle ripples,
paddle your now glassy surface –
a seeming tango, the immense sea rhythm
tickling keels.

A lull. A gull's cry and circle. Laughter.
A kahawai pulls to shake free. Blue-black.
Tangaroa gives. Blood flows.

Still you stroll waves ashore, mild and summery,
leaving for some other day your rollers' gaping mouths.

(2012)

TE KAHU ROLLESTON

Papaki tū ana ngā tai ki Mauao. Ko Te Kahu Rolleston tēnei, he uri nō Matakana, Rangiwaea me ngā moutere katoa o Tauranga moana. Ko Mauao te maunga ko Ngāi Te Rangi te iwi. Ko Ngāi Tamawhariua me Tauwhao ngā hapū. Te Kahupakea Rolleston works for the Enviroschools Foundation Te Aho Tū Roa programme and is also studying at the University of Waikato. Te Kahu is a rangatahi spokesperson for his iwi and often speaks or assists at treaty settlement, Waitangi Day and youth training events in Tauranga.

The Rena

It began. As . . . .
the essence of death, itself sept, from the monsters depths, into the sand
impacting, all creatures, from the air, sea, and the land,
she was stuck!!
Between a *'reef and a hard place'*,
jammed
like boiled fruit pulp in a jar case,
her knife-like features with a sharp, blade-like base, pierced my Moana,
while oozing, and bleeding this dark paste,
she was stuck!!
No *anchor*, nothing *butter*, dark taste,
the volatility spread, churning my once bright pantry and sanctuary into
    a dark place.

We were going wild, lives spinning,
out of control, with the wild life, killing,
that was occurring, as the government sat around, downing their *Caésar
    salad* just chilling,
how dare you,
poison the swells and the realm of Tangaroa,
then sit around and *watch . . .* as *time ticks on*, while doing nothing at all,
to those with the access and knowledge that's a food basket and store,
payments made, with the practice of Kaitiakitanga, Tikanga, and L.O.R.E
    Law,
until that day, when this *blanket* of *death lay*, on our sea *bed*, and he was
    almost a beach, dead, *for sure*,

I saw them, an army of Taniwha, surfing the waves,
in the shape of shipping containers, though nothing within them could
    be contained,
armoured in steal, stealing, taking the life of my Moana away,
unless you were raised, to be at one with the sea,
you could never see,
believe. Understand or feel this sort of pain,
while it was happening there was a culture clash,
Money vs Mana
who determines and measures success and wealth
for is wealth
the ability to be able to collect enough food to sustain yourself?
Or is the wealth
forever to be measured as the assets in your possession and cash in your
    bank account?
The sea . . . . . . Well that's a *resource* to followers of capitalism,
but what's a *re-source*, to our *Mauri-source*,
my people's very essence of living.

As soon as it happened,
we were there, an army in gumboots and latex gloves that protected
    nothing believe me,
that's the sort of power and love, shared and felt between Whānau Hapū
    and Iwi.
To overcome my anger I had to find a silver lining,
and what I ended up finding, what a unity
the one-ness that can come from such a tragedy, and that's the only
    reason I'm still smiling . . . . . .

(2013)

Forget about Guy Fawkes (Parihaka)

I'll start by stating that I am not of Parihaka whakapapa,
Taranaki is not where my maunga stands,
my maunga is Mauao, I'm from Tauranga Moana,
to be more specific Te Moutere o Matakana,

I state that,
because I'm a firm believer in de-colonising methodologies,
so I could never try to speak for them,
I can only speak on how I've personally learnt from their examples and
    philosophies,

the people of Parihaka,
a people sworn to be peaceful,
with a commitment to non-violent resistance they were bound to keep to

the people of Parihaka,
the protectors of peace and independence defenders,
the ones who manage to do it without using weapons,
their forms of passive aggressive, active resistance and protest shall
    eternally be remembered,
especially considering the sorts of law changes being made these day
    which are impeding on protestors.

We must acknowledge the visionaries with sight,
Te Whiti the shine,
Tohu the Sign.
Ngā rangatira tokorua, Tohu Kākahi, rāua ko Te Whiti O Rongomai.
Te Whiti sent men to plough, dig the lands up and mess with,
Crown land surveyors, with no intention, or mention of violence and
    aggression,
not even as Te Whiti's men who were ploughing as a means of peaceful
    protest were being arrested.

Yet still,
On November 5th, 1881 the invasion begun,

the invading squad invading waving guns,
a stand was taken, soldiers were fired upon, with. . .
shots of smiles and bombed with grenades of gracious love,
they were welcomed and embraced with hugs,
for the soldiers invading, to invade, there wasn't space enough,
so the people of Parihaka fell their own wall and made enough.

How could they, as soldiers
roll in on a people offering all they have and still confiscate their stuff,
rape and touch the women, then pillage the village and chop, everything
    from the crops to the rest of the estates until dust?

Te Whiti, Tohu and their men were imprisoned,
still they practised,
still they preached, non-violent resistance,

a challenge was posed politically,
to combat the posed political punitive policies,
by 1883, some were allowed back, Proof! The plan of a peaceful people of
    Parihaka had not failed.
Then again, in 1886, for simply holding a meeting Te Whiti was jailed,
however, by 1888 all who had survived the times, were allowed to return,
which means peace wins over war,
in the end, peace wins over all,
with examples like Parihaka why is it that we still haven't learnt
and we keep, going to war?

(2013)

ZANE SCARBOROUGH

Zane Scarborough writes, reads and loves poetry. He is a member of the South Auckland Poets Collective. He has a background in community volunteering and youth work and travels the country presenting the Attitude programme in New Zealand high schools.

[The world was your oyster]

The world was your oyster. Those oysters hung in coral orchards and you could have picked anyone. Why me?

OK. I know that sometimes I can make a good impression. In the right place I can have an entire room in stitches with stories and one liners that I've secretly told a thousand times but this time you had me in stitches. Quietly pulling the threads I seemed to unravel in front of you. Every one of our yarns would become a yarn, you collected them, wove them together, a woollen mosaic of place names, dates and moments.

You figured out how each one of my silly stories related to the next, you logic checked so they all made sense, let me embellish a bit and created a garment that you could hang my life on.

From day dot I liked the way you looked. Auburn hair and polka dot print, I used to play connect the dots with your freckles, nice frame, picture perfect. Even if you never thought you were pretty enough, dark enough, smart enough that's OK. I never wanted you to be the best anything anyway. I just wanted you to be mine. You would never have known that though . . .

I hid behind nonchalant texts, keeping cards close. Abbreviated code words, saving face in front of my bros. Maybe was code for yes. I'm chilled was code for of course. Sup was code sup-pose me and you want to get more serious . . . maybe . . . I mean I'm chilled. And then I fell . . .

Weightless. Head over heels I fell, off balance, hand-eye coordination replaced with head-heart coordination. This says (point to head) 'We make a good couple' and the other says (point to heart) 'I will never be the same.'

No surprises then we got engaged, always batted above my weight so what would you expect?

We would string together consonants and vowels that belong side by side, to make that constant vowel to remain side by side. I stared fear in the face and declared that day 'I do' because really, 'I do' love you. For better or worse, in sickness and in health, for richer . . . or more likely poorer, until death do us part . . . I do.

Every time we have a mean laugh, or a mean scrap, or a mean yarn, I now collect those memories like a yarn of wool and store them.

One day we will tell our children about these stories, they will sit there and figure out how each story relates to the next, then logic check to make sure they make sense, let us embellish a bit, about how much funnier or slimmer we once thought we were. They will see how the fabric of our family is woven into the scarves, sox and jumpers we use to keep us warm. They will see how these garments are what we hang our lives on.

(2012)

Tāmati (inspired by JKB)

I met Jesus the other day.
He appeared as a nurse.
His name was Tāmati.
He wore blue linen contradictions.
Underpaid, overworked.
You could tell he was Jesus because of his shoes.
Made for walking another man's mile.
Families comfort each other.
Hoping for the best.
He doesn't.
He says pain isn't scary, it's just honest.
And the truth only hurts – if you continue to ignore it.
He smiles without pretending everything is OK.

That's why people trust Him.
Doctors walk around the hospital, pretending to be God.
Prolonging life – delaying the inevitable.
Tāmati knows that we all go one day.
He's been there before us, shown us the way.

(2013)

KATE SHAW

Kate Shaw (Rangiwewehi of Te Arawa; 1896–1999; née Carnachan) began writing during her school days. In the 1940s she was a regular contributor to the women's pages of *New Zealand Dairy Exporter*. She wrote series for radio called *Wahine* and *Maori Legends*, which were broadcast on the National Programme, and also wrote programmes for a local Rotorua radio station. She was a member of the New Zealand Women Writers' Society, the Polynesian Society and was vice-president of the Rotorua and District Historical Society. Shaw was awarded the Queen's Service Medal for community service in 1997, and published *Hongi's Track* in her 102nd year.

To Vaughan

I see you as the Seasons –
yes, all the Seasons.
The Kōanga – gladness
of earth now kissed by gentle rain,
and sweetness building in the bud
of fun and gambolling.
The Raumati – richness
of earth now filled with wonder glow
of Eldorado fruiting, and of roses;
walks and talks and moonlight.
The Ngahuru – full of leaves,
the earth all coloured now,
red and gold and chestnut brown;
warm and wise before the storm.
The Takurua Makariri

earth lashed by Tonga and by Marangai.
Mānuka burning and the fireside
slippered ease:
achievement and content.

MICHAEL STEVENS

Michael Stevens (1954–), Ngāti Raukawa (Ngāti Kauwhata, Ngāti Huia, Ngāti Parewahawaha hapū), was born in Stratford and grew up in Taupō. He graduated from the University of Otago with a BA in social anthropology in 1976. From the 1980s he has served in a succession of roles in the Department of Māori Affairs and other organizations involved in the development of Māori assets. His poetry has been published in *Critic*, *Koru*, *Otago University Review*, *Pacific Moana Quarterly* and other literary magazines. He has written government policy papers in Māori Affairs and research papers for the Waitangi Tribunal.

Let the moon and the sea . . .

Let the moon and the still
sea conspire and rising
reclaim these shores from the
impotence of sun and men.

is this the turning

This fish has not moved through the
sea's pull, nor yet the moon's suck
wave-flooded her belly: men,
not water, brought her drowning.

is this the turning is this

Like the sea your people covered our
land: you were as *ngā tai a Kupe*
and we were not prepared. We have
become like the seabirds upon the rocks.

the turning is this

So let the moon-gathered waters
begin their rising: the tides of
sea and men change always. Let it
be known: the time for turning is come.

ko tēnei te whatinga o te mata o te tai

(1976)

BRUCE STEWART

Bruce Stewart, of Ngāti Raukawa, Te Arawa, is a fiction writer, dramatist and poet. Born in Hamilton, he grew up in the Wairarapa and was educated at Wairarapa College. He has lived mainly in Wellington, where he successfully set up the first work trust and founded Tapu Te Ranga Marae at Island Bay, creating a centre for debate and education in Māori culture and protocol and for the redevelopment of native bush. He was president of Ngā Puna Waihanga (Māori Artists and Writers Society) in 1982. Stewart's work has expressed the anger, confused loyalties and spiritual aspiration of Māori since the late twentieth century.

Pono

It is possible to quieten me
for a while by blocking your ears
At times I've been buried – hidden
for centuries
but I will always surface
. . . sometimes with a scream
for there are those
who have nothing left but
their bodies – voices
Take your hands from your ears
hear their screams.

(1989)

GEORGINA STEWART

Ko Te Whare Tapu o Ngāpuhi. Ko Whakarārā te maunga, ko Matauri te ākau, ko Ngāti Kura te hapū, ko Ngāpuhi-nui-tonu te iwi. Georgina Marjorie Stewart holds a Master of Science from the University of Auckland and a Doctorate of Education from Waikato University. Her doctoral thesis was the basis of her 2010 book *Good Science? The Growing Gap between Power and Education.* She works for the University of Auckland's Faculty of Education, based at the Tai Tokerau campus in Whāngārei.

Kitchen stool

This stool
lives in my pantry
I move it around
whenever I want something from the top shelf
or the cupboard above the fridge
or the shelf in the hall cupboard where I keep
spare blankets and pillows.

When I'm cooking I put the stool by the bench
with the scrap bucket on it, for the rubbish
that making a meal produces.

Sometimes if I'm very tired, or feeling pensive
I sit on the stool
and make a cup of tea
and look out the kitchen window.
It's also handy
if someone wants to talk to me while I'm cooking tea.

I've had this stool for about ten years
my mother gave it to me
it belonged to her mother before that
it came with another stool, and a matching table
I smashed the other stool, once years ago
when I was very very angry

I gave the table to my sister
when she needed it more than I did
and then she moved on, and gave it away.

But this stool is still here
I guess it's been in the kitchens of women like me
for over fifty years
and I don't suppose I'll be getting rid of it
any time soon.

(2000)

J. C. STURM

Jacquie Sturm was born in Ōpunake, with tribal affiliations to Taranaki iwi, Parihaka and Whakatōhea. She published poetry and short stories in periodicals and anthologies from 1947 onwards. In the early 1950s she became the first Māori woman to obtain an MA from a New Zealand university. Her first collection of short stories, *The House of the Talking Cat*, was published by Spiral in 1983 and her first collection of poems, *Dedications* (Steele Roberts, 1996) received the Honour Award for poetry in the 1997 Montana New Zealand Book Awards. She published a second collection of poems, *Postscripts*, in 2002 (Steele Roberts), and *The Glass House: Stories and Poems* in 2006 (Steele Roberts). Following the death of her husband, James K. Baxter, she worked as a librarian in Wellington for two decades before retiring to Paekākāriki. She died in December 2009 and is buried in her iwi's urupā at Ōpunake.

At Red Rocks

Better not take anything
For granted here or even
Make the usual assumptions.
The cliff towering behind you,
For instance: how do you know
It's not about to crack and crumble;
And the outgoing tide: are you sure
It can never change its mind
Then come charging furiously back?

And better not let a craving for
The smell of kelp, the taste of kina
Lead you by the nose like a dog
Over these iron-spiked rocks
Into those seaweed infested breakers.
Above all, do not allow that other
Secret hunger drive you on
Beyond recall, out of your depth
In turquoise, green and purple.

Remember, you came to see the seals.
There they are. Observe them closely.
See how easy it is to become
A smooth boulder, heaving kelp,
A vanishing mirage or simply
One's self: sprawl on a rock,
Roll over and scratch, open and close
One glinting eye, wave a flipper
Vaguely and let the world pass by.

(2000)

The last night at Collingwood

No moon and a black sea,
The daytime birds have flown
To their night time places,
The incoming tide creeps

Over Farewell Spit.
Soon waves will wash the rocks
Outside our windows,
Spraying the glass with salt.

Twenty-four hours from now
Birds, land and sea
Will repeat it all again.
We'll be gone by then

Back to that northern
Beach across the Strait,
With far fewer sea birds
But Kapiti close at hand.

There we watch the sun go down
Where the Spit lies out of sight,
Believing love, like them
Returns again and again.

(2000)

Memo for my 70th birthday

Pass lightly over this day
Take nothing, leave nothing
Do not linger, do not stay
Pass over lightly, pass on.

Do washing, do dishes
Clean toilet, wash hair.
Be kind to the cats
They are older than you.
Pass lightly over this
Pass over lightly, pass on.

After lunch visit unknown
Marae: mind your manners
Be careful, don't eyeball
The kaumatua.

Take koha, give koha
Do not linger, do not stay.

Dine out with family
Look happy surprised pleased
With their presents. Convince
Them you are fighting fit.
Taking all, loving all
Lightly pass over, pass on.

If you should think of plans
Made with him who now lies
Silenced under his stone,
Weep, if you must, but alone.
Do not linger, do not stay
Pass over lightly, pass on.

Later, keep warm loving
The living. Have no doubts
Ask no questions. Believe
It will last for ever.
Taking all, giving all
Linger on lightly and stay.

(2000)

Coming of age

for my family

I'm warning you,
After forty-two years
Of enforced domestication
And your tyrannical
Occupation of my life,
I am finally planning rebellion.

I will not, do you hear
Be bound by your house rules
Any longer, maintain myself
With unrelenting care
Like a vintage car
For your exclusive use,
Or save myself up
To be your Xmas bonus
For another Roman holiday.

Can't you see
I've come of age at last,
So give me that big gold key
Hanging round your neck
Or I swear I'll leave home
For good without it, swim out
On the next ebb tide
For that marine mirage,
Hitch a ride out of town
With a dubious stranger,
Catch the first flight
To Noumea, Bombay, Marrakech
(Your other captive chose Jerusalem
On the Wanganui, remember?)

And in the back streets
Spend myself recklessly
Down to my very last cell
In a dangerously
Extravagant spending spree
Until the debt collector
Catches up with me.

(1996)

A tricky business

A tricky business
Finding those pegs
Pulling them out
In the dark;
Come first light
Packing their owners
Theodolites and all
Over that river:

> Not of Babylon –
> No one sat down,
> Not the Rubicon –
> Some came back,
> Not the Styx – well
> Maybe for some.
> No, that river had
> Has a Taranaki
> Maori name.

Te Whiti o Rongomai
Said unto them
'Go, put your hands
To the plough.'
So they ploughed:

      At Oakura in the west
      Pukearuhe in the north
      Hawera in the south
      All the land that was theirs
      From Maunga Taranaki
      To the sea.

Then their prophet said,
'If they smite you,
Smite not in return.'
And four hundred and twenty ploughmen
Let soldiers take them away.

      Dickens would have found
      The stinking overcrowded
      Jails in New Plymouth
      Wellington, Lyttelton
      Hokitika, Westport
      Dunedin familiar
      But not the prisoners
      Half naked and brown;
      Hardly a Pakeha
      Face to be seen.
      'One or two died here
      And there' so they say.

Fencers replaced the ploughmen,
Replaced their fences destroyed
By Armed Constabulary,
Offered no resistance
To arrest. Two hundred
And sixteen joined their cousins
Quarrying stones in winter,
Building retaining walls
Around Dunedin harbour
Along the banks of the Leith

Through the Botanic Gardens
In cemeteries where later
Some were buried as paupers.

    Beside the road to
    Andersons Bay
    Caves and tunnels were sealed
    To keep out air and light.
    In nineteen eighty-seven
    Taranaki iwi placed
    A Taranaki boulder there
    Memorial to their tupuna
    Imprisoned without trial
    In the airless dark.

This is the road
That Bryce built.
He was the man
Upon a white steed
Who led the Queen's horses
And all the Queen's men
To capture Te Whiti
And Tohu Kakahi
Then sacked their kainga
Called Parihaka.

    Listen –
    Two hundred singing boys
    Are silenced.
    Look –
    One hundred skipping girls
    Are scattered.
    Can you hear –
    Children are crying
    For their mothers,
    Women are weeping

For their men,
The air is loud
With lamentation.
Can you see –
Smoke from burning whare
Darkens the face of the sun,
Maunga Taranaki
Covers his head with cloud.

Till what was done
Is undone
Injustice
Names that day.

(2000)

As the godwits fly

for Frank

After days of coming and going
Taking off, circling, landing again
So lightly and exactly dropping
Into line upon line
Settling and resettling themselves
Always facing into the wind,
Hunched low on the rocks
Like runners on their marks
Poised ready for that final
Instinctive command to
Go!
The godwits have gone
Every one, all together
Taking summer with them
To fly a private longitude

From the bottom to the top
Of the world
Where northern winters
Thaw to sudden springs.

I may never see them again.
Certainly some will fall
Down shafts of turbulence,
Or simply tumble out of
A blue and cloudless sky
Small grey and white feather bundles
Still warm,
Or falter and flutter sideways
Off course
Down a different longitude
To make a final, unplanned landfall,
While far above them
Sister hearts and brother wings
Keep on beating, beating
Without pause
Northward into the wind.

Right now I would give
Anything
To be that child again
Watching in wonder
For the first time
A cloud of white birds rising
And heading north;
To live again from then
To now exactly as it was
With no correction or variation,
Living it straight
As the godwits fly
My longitude from end to end
And keep on flying, flying

Without pause
Past my final winter
Thawing to its spring.

(1996)

Urgently

for Jim

My dear one
And only dear
My moonrise
And early morning sun

When the time comes
Will you light my way
Through the dreaded fog
Of Hine-nui-te-po

And bring me safe
To that bright place
(I believe –
I swear I believe)
Where we may be together
Again, for ever.

(1996)

He waiata tenei mo Parihaka

Have you heard of Parihaka
Between
Maunga Taranaki
And the sea

Where Te Whiti o Rongomai
And Tohu Kakahi
Preached
Passive resistance, not war?

Have you heard of Parihaka
Where Taranaki iwi
Gathered
Seeking a way to keep their land?

Non-violence was their choice
Peace their aim
Raukura their badge
Ploughs their only weapons.

They pulled down fences
Pulled out pegs
Then ploughed whatever
The settlers claimed was theirs.

Have you heard of Parihaka's
Boys and girls
Waiting outside the gates
When the mounted soldiers came

To rape and murder
Pillage and burn
To take Te Whiti and Tohu away
With all the ploughmen

And ship them south
To build a causeway
Around Dunedin's
Wintry harbour?

Have you heard of Taranaki iwi
Denied a trial,
Chained like dogs
In sealed caves and tunnels?

Ngai Tahu smuggled
Food and blankets
To the prisoners
Comforted the sick in the dark.

Kua ngaro nga tangata
Kua ngaro i te po!
Aue te mamae
That followed after!

If you haven't heard of Parihaka,
Be sure
Your grandchildren will
And their children after them,

History will see to that.
But for now,
He waiata tenei mo Parihaka –
Aue, aue, a-u-e –

(2000)

History lesson

Believe me when I tell you
With no introduction,
In spite of its beauty
The planet is an urupa.

Don't be dismayed.
Out of its concrete graves
Children grow like grass
Perpetuating us.

No language, certainly not
Yours or mine, can tell them
Anything not entered
Already in their genes.

If we are not too clever,
Some of us might help
Some of them access
The programme, nothing more.

All of us straddle
Fault lines of meaning
Waiting for the Big One
To open them up.

Meanwhile observe these dancers,
How perfectly and full of grace
They repeat themselves.
Shiva knew a thing or two

About Being. He could be
My ancestor's cousin
And yours. We share the same
Whakapapa,

Same geology too.
What is more, there is nothing
That has not been before,
The new repeats the old.

We are simply variations
On original themes.
Why are you dismayed?
We carry history in our genes

Like messages in bottles.
Surely that is enough.
Don't tell me you believe,
You want, more than this.

What, in God's name, what?

(2000)

At times I grieve

At times I grieve for you
Knowing one day you are bound
To grieve for me.
How will you be after the shock
And after shocks of my going,
When you have done what must be
Done and put me in the hole
With some small ceremony?

Be warned; my absence
In the empty house
Will hit you like a fist,
Emptiness fill you
To overflowing, silence

Wail my name in your ears,
And all the precious, useless
Things I had to leave behind
Weigh your hearts down
Like lumps of lead.

Go home; eat, drink, be
As merry as you can,
Make love as though
For the very last time
Warming each other through
And through to the still centre,
Then in the quiet that follows
After, learn how quickly,
How easily, love makes
Everything possible again.

(1996)

Splitting the stone

for John

You brought back
Carefully, nervously
A heavy grey boulder
From that other beach
Up north –
The place I call home
When I feel inclined –
A narrow iron strip
Between land and sea
With several old battlefields
Close by
And a guardian mountain.

On a clear day
If you are lucky
And really quick
You may see him
Even from here,
A small opal cone
On a blue horizon
Northwest of Kapiti.

And then
As I had dreamed
The night before
You started to make
According to instructions,
A flax pounder
Like the Old Ones
Used to use
(Some can still be found
With other missing things
In various museums)

Striking stone on stone
Carefully, patiently
While I kept away
As I knew I should
Waiting for the stone to split
As I knew it would
And let the Mauri through.

And after
Your amazed silence,
I watched you set to
Forgetting the pounder
And all those
Sad museum pieces,
And make instead

Like the Old Ones used to,
A stone dwelling
For the newcomer –
A place to call home
When he feels inclined –

Carving it steel on stone
Carefully, lovingly
In his image
So the world will know
It is meant for him
And him only.

And when it was finished
You stood there
In the small space between
The roses and the taupata,
Heavy grey rain
Soaking through your clothes
And the pores of your skin,
And looked in wonder
At what you had done,
Nursing a bruised hand.

(1996)

ROBERT SULLIVAN

Robert Sullivan, a poet of Ngāpuhi/Irish descent, is the author of a number of books of poetry, a graphic novel and a prize-winning book of Māori legends for children. He co-edited, with Albert Wendt and Reina Whaitiri, AUP's anthologies of Polynesian poetry in English, *Whetu Moana* (2003) and *Mauri Ola* (2010). In 1998 he was the Literary Fellow at the University of Auckland and in 2001 he was the Distinguished Visiting Writer at the University of Hawai'i–Mānoa, where he taught creative writing for some years. He now heads the Creative Writing Programme at Manukau Institute of Technology.

Ahi kā – the house of Ngā Puhi

We light the poem and breathe out
    the growing flames. Ahi kā. This
        is our home – our fire. Hot tongues out

– pūkana – turn words to steam. This
    fish heart is a great lake on a
        skillet. Ahi kā! Ahi kā!

Keep the fire. The sun's rays are ropes
    held down by Māui's brothers.
        They handed down ray by burning

ray to each other every
    day – we keep the home fires burning
        every day. Mountains of our

house are its pillars – I believe
    in the forces that raised them here.
        Ahi kā burnt onto summits

char in the land, ahi kā dream,
    long bright cloud brilliant homeland.
        Ahi kā our life, ahi kā

carried by the tribe's forever-story
        firing every lullaby.
                Shadows shrink in our hands' quiver

as we speak – ahi kā sing fire
        scoop embers in the childhood sun
                stare into molten shapes and see

people – building, sailing, farming –
        see them in the flames of our land
                see them in this forever light

no tears only fire for ahi
        kā no weeping only hāngī pits
                no regrets just forgiveness and

a place for the fire – it's our song
        to sing – ahi kā – got to keep
                singing the shadows away – ha!

(2005)

Voice carried my family, their names and stories

Their names and fates were spoken.
The lands and seas of the voyage were spoken.
Calls of the stroke at times were spoken.
Celestial guidance, sightings, were spoken.
Prescriptions – medical and spiritual – were spoken.
Transactions – physical and emotional – were spoken.
Family (of), leaders (to), arguments, were well spoken.
Elders (of), were well spoken.
Burials were spoken.
Welcomes at times were spoken.
Futures lined up by pasts, were spoken.
Repeating the spoken were spoken.

Inheritance, inheritors, were spoken.
Tears at times were spoken.
Representations at first were spoken.
The narrator wrote the spoken.
The readers saw the spoken!
Spoken became unspoken.
[Written froze spoken.]

(2005)

Ocean birth

With the leaping spirits we threw
        our voices past Three Kings to sea –
                eyes wide open with ancestors.

We flew air and water, lifted
        by rainbows, whales, dolphins thrashing
                sharks into birthways of the sea's

labour: Rapanui born graven
        faced above the waves – umbilical
                stone; Tahiti born from waka:

temple centre of the world;
        Hawai'i cauled from liquid
                fire: the goddess Pele churning

land from sea: born as mountains;
        Aotearoa on a grandmother's
                bone – Māui's blood to birth Leviathan;

Samoa, Tonga, born before
        the names of the sea of islands,
                before Lapita clay turned to gourd,

   before we slept with Pacific
      tongues. Chant these births Oceania
         with your infinite waves, outrigged

   waka, bird feasts, and sea feasts,
      Peruvian gold potatoes.
         Sing your births Oceania.

   Hold your children to the sky
      and sing them to the skyfather
         in the languages of your people.

   Sing your songs Oceania.
      Pacific Islanders sing! Till
         your throats are stones heaped as temples

   on the shores for our ancestors'
      pleasure. PI's sing! To remind
         wave and tree cliff cave of the songs

   we left for the Moana Nui
      a Kiwa. We left our voices
         here in every singing bird . . .

   trunks like drums – stones like babies –
      forests fed by our placentas.
         Every wave carries us here –

   every song to remind us –
      we are skin of the ocean.

   (2005)

Captain Cook

Didn't we get rid of him? There are far too many statues, operas
and histories. If only I could be a brown Orwell – a Māori Big Bro,
find every little caption card in every European museum and scrub it
out: change the wording to, 'This was given to Captain Cook as a token
of friendship and should be buried with him,' OR 'This was temporarily
given to Captain Cook and would have been expected to be returned on
his death,' OR 'Well, actually, Captain Cook stole this,' OR 'The Captain
exchanged this for something vastly inferior in value – ha ha for him!'
But even as an extra large bro I suspect the lies are superglued.
The empire that sent him to his death three times has its hero.

(2005)

Honda waka

Today I surrendered the life
of my Honda City
to a wrecker in Penrose for $30.

I bought it seven years ago for $6000.
It has rust in the lower sills,
rust around the side windows –
on the WOF inspection sheet it says:
'this car has bad and a lot of rust . . .'

That car took me to Uncle Pat's tangi in Bluff.
We stopped and gazed at Moeraki,
the dream sky, on the way.

A friend followed us in it on the way
to National Women's for Temuera's birth
(we were in her huge Citroen).

We went to Ōtaki, and Wellington,
in the Honda to visit family.

The Honda took me to Library School
perched next to Victoria Uni.

I drove Grandad across the creek in the Honda

at night after the family reunion bash.

Temuera's first car seat was in the Honda.
That Honda has seen a high percentage

of my poetry.
Now I have left it behind.

(1999)

Listen to the rhythm of the falling rain

You, her and him, are in this –
it is a jug of pure water in the likeness
of a virgin glazed with rain beside white
chickens, or a mountain pinned to a railway

station (an installation), and in this way
the rain courses through holies, idols,
people of pain and passion, chance rain
that bends heads with its drops, dissolves,

shatters light, carries logs in bending streams.
Men and women scramble to dam the wondrous rain.
They cannot understand its massive rhythm:
that such a cascade feeds on joy and not

on competition. It is grace that sets
sun moon and stars to shine. Laughter
comes from talking, pain from healing.
Rain moves the strongest hearts.

(1993)

Onehunga Bay

For Maureen Lander

The ripples on the bay are not from the wind. They
are from the traffic on the causeway. A stone perimeter
had once made this a brackish pool, but now the sand,
becoming shoal, swallows the sound of flying microlights.

Two women are wheeling their babies along the brackish beach
where the waves fling and curl the culvert weed – 'what a shitty
arse stink!' they shriek – revelling in the irony of babies
sound asleep, wrapped in nappies, that sort of disposable routine.

The weed on the bay is high today. The microlights' present height
ends by firing distress flares, adding to Daedalus' ancient special
f/x. First hesitate politely, then accept that the dog prints,
the shoe and jandal prints are very old. The local Borough Council

have opened a real turd-in-the-box. The splats of come
discovered on the causeway were spoor of man o' war
that rose too high, then died before the turning tide.
A lone heron, with silvered scissor beak, is a hero

that snips and snaps an enemy stretch of seaweed, breaking
the length. Another new filter station resembles any hacienda:
Decrabond on brick. Its owners are rich: SWITCH OFF OZONE LIGHTS
BEFORE ENTERING WET WELL: but not enough to arrest the killer

vegetation. Our heroic heron signals and lifts from the shifting
swell, spurting buckets of clag just whiskers from the man.
An airport bus bursts in, recklessly rattling the causeway asphalt
to see with sleepy eyes three white spots jettisoned from

the precipice of a dead heron's feathertips. Repeating that,
I turn my Praktika, foci circling and shooting a series
of stones' thrown images, ripples beneath our setting eyelids.
Hard to imagine this was the launch pad for the great

Manukau fleets. Aa, tōia mai, te waka! Ki te urunga, te waka!
Ki te moenga, te waka! Ki te takotoranga i takoto ai – te waka!
Aa, haul the canoe to its rest, the canoe to its bed,
the canoe to the place where it will lie – te waka!

(1990)

Waka 42

Into the new age the waka glides
through halls of mirrors

past the birthplace Rangiātea
across waves of blood – Mau,

takata Maoli, sovereignty
buried in the franchise contracts – oh

we are peoples united by more
than genes, by more than the tongues

of our ancestors reciting names
of great ones, we are united

by culture, by the psyche
of our cultures, our closeness

even in this age turned
against the sacred

(1999)

Waka 46

it is feasible that we will enter

space
colonise planets call our spacecraft *waka*

perhaps name them after the first fleet
erect marae transport carvers renew stories
with celestial import

establish new forms of verse
free ourselves of the need for politics
and concentrate on beauty

like the release from gravity
orbit an image until it is absorbed
through the layers of skin

spin it
sniff and stroke the object
become poetic

oh to be in that generation
to write in freefall picking up the tools
our culture has given us

and to let them go again
knowing they won't hit anyone
just stay up there

no longer subject to peculiarities
of climate the political economies
of powers and powerless

a space waka
rocketing to another orb
singing waiata to the spheres

(1999)

Waka 99

If waka could be resurrected
they wouldn't just come out
from museum doors smashing
glass cases revolving and sliding
doors on their exit

they wouldn't just come out
of mountains as if liquidified
from a frozen state
the resurrection wouldn't just
come about this way

the South Island turned to wood
waiting for the giant crew
of Māui and his brothers
bailers and anchors turned back
to what they were when they were strewn

about the country by Kupe
and his relations
the resurrection would happen
in the blood of the men and women
the boys and girls

who are blood relations
of the crews whose veins
touch the veins who touched the veins
of those who touched the veins
who touched the veins

who touched the veins
of the men and women from the time
of Kupe and before.
The resurrection will come
out of their blood

(1999)

Rāwiri/David

For Hone Tuwhare

I returned to Florence still on my own.
Sunday morning at the Accademia seated
next to David, writing into the tapa:

amazing or as Tuwhare said of Hotere:
speechless/euchred/eclipsed. David's enlarged
hand which killed a giant holds the stone by his right

thigh. I cannot believe in the hair up top
or down below, but veins in his arms,
creases in his belly button, nipples and strength

I believe in. Even his testicles wield
believable sacks – like rocks ready to be thrown.
Pow! He stands next to a phallic stump. His belly

juts with mana: Michelangelo's strut post-haka.
The thighs fetch slightly chubby hints
of a boy whose knees wear youthful caps.

Yet visitors play with the digital David next to
the real one. His ribs are visible on his left –
I count five – but don't see any on his right

except muscle. Adam? After moving I see one
on the right. His face shows intent but also
a reflected fear cut there facing Goliath.

The forehead slightly creases, eyebrows furrow.
Again the cheeks get chubby. He holds
the sling strap like a microphone to his closed

mouth. Sinews in that hand ridge like
a scallop shell for a Venus. The veins
from his stone-holding hand run all

the way up his right arm to
the neck. From here the strap looks
like a regal sash – his only clothing

which slips down his back. From the right
there's no fear in the face – just rugged
courage. I can only admire this man.

(2010)

Arohanui

Big love, that's what it means.
Aroha Nunui means huge love.
Aroha Nunui Rawa means very huge love.
Aroha Nunui Rawa Ake means bigger very huge love.
Aroha Nunui Rawa Ake Tonu means bigger enduring very huge love.
Aroha Nunui Rawa Ake Tonu Atu means biggest enduring hugest love,
which are some of the lengths and times of our longing.

(2006)

CHRIS TAMAIPAREA

Chris Tamaiparea is of Tūwharetoa/Ngāti Whātua descent. He was born in the Auckland suburb of Glen Innes.

Another poem about trees

a friend of mine said
that ken mair said
that at the mention of the word
green
Pākehā kids think of traffic lights and
Māori kids think of trees

apparently mister mair
is a really radical type
but no one i know
has ever stepped
on the gas
when they saw
a tree

(2003)

TRACEY TAWHIAO

Tracey Tawhiao is a writer, poet, film-maker, lawyer and visual artist. She has iwi connections to Ngāti Te Rangi from Matakana Island and Tūwharetoa, Taumarunui, as well as Whakatōhea. After receiving a law degree and BA in classical studies, Tawhiao began practising as an artist. Her writing has been widely published in magazines and journals and her paintings and poetry featured in the book *Taiāwhio* (Te Papa Press, 2002). She is the head of Artist & Repertoire for music management company Heartmusic. She is also a director of The House of Taonga, a Māori artist house of thought and creative endeavour.

Listen to me scream

The news is watching famous people
Famous for being people on the news
Sing a song, say a line, bomb twin towers
President Bush will send you flowers
Prime Minister Clark knows how to bark
Someone else said it's what's not in the heart
The journalist is quite frankly a puppet
For lowest common denominator viewer
Blame yourself for what they don't teach
Try to get what is seemingly out of reach.

Row, row, row your boat gently down the stream
Life without the sugar in it makes me want to scream.

Take off your shoes, sit on the floor
Never leave your back to the door
Take off your hat, don't get too fat
Say what you mean and stick to the facts
A tissue a tissue we all fall down
London's got some issues some issues
Don't be surprised if the Queen falls down
She has the weight of all our land to trip her
Trip her, trick her she wears the Māori Crown
Well tell her it matters the next time she's in town.

Row, row, row your boat gently down the stream
Life without the sugar in it makes me want to scream.

Māori in the wars, Māori with their low scores
Fetching, scratching, shouting at the norms
Watching, touching, fighting against the laws
Taking over the army of our most septic sores
Marching to the tune of optimism with an arrow in my back
But we're dancing, smoking and doing what we can
No point in yelling give us back our land
Shouting and belting the mouth that takes us down
Down to the river where the water flows
It's just us and a gentle breeze that blow hard and know hard.

Listen to me scream!! @#$%ˆ*!

(2010)

Blessed is blood

Came to Colonise
Called it Civilise
Impact minimise
Land no compromise
Roads chopped out
Driving into Trees
Less Leaves more Disease

Oil fuelling machine
Machine fuelling Man
Man fuelling Money
Money fuelling Greed
Greed fuelling depression
Depression fuelling disease
Disease fuelling Money
Money fuelling greed
This disease breeds

Now we realise
Less is more
And more is less

SO

Love fuels Good
Good fuels Happiness
Happiness fuels Peace
Peace fuels Love

SO

Slow down man
Your dance is insane
Break out not down

Say after me:

Best is Blessed
Blessed is Blood
Blood is Real
Real is Now.

(2010)

Māori girl

She can't get a job but she's used to that
Most of her family can't get jobs either
The man next door says she doesn't want one
A pretty girl like you must get all kinds of offers
She isn't sure why but he gives her the creeps

Last week she had an interview at Shanton's
She had had to borrow Mary's good dress
Mary said it looked too big but what else could she do
The lady at Shanton's was too busy to see
What a great shop assistant she would be

The man next door said she looked good
He asked her over for a cup of tea, she said yes
No one had ever asked her over for a cup of tea before
He talked non stop about himself as she drank the tea
He said she was too pretty to be a Māori

When she said she had to go he asked her why
She told him she had to look after her sister's kids
He told her she should get herself a real job
She left but wondered about that word real
Her sister's kids were pretty real she thought

The lady from Shanton's called back the news was bad
she was too shy the woman said, to be a sales person
That she needed to get over being shy, get confident
Get confident, real job, too pretty to be a Māori
She knew the dress had been too big but what were her choices

While she was watching her sister's kids, she cried
Why did that man make her feel bad why did he say,
Being a Māori didn't exactly get you anywhere in life
She had to stop crying because the baby was crying
She picked her up and kissed and held her tight

She closed her eyes she hummed a song, she rocked from side to side.

A lawyer and a builder

My uncle drives out to my house with his mate a builder
They talk in builder talk where a variety of grunts has meaning
I wonder whether I should do the girl thing and make a cuppa tea
Instead I dare to be unlike they were expecting and grunt too
They look a bit confused but I think they are just confused by my
    feminine accent
I try to get a grunt out with more resonance, more depth
Now they really are beginning to take a second look at me
I decide to talk in my own housewife-don't-mess-with-me voice
'I really want to get rid of those aluminium windows, I want wooden
    ones'
If my uncle's mate didn't understand grunts, he understands this less
'Why you want to get rid of those for, you have to paint the wood ones
    every five years'
He shakes his head and looks suspiciously at my uncle, who looks away
We move into another room for his inspection, no cuppa tea closer
This looks good says the builder in animated tones, no grunting at all
I imitate my uncle's no nonsense voice this time, anything for a kick, I
    am a housewife
I want all that concrete exposed and that ceiling replaced, that wall out
    but then I smile pleasantly
The grunting starts again, they don't want me to understand
My uncle takes his mate outside and I hear him say
I told you she was different, she can't just have any old builder
She needs someone who won't talk down to her, who won't mind her
    being odd
She's always been different this one, my uncle looks over to me
She might not sound all together but she's a lawyer, yeah man she is
They both look at me so I smile and say, Cuppa tea, I'll just put the jug
    on.

APIRANA TAYLOR

Apirana Taylor, of Ngāti Porou, Te Whānau a Apanui and Ngāti Ruanui tribes and also of Pākehā heritage, is a poet, playwright, novelist, short story writer, storyteller, actor, painter and musician. He has been Writer in Residence at Massey and Canterbury Universities. He has been invited several times to India and Europe and in 2012 to the Medellín Poetry Festival in Colombia. His poetry and prose has been translated into several languages. He travels to schools, tertiary institutions and prisons throughout New Zealand to read his poetry and currently teaches creative writing at Whitireia Polytechnic. The most recent of his five books of poetry is *A Canoe in Midstream* (Canterbury University Press, 2009).

The womb

Your fires burnt my forests
leaving only the charred bones
of tōtara rimu and kahikatea.

Your ploughs like the fingernails
of a woman scarred my face.
It seems I became a domestic giant.

But in death
you settlers and farmers
return to me
and I suck on your bodies
as if they are lollipops.

I am the land
the womb of life and death.
Rūaumoko the unborn God
rumbles within me
and the fires of Ruapehu still live.

(1979)

Poem for a misplaced bushman

Once you said
'Like seed planted in good earth
or left to wither on barren rock
life rides the winds of chance.'
To you a flower
was more precious
than the rarest gem.

Did the wind
plant you next to this
crematorium.
A production line
grinding out ashes
like a factory of the deceased.

Did the wind
plant you
where each tombstone
tells a story.
The rich lie in ornate oblivion.
The proud poor
queue up for their suburban plots.

You were the tūī
for whom the world held
no nectar sweeter
than hill and forest.
The bones of a bushman
will find no peace
in this city of the dead.

I feel the lid
of your casket tossed aside.
Your fingers claw the earth.

The earth on your coffin
is uneasy.

Perhaps you hear as I hear
the wind sowing seed on bush-clad hills
where once we stood
and drank
from waters
of the last pure stream.

(1979)

Feelings and memories of a kuia

These Māori today
are not Māori any more
I don't know what they are

I remember the old people
they were polite
and they liked to talk
they walked at a leisurely pace
but always got things done

Today my mokopuna always rush
yet never seem to do a thing
they hardly say a word to me
and they don't look happy

When I was a girl
we had big gardens
all us children worked in them
and the kuia and koro
used to make jokes
they cooked us a big kai in the morning
we were very happy

Sometimes
we went to the lake
we'd get some fern
and tie it into bundles
with akeake
and toss the fern
into the water

When we pulled up the bundles
we'd shake them
and lots of fish
would fall out

In the bush
there were plenty
of fat juicy pigeon
the river
was full of eels
dinner swam past
all we had to do
was catch it

The bush
got chopped down
the river dammed
and the lake polluted

It seems to me
the closer
the Pākehā got to us
the more difficult
he made it for us to live

Then came the war
I think
a lot of Māori men

who would have been
great leaders
of our people
got killed overseas
and for what

So we could live in quarter-acre sections
when once we had
more land
than my eye could see

So we could eat
hamburgers
when once we got
fresh kai

So in the end
we could be lost
and unhappy
and not know why

(1981)

Takin' words to the muso

I took my words to a musician
you're a musician man
you know the song
you've got the tune
you'll understand how
the words sound I said
and so sing please sing them
these words of mine I said

well leaning there against the lamppost
in the sun he lazily looked at me and said
'them words are good'
'how d'ya know,' I asked
'I can see 'em in yuh face,' he smiled
'I can hear 'em in yuh heart and I understand
what they are saying
but first we gotta find the tune,'
and out with his harmonica he goes and plays
I had a friend oh I had a friend
I knew he was understanding what he was saying
from listening to what he was playing

then there came a drummer
man he could rattle that snare then the rhythm and bass
got together
it was all up tempo
the brass opened up and crooned Broken Alice who sang
crooked in the armchair moon music oh music
we played and laughed
and just didn't want to stop
cause the music was in our hearts and minds
and words and music led to dancing
we danced and danced and danced
for a thousand years
the muso liked the words
I liked the song
one night the saxophonist quit years later the drummer's heart stopped
    ticking
Alice broke down completely
the muso wandered off
lost himself in wine

(1996)

Poem for a princess

once from the chiefly line
from the seed of the rangatira

there grew the most beautiful flower in all of Waikato

her petals rivalled Tama-nui-te-rā in splendour

she hauled her tribe from the jaws of Hine-nui-te-pō
she lived her life for her people, never for herself

therein lies her strength and beauty

on the banks of the Waikato River
all the taniwha call her name

Princess Te Puea, Te Puea Hērangi

he piko he taniwha Waikato taniwha rau

(2004)

Six million

'oh Api'

my friend Wolfgang weeps
as we walk up the road to Dachau
'you are proud of your ancestors
how can i be proud of mine?
my father was a Nazi
we fought over the dinner table
we've not spoken for years'

tears flood from Wolfgang's eyes

'i've never been able to visit the camps
i've lived here all my life'

brother Wolfgang weeps

his karanga to the dead rises
into the dull grey sky

the spirits listen in silence

as we walk up the road
on the corpses of six million dead Jews

(2004)

Haka

when i hear the haka
i feel it in my bones
and in my wairua
the call of my tīpuna
flashes like lightning
up and down my spine
it makes my eyes roll
and my tongue flick
it is the dance
of earth and sky
the rising sun
and the earth shaking
it is the first breath of life
eeeee aaa ha haaaa

(2004)

Te ihi

From where does it come, te hā
the life breath
and what strange winds blow
through this house
in the drift and flow
of whaikōrero
the call
ka ea ka ea
it is clear, it is clear
whakapiri tonu whakapiri tonu
hold fast, hold fast to what
te ihi, te ihi, te ihi
te ihi, what is that
te ihi, what is this word
te ihi, te ihi, what is it
kia mau, kia mau ki te aha
he pāua mura ahi ngā kanohi o Tūmatauenga
the flashing eyes of Tū
haka it is haka
lightning flashing in the sky
rapa rapa te uira
ka tangi te whatitiri
and thunder
the beat of the feet till the earth shakes
kia whakatahoki au i a au
from where does it come, te hā
the life breath, te ihi
the sobbing wailing and laughter

(1996)

Fishbone

how it must've stuck in their gullets like a fishbone
to have their plans foiled by a black little one-eyed
monkey called Tītokowaru

he could count his fighting warriors
on his fingers and toes
if he counted old women and children

Cameron gutted Taranaki
opened it up like a can of beans

he knew the cause was unjust

in search of honour glory riches and fame
they came Whitmore, McDonnell, von Tempsky
the Kai Iwi cavalry

their dreams lie buried on the battlefield

a bullet shot von Tempsky

he got a street named after him

Maxwell, his sabre thirsting for the blood of more
children, was shot on his horse charging again

blood and butchery

Whitmore, McDonnell, got hollow victory
meaningless medals empty fame

Tītoko's army, old men, women, warriors and children,
unbeaten, melted away, a fight over a woman they say
breaking of tapu

eat the rocks, chew and choke on the bones

sings Tītokowaru jailed in his cave

(2004)

NGAHUIA TE AWEKOTUKU

Ngahuia Te Awekotuku grew up in a family of storytellers and weavers in Ōhinemutu, Rotorua. She has written two collections of fiction, *Tahuri: Stories* (New Women's Press, 1989) and *Ruahine: Mythic Women* (Huia, 2003); a monograph, *He Tikanga Whakaaro: Research Ethics in the Maori Community* (Ministry of Maori Affairs, 1991); and *Mana Wāhine Māori: Selected Writings on Māori Women's Art, Culture and Politics* (New Women's Press, 1991). Her creative writing and scholarly works appear in many local and overseas collections. She was the principal author of *Mau Moko: The World of Māori Tattoo* (Penguin Viking, 2007), Māori Book of the Decade in the Inaugural Ngā Kupu Ora Māori Book Awards 2009.

Pukeroa

So wild blows the wind
          – cold
and here I sit
    against
a tree, emblem of Life
   green, growing
silent upon this hill
that was the realm,
    the fortress
  of Te Makawe
feared and avoided

That road before me stretches
far into the cool twilight –
    black tar which melts
beneath the hot sun.
Cars – modern, streamlined, vintage
   how they move
upon a road that
   once knew
only the tread of tough
   brown feet
and heard the power of the haka
the plaintive wail of

   the tangi
a call, a challenge, echo
  across our warm marae.

Still, he has come, the white man
– has come, and has conquered
wiped from beneath us
   that base we knew so well
so that it should exist no more
but be replaced, our glorious heritage
with muskets, fire and bricks
with industry, with progress
    with 1966.

(1966)

Moon poem

Do you know that I watch
the moon
and remember those nights
when the glitter of a million
 pearldrops
cast a path of silvering
light across the waters
and the waves sang
trembling in our hearts

Do you know that I watch
the moon
and remember those nights
when the long dark liquid
joy
of you richly red came
fast, filling my parched throat

Do you know that I watch
the moon
and remember those nights
when we laughed and discovered
each other, silly secrets
that were the same, the same
craving for that very touch
aching for that very moment
yet promising nothing

Do you know that I watch
the moon
and remember those nights
when your skin gleamed moist
in the shadows of
our forbidden passion
while our bodies moved breathing
like one

Do you know that I watch
the moon
and remember those nights
when I clutched the flesh firm
cliff edge of your
shoulders clawing
and swung out far across
that abyss of black pleasure

Do you know that I watch
the moon
and remember those nights
when we called her down into
our veins pumping
alive in the wisdom
and craziness of our changing
selves

Do you know that I watch
the moon
and remember those nights . . .

(2000)

For LMS 145, a bone flute at the British Museum

bone: resting lizard stretched
along the grain : bone
that once lamented and rejoiced
that once sensed the blood's
currents and rhythm : bone
that once sang bold songs
of triumph
that once lifted a warrior's arm
now
you are mute : bone
your silent eloquence
your dozing reptile
tell me more
than a million melodies
rising
above the water in the
fierce fluid moving night
bone : moe mai rā,
moe mai, moe mai.

(1994)

For 6742, a hei tiki at the British Museum

so many hands before mine : so many
lovers so many tears and
probing finger tips which

oiled your jade
curves and creases tender
pressed against their own
smoothing skin : Manawa
I call you
Ko koe tēnā, taku manawa
fanged fierce you laugh at me
pūkana eyes blank
yet bulging bold and so
many hands before mine,
after mine, through mine
Manawa, and so
we meet again

(1994)

For one trophy of the Waikato war, now in an unnamed museum

Such a face; yours, a
moulded perfection of
tilting eyes, nostrils fine and chiselled
lips; I wonder, I wonder
what did your sightless gaze
witness
that morning that day that night
when you were torn down because
your beauty, your magic
were recognised and claimed as
a prize of war
while close to the river she moved
on and the rarauwhe burned
steaming with new blood amid
the goads and shouts of obscene
triumph and destroying
they took you

bundled you into a scrim bag;
ripped you away from home. To
this, a bleak grey place where lonely
tissued by the layers of pulp and
plastic, your beauty your beauty
and our pain our pain
shine through.

(1988)

ALICE TE PUNGA SOMERVILLE

Alice Te Punga Somerville (Te Ātiawa) was born in Wellington and raised in Auckland; she is currently based at University of Hawai'i–Mānoa where she is Associate Professor of Pacific Literatures. Although most of her writing takes the form of scholarship (*Once Were Pacific: Māori Connections to Oceania* was published by Minnesota in 2012) she has never stopped writing poetry. Her work has been performed widely and published in a range of venues including *Ora Nui* (2012 and 2013), *4th floor* (2013), *broadsheet: new new zealand poetry*, *Shendandoah*, *Law Text Culture*, *Terror in our Midst*, *burn this CD*, *Mauri Ola* and *Whetu Moana*.

mad ave

i

dave dobbyn wrote a song about madeleine avenue.
dlt helped him out with it
and it's a good song.

to those of us who grew up in the area,
the street they sing about wasn't the kind of place you'd call 'madeleine
    avenue',
because it just couldn't carry off that kind of name.

to us it was just mad ave.

ii

parallel to mad ave was esperance,
the road we walked along on the way home from school.
we'd start off a big group walking slowly at the end of the day
talking and laughing and yelling 'see ya'
as kids peeled off to go in to their houses.
because my street came off the other end of esperance,
I'd walk all the way to the end.

iii

walking home down esperance was always a bit scary because of the
    dogs.
that was also part of the thrill though,
and sometimes i'd imagine a dog waiting till i was all alone
at the end of the road
and choosing that as the time to attack.

my friend stephanie's big sister saw a dog run over on esperance once.
the car ran straight over its stomach,
then the dog jumped up and kept running down the street.
we would tell and retell that story,
shaking our heads, laughing at that kind of dog
– 'those dogs on esperance man' –
impressed by the sheer resilience of the unsquashable dog
and also (secretly)
horrified by the idea the dog in question might still be out there,
dodging all reasonable efforts to kill it.

the dog that i was most scared of wasn't an unknown quantity at all, but
    was a very familiar feature:
the dog i was most scared of was Max,
the giant black dog that hid behind Mrs Mafileo's flowers,
and when Camille and i used to leave school at lunchtime

to visit our friend Tasha and baby Jessie,
we'd walk up the steps
holding on to each other
stomachs in our throats,
wondering if Max's head was going to pop up behind the
chrysanthemums.

iv

those trips to see Tasha were a big part of my last two years at school.
after i snuck from school, through mad ave, to esperance,
we'd drink diet coke, watch oprah or days of our lives,
chatter away about big and small things.
although i didn't always go back to school afterwards,
when i did i'd sometimes have a little bit of Jessie's milky sick
on the shoulder of my regulation blouse
and if it was really bad i'd cover it
with Tasha's old school uniform jumper.

i remember the time Tasha brought Jessie to school as a baby
and that principal of ours who'd been so mean and so inflexible
during the pregnancy asked Tasha if he could hold Jessie.
to our delight, which we fought hard, but failed, to hide,
as soon as she was in his arms,
Jessie turned her little head
and sicked all over his pristine shirt sleeve.

v

so why would dave dobbyn write a song about a street?

because
the flats up and down mad ave and esperance
were slowly emptied out
– there was a time when there were bits of gardens
and bits of boarded up windows all in the same street –
and then, the final insult,
they were all knocked over,
demolished.
gone.

my mum says the saddest thing
was driving through the streets
and seeing that even though the houses were gone
there were still some remaining bits of taro patches
the weedy offcuts of gardens,
resistance at the level of leaves and stems.

vi

the last time i was in new zealand i drove through mad ave,
although it's not called mad ave anymore.
it's mount taylor drive, thank you very much,
after the english name for taurere,
the mountain that's really much closer to a molehill
and sits doggedly at the end of the street.

mount taylor drive is a bit different to mad ave, aye.

each house takes up the space of about three or four mad ave families
there aren't any cars on blocks in the front yard,
there are no taro patches in the back

old ladies chatting as they walk up the road
kids walking home from school
or chrysanthemums.
and even though i'm sure the new places don't have the problems of rot,
burned-out kitchens,
worn-out-ness from overcrowding
that the old places had,
to me they look like a gust of wind might make
the walls topple over
the roof fall in
the windowpanes crash to the ground.

'mount taylor drive' isn't really a change of name for the same street,
    then,
as much as it's a new name for a new thing.

vii

when i was 14
i was in a school production about taurere
and the stories told about the people who'd known the landscape
before mad ave, before mount taylor drive.

I'm still not sure who has the right to mourn
who has the right to say
that their place was taken away.

(2003)

Daddy's little girl

Hours and hours in the back seats of family cars,
long trips and waking up:
snuggled in giant jumpers and sleeping bags,
wrapped in night and stars and sleepy breath.

Dreams and conversations mix, then fade,
and Dad's listening to the radio news:
he's softly clicking and flicking a switch,
a lullaby for young late night travellers.

Years later when I learned to drive
I was surprised to rediscover the sound
which I'd grown to link with Dad
and sleeping bags and warmth.

An adult now, I drive through the dark,
long long trips wrapped in stars and night:
I think of Dad and his hours of gentle courtesy,
lights dipping and bobbing for passers by.

(1998)

First draft of a waiata tangi

For Te Rangihīroa

it's hot here:
without electric fan, open window, bare legs
i'd be lying in the dark, heavy limbed and drowsy

as it is, i can feel an ache of warmth at the back of my neck
where hair falls in a tight curtain around an already moist little nook

i'm lying on my tummy, skin pressing into a warm patch of blanket
working on the first draft of something i'll never finish

although warmed milk and sheets are supplied at nighttime
to wide-awake children in the islands of our births
warmth has the opposite effect here:
it's too hot to fall quickly to sleep tonite

i visited your whare 'te pātaka o pīhopa' today

before heading to the archive in the back of the building
i walked through front doors, up stairs, over carpet
to greet the small Māori display at the end of the mezzanine

laid a handful of leaves beside the whakairo there
quietly sang to them under my breath,
a small one-sided karanga
surprising the other occupants more than the other visitors

wondered if you used to visit these cabinets too
if you looked across the carpet as i did and felt them looking back,
appraising,
gluing feet to floor and tumbling body into air,
all at the same time

walked along corridors you paced for years,
a precise producer of catalogues:
a scientist working with the test-tubes and bunsen burners of culture
before it was embarrassing to treat people like lab rats,
to steal things and ideas for safekeeping on airconditioned shelves

the relief it must have been to return here after your last trip home,
but also the grief:

did you visit the whakairo more or less after your final wrenching?
does spending time with those things of our own provide solace or
    discomfort?
do things behind glass feel enclosed, cut off, pristine, or do they keep you
    company?

e te rangihīroa

still hot, still sticky:
was it like this the night you died?

i wonder if you felt more at home as your body turned cold after last
    breaths

i wonder if your wairua found a path to follow to hawaiki,
departing as it did from this wrong end of our marvellous watery
    hemisphere

(2010)

NORMAN TE WHATA

Nōmano Makarini Horomana Remana Te Whata (Norman Te Whata) was born on 7 July 1932 and is affiliated with Ngātokimatawhaorua (waka), Pūhanga Tohora (maunga), Hokianga-whakapau-karakia (awa/moana), Ngāpuhi (iwi), Māhurehure (hapū) and Taheke (tūrangawaewae). He has a background in sculpting, carving and painting and began writing poetry while in isolation in Mt Eden Prison in 1969, where he says all his creative energies were generated. He cares for his wairuatanga (spiritual health) through his artistic expression, his sense of humanity with others and his contact with Te Ao Māori.

This street

I have
walked this street
making great holes

in my feet
got to tell you
you're on this street too
on that bypass
hey man you won't last
too long on this street

    walking great holes in my feet
    wearing big soul holes man
    wearing big soul holes man
    I'm walking this street
    making great holes
    in my feet

See that
guy over there?
his Afro hair now grey
he lives like a cowhide drying
wrinkled old and hiding
from his shame
even from his name

    I keep walking this street
    making great holes
    in my feet

See that
young chick?
looks old and lost
she's looking for a living
don't turn away
we all walk this street man
hear what I say man?

    walking great holes
    in my feet

wearing big soul holes man
wearing big soul holes man
I'm walking this street
making great holes
in my feet

MAHINĀRANGI TOCKER

Mahinārangi Tocker was a singer, songwriter, performing artist and poet of Ngāti Raukawa, Ngāti Tūwharetoa, Ngāti Maniapoto, Hebrew and Celtic ancestry. Her poetry and music are about identity, love, loss and cultural background; she recorded seven albums and collaborated with many other musicians. She was working on her eighth album, *Worksmiths*, when she sadly passed away at the height of her career in 2008. Mahinārangi became a member of the New Zealand Order of Merit for services to music in the 2008 New Year's Honours List, and her music continues to be played in Aotearoa and throughout the world. These poems are from her first book of poetry, *lyrics without melody* (Street Women Press 2001).

My eyes close to see you

i saw you again
    when i closed my eyes . . .
i saw you look at me . . . and i . . .
    i closed my eyes again . . .
to remember what it is
    that i haven't yet learned
and i heard you . . .

a tape winding around
    in my head
a melody
    challenging my throat
a sigh
    clutching at my heart

i close my eyes again
    and again ... and again
so that i can have you
    to myself
i close my eyes to see you
    so that i can see

(2001)

privilege

I walk the maze
of streets
in crowded thought
          ko Tongariro tōku maunga
and catch
a blaze of sun
through sky
high concrete
          ko Taupō tōku moana
in search of something
wildly wicked
hopeful
and
strong in touch
with everything
i've seen before
i see again
          ko Kauriki tōku marae
war less fugitives
of reason and hope
in trust
that this is paved
and marked
for destiny sake

where cracks the ground beneath
my footstep
    ko Rihitapuwae tōku māmā
no revolution in this atmosphere
where surrounds the chaos
of quiet disrespect
desire is a many splendoured
hemisphere
between sky
and earth
the first breath
and
the last
    ko Ngāti Tūwharetoa tōku iwi
where watches an hour glass
to take us
nowhere
    E tū! E tū!
where catches a second
to make believe
that this city
is united
in a colourless
sigh
    He aroha He aroha

(2001)

HONE TUWHARE

Hone Tuwhare (1922–2008) was a poet of Ngāpuhi iwi – hapū Ngāti Korokoro, Ngāti Tautahi, Te Popoto and Te Uri-o-Hau. Tuwhare burst on to the New Zealand literary scene with his first collection of poetry, *No Ordinary Sun* (Blackwood and Janet Paul, 1964). Over the following four decades he published twelve further collections of poems, short stories and a play, and immersed himself in writing, performing and touring both in New Zealand and overseas. He was the recipient of many awards and fellowships and was twice winner of the Montana New Zealand poetry award. Tuwhare was Te Mata Poet Laureate in 1999 and received two honorary doctorates in literature. He was named one of New Zealand's ten greatest living artists in 2003. Hone Tuwhare passed away in Dunedin on 16 January 2008. His poetry is now available in *Small Holes in the Silence: Collected Works* (Godwit, 2011).

O Africa

On bloody acts
that make less human
mankind's brighter sun,
let revulsion rise.
Eclipse
the moon's black evil:

so that innocence
and the child shall reign
so that we may dream
good dreams again.

(1964)

No ordinary sun

Tree let your arms fall:
raise them not sharply in supplication
to the bright enhaloed cloud.
Let your arms lack toughness and
resilience for this is no mere axe
to blunt, nor fire to smother.

Your sap shall not rise again
to the moon's pull.
No more incline a deferential head
to the wind's talk, or stir
to the tickle of coursing rain.

Your former shagginess shall not be
wreathed with the delightful flight
of birds nor shield
nor cool the ardour of unheeding
lovers from the monstrous sun.

Tree let your naked arms fall
nor extend vain entreaties to the radiant ball.
This is no gallant monsoon's flash,
no dashing trade wind's blast.
The fading green of your magic
emanations shall not make pure again
these polluted skies … for this
is no ordinary sun.

O tree
in the shadowless mountains
the white plains and
the drab sea floor
your end at last is written.

(1964)

Hotere

When you offer only three
vertical lines precisely drawn
and set into a dark pool of lacquer
it is a visual kind of starvation:

and even though my eye-balls
roll up and over to peer inside
myself, when I reach the beginning
of your eternity I say instead: hell
let's have another feed of mussels

Like, I have to think about it, man

When you stack horizontal lines
into vertical columns which appear
to advance, recede, shimmer and wave
like exploding packs of cards
I merely grunt and say: well, if it
is not a famine, it's a feast

I have to roll another smoke, man

But when you score a superb orange
circle on a purple thought-base
I shake my head and say: hell, what
is this thing, called love

Like, I'm euchred, man. I'm eclipsed

(1970)

To a Maori figure cast in bronze outside the Chief Post Office, Auckland

I hate being stuck up here, glaciated, hard all over
and with my guts removed: my old lady is not going
to like it

I've seen more efficient scare-crows in seed-bed
nurseries. Hell, I can't even shoo the pigeons off

Me: all hollow inside with longing for the marae on
the cliff at Kohimarama, where you can watch the ships
come in curling their white moustaches

Why didn't they stick me next to Mickey Savage?
'Now then,' he was a good bloke
Maybe it was a Tory City Council that put me here

They never consulted me about naming the square
It's a wonder they never called it: Hori-in-the-gorge-at-
bottom-of-Hill. Because it is like that: a gorge,
with the sun blocked out, the wind whistling around
your balls (your balls mate) And at night, how I
feel for the beatle-girls with their long-haired
boy-friends licking their frozen finger-chippy lips
hopefully. And me again beetling

my tent eye-brows forever, like a brass monkey with
real worries: I mean, how the hell can you welcome
the Overseas Dollar, if you can't open your mouth
to poke your tongue out, eh?

If I could only move from this bloody pedestal I'd
show the long-hairs how to knock out a tune on the
souped-up guitar, my mere quivering, my taiaha held
at the high port. And I'd fix the ripe kotiros too
with their mini-piupiu-ed bums twinkling: yeah!

Somebody give me a drink: I can't stand it

(1972)

Kitten

the phone didn't ring
yesterday.

it never even looked like
starting

and no letters've come
today, either – except

a stray kitten

i have given it milk;
it has adopted me

we've had a brief talk
about his mum? his dad?

you might say it was
a one-sided chat about cats:

but nothing's come of it

kitten knows only two
words and one of them is:

slurp

it is making love to my
feet: it understands

my loneliness . . . miaow?

(1992)

On a theme by Hone Taiapa

Tell me poet, what happens to my chips
after I have adzed our ancestors
out of wood?

What happens to your waste-words, poet?
Do they limp to heaven, or go down easy
to Raro-henga?

And what about my chips, when they're
down – and out? If I put them to fire
do I die with them?

Is that my soul's spark spiraling; lost
to the cold night air? Agh, let me die
another hundred times: eye-ball

to eye-ball I share bad breath
with the flared nostrils of the night.
For it's not me I leave behind: not me.

Only the vanities of people;
their pleasure, their wonder and awe
alone remain.

Bite on this hard, poet: and walk careful.
Fragmented, my soul lies here, there: in
the waste-wood, around.

(1974)

Haiku (1)

Stop
your snivelling
creek-bed:

come rain hail
and flood-water

laugh again

(1970)

Salvaged

I too, am not inured to pain –
      the pangs of jealousy – the huff
      the puff, of cry-wounds.

We refashion newly, the misshapen
      allegories of love – with one
      red rose – furtive,
      among the groceries.

And may I divulge that I, craftily
      have hid that special tankard
      rich, brimful

of memories – from which no other
      lips but ours, have sipped: no
      other love, eclipsed.

(1997)

Rain

I can hear you
making small holes
in the silence
rain

If I were deaf
the pores of my skin
would open to you
and shut

And I
should know you
by the lick of you
if I were blind

the something
special smell of you
when the sun cakes
the ground

the steady
drum-roll sound
you make
when the wind drops

But if I
should not hear
smell or feel or see
you

you would still
define me
disperse me
wash over me
rain

(1970)

Heemi

For James K. Baxter

No point now my friend in telling
you my lady's name.
She wished us well: offered wheels
which spun my son and me like
comets through the lonely night.
You would have called her Aroha

And when we picked up three young
people who'd hitched their way
from the Ninety Mile beach to be
with you, I thought: yes
your mana holds, Heemi. Your mana
is love. And suddenly the night
didn't seem lonely anymore.

The car never played up at all.
And after we'd given it a second
gargle at the all-night bowser
it just zoomed on on gulping
easily into the gear changes
up or down.

Because you've been over this road
many times before Heemi, you'd
know about the steady climb ahead
of us still. But once in the tricky
light, Tongariro lumbered briefly
out of the clouds to give us the old
'up you' sign. Which was real friendly.

When we levelled off a bit at the top
of the plateau, the engine heat couldn't
keep the cold from coming in: the fog
swamping thick and slushy, and pressing
whitely against tired eye-balls.

Finally, when we'd eased ourselves
over a couple of humps and down down
the winding metalled road to the river
and Jerusalem, I knew things would be
all right. Glad that others from the
Mainland were arrowing toward the dawn
like us.

Joy for the brother sun, chesting over
the brim of the land, and for the three
young blokes flaked out in the back seat
who would make it now, knowing that they
were not called to witness
some mysterious phenomenon of birth on
a dung-littered floor of a stable

but come simply to call
on a tired old mate in a tent
laid out in a box
with no money in the pocket
no fancy halo, no thump left in the old
ticker.

(1974)

The New Zealand land march on Wellington, Hepetema 14–Oketopa 17, 1975

What will I wear? What can I afford to wear? And will my
    landlord keep my flat for me in Dunedin? This long
    walk: what a hell of a thing.

I need a haversack. Who will lend me one? I might have to
    carry my gear in a sugar-bag with flax tied to the bottom
    corners: no sweat. But I need a raincoat. Who will

    trust me with one in the immense time of Spring when
    showers bless the earth, eh? I am old. Already wrinkles
    spread inexorably: inching, inching. They're not all of

    them laughter-lines. Agh, what a hell of a thing. But it
    won't be a lonely walk. People all around and mostly
    young: from blue-brown with bits more added right on

    up to off-white? *Jesus, how self-conscious can you get.*
    Like man, I only want to last the distance, right?

Yeah: and all the different people worrying differently and
    separately about the decision and the action of commitment
    they each have taken to grab the burning but elusive

    star together. And together not knowing what lies at the end
    of the star's reach. Together, not knowing whether they will
    get a punch in the face at the end of the

    road, or, with much pain learn that it is just beginning . . .
    My feet are beginning to ache already. The cracks on my
    Maori feet are beginning

    to widen, my blood turned on. Do not laugh.
    Laugh only when the blisters fade with the jaded politicians
    and their cunning.

Laugh only when the small spies soft-pies pie-eyed freckled ladies
    and their mafia-men with dark glasses are dug out like
    bed-bugs from among us. Be watchful, watchful . . .

I need a haversack. Who will lend me one? I need a raincoat.
    Who will trust me in a time of Spring when flowers clamour
    for the yellow and the blue, the

red the green of the life-giving earth? What a good time to take a walk.

(1978)

Rain-maker's song for Whina

I'll not forget your joints creaking as you climbed into
  the bus at Victoria Park to bless the journey.
  When you broke down in the middle of the Lord's Prayer,
  I thought that what you left unsaid hung more tangibly
  uncertain above us all than some intangible certainty
  that we would all get a comfortable berth in the
  hereafter.

Saint Christopher in the rain at night, just before Mangamuka
  Gorge. People wearing Saint Christopher badges getting
  off the bus and helping to put an overturned vehicle right
  side up. No one hurt. I finger the cheap badge you gave me
  of the saint. *Will it be, alright?*

A couple of days later in bright sunshine, we hit the road
  leaving Te Hapua behind. And all the way south – to the
  'head of the fish,' I picked up some hard truths embedded in
  your hilarious speeches on the marae:

> *No more lollies! We been sucking the pakeha lolly*
> *for one hundred and fifty years.*
> *Look at what's happened. Look at what we got left.*

> *Only two million acres. Yes, that's right. Two million*
> *acres out of sixty-six million acres.*
> *Think of that. Good gracious, if we let them take what*
> *is left we will all become taurekareka. Do we want that ?*
>
> *So you listen, now. This is a sacred march. We are*
> *marching because we want to hold on to what is left.*
> *You must understand this. And you must think of your*
> *Tupunas. They are marching beside you. Move over, and*
> *make room. We are not going to Wellington for nothing.*
> *And don't be mistaken: Kare tenei hikoi oku, he hikoi*
> *noa-aha ranei ki te miri-miri i nga paoro o Te Roringi.*

E, kui! What a way to bring the 'House' down. You could not
have lobbed a sweeter grenade. I'm all eared-in to you,
baby . . . Kia ora tonu koe.

(1978)

We, who live in darkness

It had been a long long time of it
wriggling and squirming in the swamp of night.
And what was time, anyway? Black intensities
of black on black on black feeding on itself?
Something immense? Immeasureless?

No more.
There just had to be a beginning somehow.
For on reaching the top of a slow rise suddenly
eyes I never knew I possessed were stung by it
forcing me to hide my face in the earth.

It was light, my brothers. Light.
A most beautiful sight infiltered past

the armpit hairs of the father. Why, I could
even see to count all the fingers of my hands
held out to it; see the stain – the clutch of
good earth on them.

But then he moved.
And darkness came down even more oppressively
it seemed and I drew back tense; angry.

Brothers, let us kill him – push him off.

(1987)

Bird of prayer

On the skyline
a hawk
languidly typing
a hunting poem
with its wings.

(1992)

The old place

No one comes
by way of the doughy track
through straggly tea tree bush
and gorse, past the hidden spring
and bitter cress.

Under the chill moon's light
no one cares to look upon
the drunken fence-posts
and the gate white with moss.

No one except the wind
saw the old place
make her final curtsy
to the sky and earth:

and in no protesting sense
did iron and barbed wire
ease to the rust's invasion
nor twang more tautly
to the wind's slap and scream.

On the cream-lorry
or the morning paper van
no one comes,
for no one will ever leave
the golden city on the fussy train;
and there will be no more waiting
on the hill beside the quiet tree
where the old place falters
because no one comes any more

no one.

(1964)

Old man chanting in the dark

Where are the men of mettle?
   are there old scores
   left to settle?
   when will the canoes leap
   to the stab and kick
   the sea-wet flourish
   of pointed paddles?
   will the sun play again
   to the skip of muscles

    on curved backs bared
    to the rain's lash
    the sea's punch?
    to War! to War!

where are the proud lands
    to subdue – and women?
    where are the slaves
    to gather wood for the fires
    stones for the oven?
    who shall reap
    the succulent children whimpering
    on the terraced hill-top?

no more alas no more
    no raw memory left
    of these
    nor bloody trophies:
    only the fantail's flip
    to cheeky war-like postures
    and on the sand-hill
    wry wind fluting
    the bleached bones marrowless

(1964)

Pupurangi

(Kauri snail shell)

On the ground
that was densely
populated by
the Kauri,
I, Pupurangi once
thrived there also.

The Kauri forest
is gone. It is no more.
But you may yet chance
upon my spiral-conical
house, intact, untenanted
unshattered and unshat-upon
by carefree, fourfooted cattle.

    I am no ordinary snail.
    I, Pupurangi – a long time
    fugitive from the Sea, have
    adapted to this sad environ
    of depletion, where the Kauri
    and me, are merely listed as endangered.

        In a time (when trees were plentiful)
        overactive fledglings that have fallen
        out of the nest, distract me by their
        feeble peeps, their helpless twitchings
        on the ground. I travel toward my target
        with great elan and swish. Moments like this
        do not find me gummily glum. There is a special
        lilt to the turbulence of air flowing over the dome
        of my house, as I lift my speed just a wee bit
        over familiar terrain. But now the Kauri and me
        in number – are diminished.

            And now, if you should hold me up to your ear
            you may yet hear (painfully) the rising, agonised
            shriek of the rip-saw biting – the thump-bump
                    of the hammer on the nail – driven.

(1997)

On becoming an icon (!)

Except for a couple of absentee
>	Icons, together, we stand –
>	all ten of us comically sardonical;
>	sartorially
>	succeeding only in being
>	dark-suited –
>	bow-tied & white-shirted,
>	but secretly stretched
>	in bowel and
>	bladder control, as

the Governor-General,
>	Dame Silvia pins
>	a round, green-stoned-
>	cored badge, on our
>	plumped-up chests to a series
>	of comedically repressed 'Ow-ouches'
>	and discovering politically that
>	we are all 'Lefties'
>	as the pin lances
>	a left nipple.

We become more phylosophically
>	dead in the face, as
>	our lips curl to a
>	comedically heroic, tight-
>	lipped silence of
>	painful acceptance,
>	laconically iconical!

(2005)

TRACY WATSON

Tracy Watson lives with her three children in Moreton Bay, Queensland, Australia. She is of Celtic and Māori descent. Her father is Te Ātiawa with ancestral links to Ngāti Raukawa, Ngāti Kahungunu and Ngāti Porou. Her mother is Te Whānau a Apanui with ancestral links to Ruawaipū, Uepōhatu, Ngāti Porou, Ngāpuhi, Tainui, Kāi Tahu and Kāti Māmoe. In 2013 she was Moreton Bay Region's Citizen of the Year and since 2011 has been holder of its writing portfolio. In 2013 she won a Queensland Achievement Award for arts and culture.

Kōauau (NZ Māori flute)

Light to the touch
I raise you to my nostrils and take in your wooded scent
familiar . . . of musty almond

My fingers wrap around your flesh
like the hongi
in honour of each other's presence

Ancient marks are memories
a tāmoko tapestry
blueprints of yesteryear

Bellowing a chiefly sound
your notes waiata stories of old
that penetrate six generations

Page after page, note after note
the shrill pitch transcends form
A pōwhiri to, your new owner, the *seventh* keeper I am.

(2010)

Kōpū (Venus)

Kōpū, North Star, large and bright
lingering in the sky tonight

Those on Earth look up and wonder
at your greatness we tend to ponder

Are you the one who brings in the day
allowing us to jump and play?

Of course you are I must be blind
bringing near end to this rhyme

You are the dust and the dawn
Your name is Kōpū the star first born.

(2010)

REINA WHAITIRI

Reina Whaitiri, Kāi Tahu, is of Māori and Pākehā descent. She is a teacher, researcher and editor of Māori, Pacific and indigenous literature. She taught English literature at the Universities of Auckland and Hawai'i, and co-ordinated the former's Tertiary Education Foundation Programme. She has published articles on being Māori, and on Māori women's poetry, and has co-edited three anthologies, *Homeland: New Writing from America, the Pacific, and Asia* (University of Hawai'i Press, 1997), *Whetu Moana* (AUP, 2003) and *Mauri Ola* (AUP, 2010). She was one of the judges for the 2012 New Zealand Post Book Awards and for Huia Publishers' Pikihuia short story annual competition. She is retired and lives in Auckland.

Lincoln Hall – Hawai'i

September 1999

A banyan tree outside my window
fills two frames and more
spreading shade
and dappling light.

Its size commends it
to this place

of mighty mountains
adzed by playful Atua

who've crammed as much
as thought allows
onto this tiny island
afloat Moana-nui-a-Kiwa.

The trees at home
grow up towards the light and straight
a deeper green
than this

but when I wake
and see the sky
through leaves
ablaze with light

and smell the heavy
heady scent of
pīkake and rainbow showers
my thoughts return

to Aotearoa
much further south
where sunlight
filters through the bush

which breathes and
throbs with birdsong
and incessant drone
of insects.

Held fast by
Hawai'i's northern star
and Aotearoa's southern cross
Polynesia's dazzling maro

peopled still
by those who have the gift
of not forgetting
those powerful ancient ones

who've restored to them
their rightful place
and chanted back
their potency.

(1999)

Ka tangi

Taitokerau
I didn't make it to his tangi
Dad did though and he recounted
what he saw and what he felt
I knew his pain was deep at the death
of his old commander in chief – James Henare
those warriors of the Battalion
were more than just a fighting force

Murihiku
'Māori Battalion march to victory
Māori Battalion march to war
Māori Battalion march to the enemy'
the Battalion hymn pipes
his casket inside the church
the marching beat stirring
one last time his soldier's heart

Taitokerau
Dad travelled by car to the base of the hill
where hundreds of people milled expectant

in the hot and dusty chaos
his body had not yet arrived
so few remained of those who fought
but enough for a reunion
as they waited heavily for their leader

Murihiku
Zippy dinghies ferry people ashore
surfing the mighty southern ocean swells
and dumping them on the beach
where, hunched against the cold
they congregate at a single point
on the sweeping curve of bay
to await their Upoko – Robert Whaitiri

Taitokerau
Finally, he comes to a welcoming haka
performed to a faltering shaky rhythm
by soldiers old now and weary
but fiercely strong in aroha and deep respect
as they fall in behind one last time
to begin the stumbling struggling
climb to the top

Murihiku
The howling wind and pounding surf
lend mana to the warriors' haka
calling, hauling in the waka
which bears my Dad
as he rides alone
with just one man to steer him in
to his beloved tūrangawaewae

Taitokerau
Once there they carefully place
his mate on the paepae

while all around his women gather
decked in black and green
to mourn the man who'd led
those men, those magnificent men
of the 28th Māori Battalion

Murihiku
Broad, strong Kāitahu men
bear the heavy coffin
up the uneven rock-strewn path
the kai karanga calling calling
urging them on as they trip and stumble
while we with eyes cast down
tramp unwillingly behind

Ka mahi te mea i tohia ki te wai o Tū-tāwake
the kauri of te Ika a Māui
the tōtara of Te Waipounamu
have fallen

(*2009*)

One times three

Three boys, three times one boy
each unlike the other
and so much more
than brothers

The tuakana
first for food and affection
named after his tipuna
the fighting chief – Te Wera

Hōhepa the gentle
one between
who seeks to know
the why and how

The loudest one
invades the space
connecting him
to Tahu Pōtiki

With time and luck
they'll grow into
the men their Pōua
dreamed they'd be

(2005)

HAARE WILLIAMS

Haare Williams, Te Aitanga a Māhaki, Rongowhakaata and Tūhoe, was raised by his grandparents in Ōhiwa Harbour near Ōpōtiki. He has worn many hats during his long and distinguished career including that of school teacher; lecturer in education and curriculum development and later Māori studies; and registered minister in the Ringatū Church. After his work in education, he moved into television news and current affairs and was a pioneer in Māori radio as the general manager of Aotearoa Radio. He won the prestigious Director General's Award for broadcasting excellence and has recorded and archived Māori oral histories. Haare has been a judge for the Wattie Book Awards, has published his poetry widely and had also had many solo art exhibitions.

Koroua

E Koro – kaua e haere
Don't leave
who will make
fresh footprints
tracing our own
in the sand

E Koro – kaua e haere
Don't leave
who will kindle
the fires
smoke
to tease the nostrils

E Koro – kaua e haere
Don't leave
who will sing the melody
from beyond the shore
to linger
in the corridors of the mind

E Koro – kaua e haere
Don't leave
who will growl
when we're out of tune
so that music flows
from broken guitar strings

E Koro – kaua e haere
Don't leave
who will paddle us
through the misty
drift of
inconsequential tides

E Koro – kaua e haere
Auē taukiri ē
E Koro
Don't leave

(1981)

Bellbird and flax flower

'Unuhia te rito o te harakeke
Kei hea te korimako e kō'

We found our pleasure
listening that morning
to the song of the korimako

For the korimako
pleasure is gathering nectar
from a flax flower;
it is a pleasure too
for the flower to yield

Neither the korimako
nor the flower
can store away
today's desires
for tomorrow's coming

In praise of the flower
the korimako sings
bringing music
like nectar
to a confused day

To the korimako
the flower is
the bringer of life;
And to the flower
the korimako is
the messenger of love

(1981)

Patches hide no scars

They bear patches
on their jackets
hiding scars and wounds
finding their own
direction, discipline
orders

How do we prosecute
those already punished
how do we fine
those lost in the streets
of no direction

How do we heal
those slashed
in the flesh
when they are
slashed in spirit

To a fish in the sea
to a bird in the sky
to a deer in the forest
all men are dangerous,
brutes, intruders,
vagrants

Gone the steady
roar of the sea
the echo of the hills
the voice of the elder
invoking the ancestors
rebuking the young
the tracks that cling
to the hillside
where barefooted

they walked out
and rode away
on bikes

Gone

The tohunga
who healed from within
with his remedy of aroha

Gone

Their boots
their jackets
no longer hide
their scars

(1981)

Kūmara

E kare
Can I have my mokopuna
help me dig out my
kūmara

We'll do better,
we'll all come
tomorrow and tomorrow
to dig out your
kūmara

We watched her old hands
fondle the kūmara
on the brown earth
children sorting and counting
kūmara

There, she sat and smoked
one arm akimbo, skirt gathered in
children gathering the first fruits
into the kits of Pani
kūmara

These we eat now
these for the tangi
these for seed
and these, e kare mā, are your
kūmara.

(1981)

Koha

Our
Nanny Wai
sang
to orchard trees
calling each
by name

We didn't really know
why
'Trees give their best
for trees
to hold back is to
die

You give little
when you give
things
give of yourselves
like trees

that's giving
learn from them

With Earth
for Mother
Sky
for Father
they hold back
nothing!'

The year
Nanny Wai went
the trees grew old
and died
we didn't really know
why

(1981)

VERNICE WINEERA

Vernice Wineera, born in New Zealand to Māori and English parents, traces her heritage to Ngāti Toa and Ngāti Raukawa. She grew up in Takapūwāhia Pā, Porirua, and earned her BA in English and Art from Brigham Young University–Hawai'i. She received her MA and PhD in American studies from the University of Hawai'i. Her poetry has appeared in books and journals in Papua New Guinea, New Zealand, India and the United States. She worked for the Polynesian Cultural Center (1980–92) and for BYU–Hawai'i (1978–80, 1992–2008). Her books include *Mahanga: Pacific Poems* (BYU–Hawai'i, 1978), *Ka Po'e o Laie* (Polynesian Cultural Center, 1979) and *Into the Luminous Tide: Pacific Poems* (BYU–Hawai'i, 2009). She and her family live in Laie, Hawai'i, where she is working on a series of contemporary paintings exploring Māori themes.

Song from Kapiti

Some people there are
who survive
on the promise of summer.

Such are the inhabitants
of the Paekākāriki coast,
in dwellings nestled against
cliff-face and ragged clay
in the full winter fury
of the open ocean.
I watch a lone seabird
who sits woodenly
on a wind-ravaged crag,
his feathers ruffled
by the cold southerly
straight from the Antarctic.
The sparse toetoe
lean with the wind,
and trail feathered fronds
over the wild, grey beach.
They reach chill fingers
into my heart.
I am that bird
frozen by the southern wind,
my wings wooden
in the cold salt air.
I am the child of the Ngāti Toa,
seeking my place
in a mainland society.
I am she learning to sing
the sad-sweet songs of a people's soul.
I am the lone bird
alive in a limbo of longing,
enduring the winter world,
surviving
on the slim promise
of a future summer.

(1982)

Wellington, circa 1950

The winds were always there.
The southerly, up from Antarctica,
baring teeth that tore your clothes,
hair, skin, even flesh from off your ribs
then licked your bones
with that infinitely cold tongue.
And sometimes the northerly,
no less cruel, snarling down the gorges
north of the pā, clawing branches
off the eucalyptus trees, roofs
from wooden houses, frail, every nail
creaking in the onslaught.
Then we'd hate to go outside
for more wood, the few lumps
of coal you bought with shillings
kept safe within your coin purse.
Someone had to though,
and I avoided the guilt of seeing you
trussed in that thin overcoat
in the brute wind, the flimsy scarf
whipping about your grey hair,
the axe ever-poised in the air
as you fought to let it drop
against the wet logs
on the chopping block.
So I'd go, stepping beyond
the slamming of the time-lock door
into the animal day,
the whole world writhing,
snakes in the trees,
dogs howling down the sky,
the picket fence rocking, possessed
of something terrible, unseen.
Then the empty rooms of that house,

damp with their view of the grey sea,
the bleak sky, became
the only womb of warmth left
for a fifteen-year-old adrift
in a storm, a grandmother's fading year
the sole companion.

(1982)

At Laieloa

Under the bridge where paint
is sprayed in pictures on the rock walls,
where the tide washes storm water overflow
back into a large black pool,
where boys probe with sticks for treasures
going to and from the elementary school,
the turtle lay.

Covered with tar, oil-slick second skin
thick about his wrinkled neck,
eye unseeing for the black hood
dripping from his drooping head,
motionless in the greasy water
beside the auto tyre, the clotted cans,
the thatch of rubber slippers, plastic diapers,
lumps of grey detergent soap,
the turtle lay.

'Oh no!' the children said, 'He is so beautiful,
is he dead?' We do not, cannot answer
'Dying – a slow death,' noting as we do
his foaming eye and mouth,
the laborious inching of one flipper,
a broad arrow pointing south.

South to green islands, clean waters, blue
air, south to where, an age ago, he inched
his way seaward from the beach, new-hatched.

(1982)

Hokuleʻa

We have all watched
with some misgiving
the ocean of possibilities
beyond our doors,
wondering, in our complacency,
whether we had courage enough
to chart a course
to farther islands.
No one of us
can yet walk on water,
and so few ever try,
knowing the fragility
of the sea's soft skin
and the hook of fear we feel
within our very human lives.
So it was with some rationalisation
that we watched your proud sails
turn toward Tahiti.
We were not with you
for a multitude of reasons,
yet we watched, fascinated,
and something deep within us
stirred with pride
and we put aside
the mundane happenings
of our comfortable lives
to watch the Star of Gladness

tack across the sky.
We watched.
We saw the rain we had not seen
for many balmy weeks
come slanting off the ocean,
its arrival appreciated as always
for the promise of sustenance
it brings to these islands,
and no less for its blessing
on the launching of Hokule'a.
We watched
as an ocean
whipped suddenly to spray that stung
the salt-caked flesh of men
leaning against waves
steep as the Ko'olaus
risen abruptly from deep green valleys
and safe, placid fields,
muscles roped across their backs.
Āe, we watched.
And watching, felt at once
the poignancy of guilt,
the shattering of smugness
in lives that now know triumph
born of pride in Hokule'a.

(1982)

The farm-boy rides a Yamaha

Skinny shoulders blistered by the sun,
freckles prominent across his serious face,
the ten-year-old herds slow cows
towards the milking-shed.
Back and forth behind them

the eager dogs bound and skip
watching for a sign
but he gives none.
– He is wearing blue and gold,
silk and leather,
numbered helmet that glitters in the sun.
The guttural lowing of the cows
are roars from great excited crowds
of watching people.
These tufts of tussock
veering his machine aside
are hillocks on his dangerous
and lonesome victory ride,
when, the gate ahead a checkered flag,
he guns into the cloud of dust
to roar across the finish line
bettering the record time.

Then,
wiping his face
on his scarf of silk,
he bails the cows
and prepares to milk.

(1982)

Boy in a sleeping bag

First he lays it flat along the ground,
making sure there are no rocks beneath.
Then, legs together, sliding carefully,
he inches between its quilted folds,
aware that any jut of knee
or elbow will disturb
the perfect symmetry

that is his private bed.
Once in,
he reaches sleepy fingers
to tug the awkward zip
up to his chin.
One last glance beneath the chairs
assures him that there are no bears
then, snug and warm in his bright cocoon,
my son camps out in the living room.

(1982)

Tāniko

Looped about my fingers,
a single thread,
silk-soft
weaves the fabric
of my life,
patterned by culture
and a coloured view
of the give and take,
twist and loop,
stretch and ease
of reality.
Passive warp,
active weft,
each formless individually,
combine to shape
my own design,
the art
I own within my mind
and heart.

(1982)

BRIAR WOOD

Briar Wood grew up in Māngere in Auckland. She is a graduate of the University of Auckland and has a DPhil from the University of Sussex. Her poetry and critical writing has been widely published. Her recent poetry collection *Welcome Beltane* was published by Palores Press in 2012. *Glorified Scales* (2001) includes poems written for the installation by Maureen Lander at Auckland War Memorial Museum, which referred to their Ngāpuhi whakapapa. Recordings of her work are online at the Poetry Archive and Aotearoa New Zealand Poetry Sound Archive.

Rotomahana

Two lakes made this stretch of water –
one hot, one chill, though now we're told
the water's mostly cold, except around the edges
where cliffs steam and the earth rumbles.

Visitors, we float on a solid boat, the *Ariki Moana*,
across the site of Ōtūkapuarangi,
coloured by amorphous antimony sulphides in sinter.
Te hana o Tarawera – buried terraces, villages and all.

The pretty tranquil town of Te Wairoa
where the tohunga Tūhoto Ariki was left
among ash and mud in his whare for four days
since his predictions were mistaken for a cause.

Ah, the cost of prophecy,
though Hochstetter got away with it
and Guide Sophia's mana grew. All respect
to Te Arawa, whose wāhi the gathering visits.

Calmer days now, the kānuka grows
but in Fumarole Bay, the steaming cliffs
and the fracture of a fault line suggest
restless temperatures, tremulous vents.

'If this place goes up again' the captain says,
'and it's only a matter of time,
this lake in this boat is the last place I'd want to be.'
After that we trundle uphill in the bus asap,

past Rūaumoko's Throat, now labelled
Inferno Crater Lake – baby blue, azure –
and its symbiotic, Papatūānuku
down up relationship with Frying Pan Lake.

There and now, we could easily be in hot water
whatever newness earth has to create.
Despite the names, science and mythology alone
can't explain this place. Rotomahana.

(2010)

Rangiputa

Clouds, white sand and blue
expanse of seasky reflecting
each other seeming to go on
and on forever. The transport,
a catamaran floats close to shore.

The dolphins do not appear
although they were here
only yesterday, swimming
among the rocks, playing
with the snorkel faced children.

I search without expectation
for my father, understanding
I will not find him in the dinghy
he rowed to the horizon in
on that stormy bay one day

over forty years ago long
before the manicured motels
now here. That time he came back,
with his friend, a diver,
holding up bundled crayfish.

Ngatote's gift to Joseph
except not in perpetuity.
Now the iwi want it back
and wouldn't you? Who'd
trust a missionary's version?

Today the ship loads up
with business and bonhomie;
not much sign of the god
except the sky rolling on and on,
long and deep as a song.

(2010)

Kūmara hōu

Kūmara hōu – new kūmara –
also kūmara tawhito – old kūmara –
brought on waka from Hawaiki
maybe Mexico, Peru, the Kontiki
sailed thousands of miles across
Te Moana-nui-a-Kiwa seeking
your roots, your tubers
ipomoea batatas, earth banana.

Those of us living in London
how we miss you. We dream
of hangis, roasts and bakes,
chips with cold beer – soul food.

After years and years here kūmara
some of us still worship you.

How did we leave Aotearoa
where the kūmara is legendary –
Rongo's gift to his wife Pani
passed on to us, lush leaved, lucky
like on the slopes of Te Upoko o Mataaho?

Wars have been fought over you
cause of fast and feast.
In the pits – a great place to hide,
riding on toroa or waka rererangi
kūmara have travelled
to Rānana where the sweet potatoes
sometimes leave us wanting homegrown.

Descendants of Owairaka red
dreaming our favourite varieties
purple jewelled skin and tender
creamy yellow wriggle squirm
made flesh, peeled and dressed
into harlequin stripes, a joker
as the saying goes – Kāore te kūmara
e kōrero mō tōna ake reka.

But I do, kūmara, proclaim
your sweetness, your links to
the future, may you prosper
spread your wāina tendrils –
and grow around the glowing globe.

(2010)

Whenua uenuku

It was that green summer
after your mother retired.
Janine was undisputed queen
of the ice-cream parlour.
Shane and Evan were away.
Māia wore neon peach jeans
and the New Year barbecues
got rained off. Waharoa.

A rainbow rose at Taipā
while pōhutukawa bloom
gave memory that red tinge
and waves of violet curve
to infinity at least –
an observer's perspective –
who faces kōwhai falling
rain with evening sun behind.

Sunlight's refraction refracts
as it enters roimata
causing different wavelengths
of visible light to split,
to separate the blue dew
and indigo skittering
of swallows at the Sail Club
angles off a globed surface.

(2013)

REWA WORLEY

Rewa Palliser Worley is a young poet of Pākehā and Māori descent, 'nō Ngāpuhi me Ngāti Porou'. He began writing poetry seriously after his involvement in the Rising Voices Poetry Slam 2012, created by Grace Taylor and Jai MacDonald. He is a member of the Waxed Poetic Revival, and is currently working on a Master's thesis that involves spoken word poetry and its relationship to well-being.

The separation

In kōhanga reo,
the language nest
when I was still small maybe three or four
they told all of us,
the children who listened,
the story of how our world was made
and in it,
the void, Te Kore,
an empty silhouette of what would be
filled its emptiness with the essence of the night,
Te Pō-tahuri-mai-ki-taiao.

Time and distance spiralling down its spine
leaving dreams and ripples of what may come In Its memory
and reaching its depths,
casting from this womb's lips
the star-crossed lovers,
Ranginui the sky father and the earth Papatūānuku beneath him
kissed into existence,
side by side
and their love was one
without time or limits,
there was no line where one began and the other finished,
wrapped in the dark by a shroud,
a cloak, that bound them so close
that as they slept he would breathe her breath
as she felt his chest move up,

and down, against hers
Filling his lungs with the taste of her dust,
just long enough,
to give it back again.

And once
as if ploughing through a field
he would plant their son,
a Seed, Tāne, the Forest.
But in need of space and sun,
sprouting out from my mother
my legs like tree trunks,
my feet branching into the sky as I
pushed away at my father,
so that the light and cold could stream into the space between.
Separation must have been hard for them,
divorce is not something we like to talk about.

Even now,
I still see my father sometimes
in a world of his own
his head, somewhere in the clouds
and even though I never saw it I knew from the look in his eyes
like the colours in the sunset
that he had shed and cried tears for that he had lost.
Like a myth, or a legend
a story I never forgot.

(2012)

E kore e hekeheke he kākano rangatira.

SELECT GLOSSARY

āe	expression of agreement or assent
ahi kā	home-burning fires signifying rights of occupation
ake; ake, ake, ake	upwards, away; forever and ever
akeake	a small tree with long, sometimes reddish leaves
āmine	amen
Aotea	Taranaki waka, especially connected to Pātea
Aotearoa	New Zealand, 'long white world/land'
ara	pathway; to rise up, awake
Arahura	river on the West Coast of the South Island
ariki	paramount chief, leader, aristocrat
Ariki Moana	passenger boat used on cruises of Lake Rotomahana
aroha ki ngā rangatahi e	caring for the young people
aroha; arohanui; Aroha	love, respect; great love or respect; also used as a personal name
ata-kahurangi	blue dawn sky
atua	ancestor, god, demon, deity
Atutahi	'first light' or 'first born'. Used as a personal name; also the name given to the star 'Canopus', the second brightest star in the sky.
auē	exclamation of pain, surprise, shock or grief
auē te mamae	oh, the pain
auē, taukuri ē	oh, my sorrow
Awahou	'new river'; the name of a stream that flows into Lake Rotorua, sacred to Ngāti Rangiwewehi of Te Arawa
Bastion Point	In the 1970s Māori occupied this site on the Auckland coast for 507 days, determined to stop the development of Ngāti Whātua land. This occupation was a watershed moment in Māori politics and resistance.
DOC	Department of Conservation
Don Brash	Politician and leader of the National Party between 2003 and 2006. He made controversial speeches on race relations and Māori identity.
e hoa	friend
e kare mā	affectionate term for a friend, used mainly by those connected to the Mātaatua waka
E kore e hekeheke he kākano rangatira	I will never be lost for I am of the seed of chiefs

E kore e mutu mai ngā wawata e Me waiho i roto, te manawa e	No end to the dreams/desires Let them remain in the heart
E kore e mutu, te aroha e, Ka pūmau tonu rā, I ngā wā katoa, ngā wā katoa	No end to the love For ever and ever
E kore te aroha e taka e I waho i taku Manawa	Love will never leave my Heart
E Koro – kaua e haere	Grandfather – please don't go
e mōhio ana ahau	I know
E ngā iwi o ngāi tahu	The people of Ngāi Tahu
E noho rā, Tongariro E noho rā, Te Taupō-nui-a-Tia E noho rā, Tūwharetoa	Farewell, Tongariro Farewell, Te Taupō-nui-a-Tia Farewell, Tūwharetoa
E taonga tū mai, tū mai, tū mai	A treasure that remains for ever
E tū rā!	Stand there!
E tū, e tū, e tū, Tānemahuta!	Be upright, be upright, Tānemahuta!
Eva Rickard	An activist who championed Māori land and women's rights. Best known for fighting to regain the Raglan Golf Course which was unjustly taken during World War II.
fa'aniusila	(Samoan) the New Zealand way
fale	(Samoan) house
faleo'o	(Samoan) small house
haere mai	greetings, come hither, welcome
haka	dance of defiance, challenge, show of unity and strength accompanied by incisive words chanted by the performers; traditionally performed before battle
haka pōwhiri	haka to welcome visitors
hamuhamu māia	bold scavenger
Hana Te Hemara	An activist who fought for the teaching of te reo and against injustices to Māori in the 1970s. Became famous for reportedly saying 'Māori should kill a Pākehā and become a hero' after visiting Pāremoremo prison and witnessing the high number of incarcerated Māori men.
hāngī	earth oven used to cook food with steam from heated stones
hapū	subtribe, kinship group, those connected to a common womb; also means pregnant
harakeke	flax; an important plant used for weaving
haramai te toki, hui e, haumi e, tāiki e	coming together, joining, uniting
Hawaiki	spiritual homeland of Polynesians, exact location/locations unknown
Hawaiki-nui-ki-Aotearoa	Hawaiki to Aotearoa

Hāwera	place name meaning 'hot breath'
he hōhā	a bore, a nuisance; tiresome
He piko he taniwha Waikato taniwha rau	On every bend of the Waikato there is a taniwha
He rā ka whiti he rā ka tō he rā ka whiti	The sun rises the sun sets the sun rises again
he waiata tēnei mō Parihaka	this song is for Parihaka
he waiatanui kia Aroha	great love song to Aroha
hei tiki	carved figure, ornament, post to mark a sacred place
Hēmi / Heemi	Māori name for James; used especially to refer to New Zealand poet James K. Baxter
Hēni Pūtia	personal name, 'Hēni the Butcher'
Hepetema	September
Hikurangi	Ancient name from Hawaiki meaning 'mountain' or 'peak'. Name of a mountain in the Raukūmara Range.
hine; Hine	girl; daughter; younger woman; also used as a personal name
Hine Kōrako	a taniwha guardian who fell in love with a human man; can also refer to the moon
Hine Te Ariki	Hine The Highborn One
Hineahuone	mythical figure; together with Tāne she created the first woman, Hinetītama, who later became Hine-nui-te-pō
Hinemanu	'bird woman'
Hinemoana	a sea goddess; also the name of the legendary lover of Tangaroa, god of the sea
Hine-nui-te-pō	'mighty lady of the night', the goddess of death, who lives in the underworld where she waits to receives human beings when they die
Hinepare	personal name
Hinepare, tuwhera mai ki tō iwi marara nei!	Hinepare welcomes all the scattered members of the tribe!
Hinerangi	An early ancestor of Te Kawerau o Maki. She married a young Karekare chief and settled with him before a tragic accident occurred. On a fishing trip at a particularly dangerous spot, Hinerangi's husband and his friends were washed from the rocks and swept away. It is said that Hinerangi, disconsolate and heartbroken, sat on the headland above until she died of a broken heart.
Hinetītama	Mythical figure, known as the dawn maiden, who was the daughter of Tāne and Hineahuone and became, in time, another of Tāne's wives. When she realised Tāne was also her father she decided to leave the world of the living and become Hine-nui-te-pō, the goddess of death.

Hiroki	refers to Wiremu Hiroki, possibly of Taranaki descent, who was unjustly hanged for murder in 1882
hoa	friend
hōhā	to annoy, to irritate; a nuisance
Hōhepa	Māori transliteration of the name Joseph
Hokianga	the Hokianga Harbour, on the west coast of the North Island; also known as Hokianga-nui-a-Kupe or 'great returning of Kupe'
hōkioi	an extinct New Zealand bird
Hokuleʻa	an ocean-going waka built using traditional Hawaiian methods and materials which helped inspire the recent revival of Polynesian navigation methods
Hone Taiapa	a master carver of Ngāti Porou
hongi	to press noses and foreheads in greeting; an exchange of breath
horoi	to wash
Hotere	refers to painter Ralph Hotere, one of New Zealand's most distinguished artists
hou / hōu	new, recent, modern
huhu	wood grub found in decaying logs (a delicacy on the tongue, but perhaps not in the imagination)
hui	gathering, meeting; coming together
huia	extinct New Zealand bird, highly prized for its white-tipped feathers which were used as ornamentation
iwi	tribe, extended kinship group
Ka ao, ka ao, ka awatea	The dawning of a new day
ka ea	clear; satisfactory; avenged
Ka kōrero mai tōna ngākau, waiho rā, taria te wā ka hoki mai te wairua!	His heart tells him to leave it after a while the spirits will return!
ka mahi te mea i tohia ki te wai o Tū-tāwake	fulfilling their destiny
ka mau te wehi	low; terrible; awesome; frightening
ka pai te pōtae	that's a nice hat
ka patupatu taku manawa	my heart beats
ka raungaiti au	to become diminished; I despair
Ka rere te maramara Ka rere ki te pūtake Koia i piri ai Koia i tata ai E tūpā whaiā	The chips fly The chips fall to the base of the tree They gather and cling Joining together An incantation to whaiā
ka tangi	to weep; weeping
ka tangi te ruru	cry of the owl

Ka whawhai tonu mātou, ake, ake, ake	We will struggle without end, forever and ever and ever
kahawai	a feisty, silvery-blue New Zealand fish; the first caught each day is offered to Tangaroa, god of the sea
kahikatea	a slow-growing, fruit-bearing tree found in semi-swamp land; once heavily milled for timber
Kahungunu	refers to the ancestral figure of Ngāti Kahungunu, a tribal group of the central and southern North Island east of the ranges
kai	food; to eat
Kai Iwi	place name; one meaning is 'the eating of people'
kai karanga	women who call visitors onto the marae
kai te pai	dialect phrase for kei te pai, meaning 'I'm good'
Kaihu	river valley in Northland
Kaikōura	town on the north-east coast of the South Island
kāinga	home; village; residence
Kaipara	district and harbour in Northland
Kāitahu / Kāi Tahu / Ngāi Tahu	the principal iwi in the South Island
kaitiaki	guardian, minder, keeper
kaitiakitanga	trust, guardianship, stewardship
kākā	a parrot with olive-brown feathers which were once used for adornment
kānga pirau	fermented corn
kānga waru	grated corn
kānuka	native scrub-tree, similar to but taller than mānuka
Kāore te kūmara e kōrero mō tōna ake reka	The kūmara doesn't speak of its own sweetness; meaning 'don't speak in your own praise'
Kapiti / Kāpiti	island off the west coast of the lower North Island; final home of the fierce fighting chief Te Rauparaha of Ngāti Toa
karakia	prayer; poem; incantation; chant
karanga	call of welcome, usually made by women
kare	dear friend, companion
Kare tēnei hīkoi ōku, he hīkoi noa-aha rānei ki te miri-miri i ngā paoro o Te Roringi	My walk is not without purpose but to caress the scrotum of Te Roringi
Karori	Wellington suburb
katipō	venomous spider with red spot on its back
kaumātua	elder, old person

kaupapa	proposal; subject; theme, topic, policy
kauri	Coniferous tree whose straight tall trunks served as masts and spars in the nineteenth century. Only small pockets of kauri, not burned by Māori or logged by later immigrants, remain.
kāwanatanga	governorship
kēhua	ghost; spirit that lingers after death
kei te wawā roa	long noise; external noise
Ken Mair	a political activist and politician; spokesperson for the people of the Whanganui River and one of those responsible for the occupation of Moutoa Gardens
Kēnana	refers to Rua Kēnana, prophet, faith healer and land rights activist of Tūhoe, who wore his hair long
kererū	New Zealand wood pigeon
kete	woven basket
Key	refers to John Key, New Zealand Prime Minister elected in 2008
ki āku tipuna Māori	to my Māori ancestor
ki te Ao Mārama	to the World of Light
ki te Kaha Rawa	to almighty God
ki te Pō, ki te Pō	to the Darkness
ki tō iwi marara nei	to the scattered tribe
kia Aroha	for Aroha
Kia hora te marino kia whakapapa pounamu te moana kia tere te kārohirohi mua i tōu huarahi āianei, ā ake tonu atu	a tauparapara used to introduce oneself or to begin a formal speech
kia manawa nui	be steadfast, big hearted
kia mau, kia mau ki te aha he pāua mura ahi ngā kanohi o Tūmatauenga	hold on the eyes of the God of War are aflame
kia ora	greeting meaning 'good health'; hello
kia ora ki a koe	greetings to you
kia ora tonu koe	continue living
kia whakatahoki au i a au	a chant used in a haka
Kihei aku mihi i pau atu, e hine, Rokohanga koe ka pikauria e	My greetings to you are not complete It is left to you to carry on
kihikihi	cicada
kina	sea urchin or sea egg
kite	to see, find, discover

kiwi	native flightless bird once prized for its feathers
ko Kauriki tōku marae	Kauriki is my marae
ko koe tēnā, taku manawa	you're there, my heart
ko Ngāti Tūwharetoa tōku iwi	Ngāti Tūwharetoa is my tribe
ko Rihitapuwae tōku māmā	Rihitapuwae is my mother
ko Taupō tōku moana	Taupō is my lake

Ko te iwi Maori e ngunguru nei!
  Au, au, au e ha!
Ko nga iwi katoa ra, tau tangata e
  taoho ai koe,
Taoho!
	a haka

ko tēnei te whatinga o te mata o te tai	breaking the waters, slapping tidal waters
ko Tongariro tōku maunga	Tongariro is my mountain
Ko wai tērā … huri rā i ngā rori? Ko te kihikihi … haere ora i te ao e!	Who is that moving around on the road? It's the cicada alive!
Koʻolau	mountain range on the island of Oahu, Hawaiʻi
Kōpū	Venus, the North Star
kōanga	spring; time for planting
kōauau	nose flute
koha; Koha	offering, gift, donation; name of TV programme
koha o ngā kupu ki aroha	gift of words of love
kōhanga reo	Literally 'language nest', an initiative to save te reo Māori from extinction. Elders and teachers fluent in te reo pass on the language to preschoolers in special schools.
Kohimarama	Auckland beach suburb
kōkā	mother, aunt
kōkako	large New Zealand bird with dark bluish-grey feathers
kōkōwai	red ochre
kore	void; nothing; nil
korimako	a bird with olive-green feathers and a beautiful bell-like song; bellbird
koro	old man; grandfather
koroua	elderly man; elder; grandfather; granduncle
korowai	cloak ornamented with feathers or tags
koru	juvenile fern frond; carved spiral pattern based on this
kōtiro	girl, young woman

kōtuku	The white heron; their long white feathers were once used for adornment. Also a term used for an unusual and important visitor.
kōuka	the cabbage tree; used as a food source
kōwhai	a native flowering tree with bright yellow blossom
kōwhaiwhai	traditional curvilinear painting, used as ornamentation on house rafters
Kua mate taku Māmā	My Mother is dead
Kua ngaro ngā tangata	People have died
kuia; kui	old lady; grandmother; senior female
kūmara	sweet potato, a staple food of early Māori
kūmara hōu	new kūmara
kūmara tawhito	old kūmara
Kupe	Polynesian discoverer of Aotearoa
Kurahaupō	Rangitāne and Muaūpoko waka
kutu	head lice, vermin
Lapita	prehistoric Pacific Ocean people who lived around 1600 BC to 500 BC
lavalava	(Samoan) rectangular piece of fabric worn as clothing by many Pacific Island people
Mai ngā pōhatu katoa . . . Kua takahurihuri nei Mai Kakepo ki te tihi o Tawhiti nui . . .	From all the stones spinning around from Kakepo to the top of Tawhiti nui . . .
mamae	sadness, hurt; sore, painful
mamaku	black tree fern; giant tree fern
mana	spiritual power; prestige, authority, status
mana kupu	powerful words; the power of words
mana Māori motuhake	separate Māori identity; autonomy
mana wāhine	authoritative, effectual, powerful women
manaakitanga	hospitality; kindness
manaia	sea horse, a stylised figure used in carving
manawa	heart
manawa-nui	big heart; brave
Mangaiti	place name meaning 'small stream'
manuhiri	visitors; guests
mānuka	native scrub-tree with pink, white or red flowers
māoritanga	Māori culture, practices and beliefs
marae	central place of community; the open area in front of the wharenui

SELECT GLOSSARY

marangai	the east wind; a storm
maro	apron, short kilt, loincloth
Mātaatua	a waka, which Tūhoe, Ngāti Awa, Te Whakatōhea and Te Whānau a Apanui whakapapa back to
Matariki	The Pleiades or Seven Sisters; also the brightest star of that cluster. The rise of Matariki signifies the new year.
mate	dead; ill; defeated
mate kite	seer, one who can see the future
matua; mātua	parent; parents
Matuatiki	river name
Mau	Samoan independence movement against New Zealand in 1920s
Mauao	Mount Maunganui, Tauranga
Māui / Māui Tikitiki	The great hero of Māori mythology, 'Māui of the Topknot'. Māui's mother, mistakenly thinking he was stillborn, made a nest of her hair and set him afloat in it on the sea.
maunga	mountain; peak
mauri	life force; source of emotions; symbol of life
me	and; with
me aro koe ki te hā o Hineahuone!	take guidance from the breath of Hineahuone!
Me tū tahi ahau hai mānuka	I must stand alone like a mānuka
mere	short, flat weapon of stone or pounamu
Mere	Māori transliteration of the name Mary
mihi	introduction; to acknowledge, thank, greet
Miritene	Māori transliteration of the name Milton
moana	ocean; sea; large lake
Moana-nui-a-Kiwa	Pacific Ocean; 'the great ocean of Kiwa'
moe mai rā, / moe mai, moe mai	rest now / rest forever
Moeraki	'a place to sleep by day'; beach on east coast of South Island famous for its large spherical boulders
Moetu	place name; personal name
mokemoke	be lonely, solitary
moko	tattoo; shortened form of grandchild (mokopuna) or grandchildren or descendants in general
mokopuna	grandchild, grandchildren
Motutapu	ancient place name from Hawaiki meaning 'sacred or forbidden island'
moumou kai	wasted food

Muldoonery	refers to Robert Muldoon, Prime Minister of New Zealand from 1975 to 1984, who had a particularly abrasive style of leadership
Murihiku	place name meaning 'rear anchor', used for the deep south or Southland
Muriwai	place name or personal name meaning 'backwater' or 'junction of streams'
muru raupatu	to conquer, wipe out, overcome; take revenge by taking land
nau mai	draw near, come; welcome
ngā mihi ki a koe	greetings to you
Ngāpuhi / Ngā Puhi	iwi name; the northern and largest tribe of Aotearoa
ngā rangatira tokorua, Tohu Kākahi, rāua ko Te Whiti O Rongomai	the two great chiefs of Taranaki
ngā tāne atua	male gods, male ancestors
Ngā waka e whitu e tau nei Hoea hoea rā Tainui, Te Arawa, Mātaatua Hoea hoea rā Tokomaru, Tākitimu, Kurahaupō, Aotea rā, Ngā waka ēnei hoea rā, E ō tātou tūpuna	Seven canoes headed this way. Sail on, sail on Tainui, Te Arawa, Mātaatua Sailing, ever sailing Tokomaru, Tākitimu, Kurahaupō and Aotea These are the seven canoes that sailed here with our ancestors
ngahere	forest
Ngahuru	autumn; tenth month of Māori calendar
Ngāi Tahu	iwi name meaning 'descendants of Tahu'; the main tribe of Te Waipounamu, the South Island
ngaio	A native tree. Rona is said to have tripped over a root of this tree in the dark, causing her to curse the moon whose light had been shadowed by a cloud. Rona and the ngaio tree were spirited up into the moon as punishment.
ngaro	to be lost, missing, gone, consumed
ngā tai a Kupe	'the coast or sea of Kupe', or a king tide
Ngāti Toa	iwi name; the tribe associated with Te Rauparaha who led forays against Te Waipounamu
Ngatote	personal name
Ngāwhā	place name, known for natural hot springs, and, more recently and controversially, as the site of a private prison
ngeri	short haka performed without weapons
nīkau	iconic native palm tree

Numiamatumua	personal name
Ōkarito	place name, West Coast of Te Waipounamu
Oketopa	October
Ōrākau	place name meaning 'place of trees', the site of a battle between Ngāi Tūhoe and government troops in 1864
oriori	lullaby; to chant, lull to sleep
Ōtemātātā	village in Waitaki district of North Otago
Ōtūkapuarangi	site of famous pink and white terraces on the banks of Lake Rotomahana, destroyed in the 1886 eruption of Mount Tarawera
Owairaka	An ancestress of the Ngāti Awa people, Wairaka is famous for having saved the Mātaatua waka from bring dashed against the rocks. The Auckland suburb of Owairaka is possibly named after her.
pā	fortified village
pā mai tō reo aroha	to feel the love
paepae	front of the whare; orators' bench; threshold of house
Pākehā	foreigner; different; New Zealander of European descent
Pākiri	place name
Pani	goddess of Kūmara; leading female mourner
papakāinga	home place, village
Papatūānuku / Papa	Mother Earth, wife of Ranginui the sky father
parāoa	bread, flour, dough
Parata	refers to Hekia Parata, Minister of Education in John Key's National Government
Pare	abbreviation for Pāremoremo
Pāremoremo	New Zealand's largest and most notorious maximum security prison
Parihaka	Village on the slopes of Taranaki, famous for its people's peaceful resistance against colonial takeover of land in the mid-nineteenth century. Infamous for the vicious attacks there by British military who were sent to destroy Māori trying to defend their land.
paru	dirt; polluted, soiled
Patupaiarehe	fairy folk, fair-skinned people who live in the bush
pāua	Edible shellfish of the abalone family. When polished the shell reveals a blue-green mother-of-pearl iridescence.
Pele	(Hawaiian) powerful goddess of volcanoes
pīkake	(Hawaiian) fragrant flower
piki mai, kake mai, homai te wai ora / ki ahau	'welcome, give me the healing waters of life'; part of a well-known waiata
pīngao	golden sand sedge
pipi	New Zealand shellfish

piupiu	comparatively modern form of clothing made of dried and patterned flax
pōhutukawa	large coastal native tree with large red flowers which bloom around Christmas
pono	right; correct; truth; valid, honest
poro te waero	chop off the tail
pou tokomanawa	central pole of wharenui which supports the ridge pole; heart of the family or the community
pōua	South Island dialect term for 'grandfather'
pounamu	greenstone, New Zealand jade; something of great value
poupou	carved panels adorning walls of wharenui, usually representing ancestors, elders, people of importance to the community
pōwhiri	formal welcome ceremony
Pōwhiritia atu! Haere mai!	Welcome! Come hither!
pūhā	Sour thistle, a wild food that sharpens the Māori 'boil-up', a dish that can include pork bones, kūmara and potatoes. Rona's curse at the moon referring to pūhā is particularly brutal, mingling a common vegetable with the head, sacred within Māori lore.
pūkana	showing as much of the whites of eyes as possible to emphasise certain words in the haka
puke	hill
Pukearuhe	place name meaning 'hill with ferns'
pūkeko	swamp hen
Pukeroa	'Long Hill', a rhyolitic mound, and in the past a well-fortified pā of Ngāti Whakaue, Rotorua
puku	stomach, gut
pukutere	runny tummy
pūpū	winkle, cat's eye, univalve
pūpūrangi	kauri snail
Pūrakanui	inlet in Dunedin area
pūriri	New Zealand tree with red fruit beloved by kererū
pūtātara	conch shell; trumpet used to call or warn the people
Rakiura	name for Stewart Island, the third largest island of Aotearoa, meaning 'shining/glowing skies'
Rānana	London
rangatira	leader; to be rich, noble, esteemed, revered
rangatiratanga	leadership
Rangiātea	sacred name from Hawaiki, referring to an island of Tahiti thought to be the originating site of the Māori migration; also the name of much loved carved church which recently burned down

Ranginui / Rangi	the sky father
Rangiputa	place in the far north of Aotearoa
Rangitoto	name for island in the Hauraki Gulf meaning 'bleeding skies', after the eruption of the volcano which created the island and threw ash into the sky for many days
Rangitukia	place name meaning 'the day of the attack'
Rangitukia-Te Uranga	Rangitukia-The Rising Sun
rapa rapa te uira ka tangi te whatitiri	flash of lightening boom of thunder
Rapanui	Polynesian name for Easter Island
rarauwhe	bracken, common fern
Raro-henga	realm of the spirits, the underworld
rātā	large forest tree with crimson flowers and hard red timber
Raukūmara	area north of Gisborne
raukura	albatross feather worn as symbol of peace by people who resisted the illegal takeover of their land in Taranaki
raumati	summer
raupā	calloused, cracked, chapped
Rāwiri	Māori version of the name David
Rena	the container ship *Rena* which grounded off the coast of Tauranga in 2011, causing a major oil spill
reo	language; voice
Rewi	personal name
rimu	native tree, red pine
ringawera	kitchen workers
roimata	tears; to cry
Rokohanga	place name
Rona	legend has it that Rona cursed the moon for hiding behind clouds; as punishment she was taken up to live on the moon
Rongo	god of peace and of cultivated plants and medicine
Rotomahana	the 'warm lake', lying at the foot of Mount Tarawera
Rotorua	Town in the Bay of Plenty on the southern shores of the lake of the same name. A geo-thermal wonderland and popular tourist destination.
rua	two; pit
Rua	could refer to Rua Kēnana, prophet, faith healer and land rights activist of Tūhoe
Ruapehu	one of the three maunga on the central plateau of the North Island

Rūaumoko	Papatūānuku's unborn child, the god of earthquakes and volcanoes
ruru	morepork, New Zealand owl
tā moko	body tattoo
Tahu Pōtiki	Tahu the 'Last Born'; founding father of Ngāi Tahu and the younger brother of Porou (of Ngāti Porou). According to legend the two brothers loved the same woman but, as the elder, Porou was entitled to take her as his wife. Disappointed, Tahu took his followers and travelled south to establish Ngāi Tahu.
tai	the sea, tide, coast
taiaha	long weapon of hard wood
Taiepa	personal name
Tainui	iwi name; waka name
Taipā	place name
Taitokerau	region of the far north, home of Ngāpuhi
takurua	winter
Takurua Makariri	the Winter Star
takata Maoli	indigenous people of Tahiti
Tākitimu	waka of Ngāti Porou and Ngāi Tahu
Tako ki to kai rangatira! Tako!	phrase that refers to the practice of holding food in the cheek while in battle, thus avoiding the need to return to the pā for sustenance
tākou	red ochre
taku hoa wahine	my wife
Tama-nui-te-rā	the sun
Tamatekapua	Chief who led the canoe bearing the Te Arawa people to New Zealand. At the launching of this waka, Tamatekapua is said to have kidnapped Whakaotirangi, the beautiful young wife of Ruaeo, and carried her with him to New Zealand. In Māori mythology Tamatekapua's name is synonymous with 'stratagem'.
Tāmati	personal name
Tame Iti	well-known activist of Tūhoe who bears full facial moko; one of the most recognisable faces of Māori fighting for justice
tāne	man; male; husband
Tāne / Tāne Mahuta	God of the forest, birds and insects, responsible for separating his parents Papatūānuku and Ranginui. Also the name given to the largest known kauri tree.
Tāne-nui-a-rangi	Mighty man of the heavens
Tāneroa	personal name
Tangaroa	the god of the sea
tāngata whenua	people of the land
tangi	funeral; to weep, mourn, cry

SELECT GLOSSARY

tāniko	woven border of cloaks; to weave, embroider
taniwha	guardians of water, rivers, lakes, bodies of water
taonga	treasure, prized object; anything of value
taonga whakairo	carved treasure
Taonui	personal name
tapa	margin, edge
Tapere-nui-a-Whātonga	place name; marae name
tapu	sacred, holy; restricted, prohibited
Taranaki	the region on the west coast of central North Island or the mountain of the same name
Tarawera	the mountain which erupted in 1886 causing the destruction of the world-famous Pink and White terraces
tatau	(Samoan) body carving; tattoo
taukiri ē	an exclamation of surprise meaning 'oh dear'
taupata	large New Zealand shrub; creeper-like plant
Taupiri	Tainui's sacred mountain where they bury their dead
Taupō / Te Taupō-nui-a-Tia	New Zealand's largest lake, ancestral to the iwi Tūwharetoa
taurekareka	to be enslaved; shameful, low, captive
Taurere	Taylor's Hill
taurite he taonga	like a treasure
taurite ngā moehewa o Aroha	like the dreams/desires of Aroha
Tāwhirimātea	god of the winds and storms, who disagreed with his brothers as to the separation of their parents Ranginui and Papatūānuku
Tawhiti	ancient name from Hawaiki
tawhito	old
Te Ao Mārama	The World of Light
Te Ao Hou	The New World
Te Arawa	iwi name; waka name
Te Arikinui	paramount chief; title of the Māori queen
te ariki o te ao	world leader
te aute tē whawhea	whakataukī with the meaning 'when peace reigns, even the paper-like bark of the aute (mulberry tree) is not disturbed by the wind'
te hā	breath; the breath of life
te hana o Tarawera	the red skies of Tarawera; probably referring to the eruption of 1886
Te Hāpua	community on the shores of the Pārengarenga Harbour in Northland, New Zealand; the starting point for the hīkoi instigated by Whina Cooper

te hau	the wind
te haunui o te wairua	the gushing of the spirits
te ihi	essential force, power
te kawanga	house-opening ceremony
Te Ika a Māui	'the fish of Māui', name for the North Island
te kawaranga	protocol
te kōkā, te whare tangata	the mother, house of the people
te kore	darkness; the void; nothing, nil
te kōrero te kai a te rangatira	talk is the food of chiefs
Te Makawe	a protecting spirit and custodian of Ngāti Whakaue; his presence symbolised by a great tree of intense tapu on Pukeroa hill
te marae o te whānau	the family marae
te marama	the moon
Te Moutere o Matakana	place name
'te pātaka o pīhopa'	'the storehouse of pīhopa', or the Bishop Museum
te Pō-tahuri-mai-ki-taiao	the Night turned to light
te pō, te pō, te pō aroha	the night, the night, the loving night
Te Puea Hērangi	Inspirational leader of the Tainui people, responsible for building Tūrangawaewae on the banks of the Waikato River which was opened in 1929. The first leader to form kapa haka groups in order to raise funds. She was also responsible for the way manuhiri are hosted on modern marae.
Te Rangihīroa / Te Rangi Hīroa	Sir Peter Buck, a prominent member of Ngāti Mutunga, Taranaki. Author of important anthropological books on Māori and the Pacific and long-time curator of the Bishop Museum, Hawai'i.
te rerenga kēhua	white flight
Te Rerenga Wairua	Cape Rēinga in Northland, 'Leaping Place of Spirits'. Traditionally the dead travel north to this place before plunging into the ocean for the final journey to Hawaiki.
Te Roringi	personal name; used especially to refer to New Zealand politician Bill Rowling
te tangi a te rito	young centre shoot of harakeke, 'where will the bellbird sing if you pluck out the centre shoot'
Te Taupō-nui-a-Tia	see Taupō
Te Upoko o Mataaho	name of mountain meaning 'the head of Mataaho', the god of volcanoes
Te Uranga	place name meaning 'the sun rising'
Te Uri o Hau	name of a tribe
te waero	tail of an animal

Te Waipounamu	the South Island, the only place where the highly prized pounamau is found
Te Wairoa	Village destroyed by the Tarawera eruption and where a tohunga who predicted the disaster was buried in his whare by the ash. The people refused to dig him out because they held him responsible for the eruption.
Te Wera	an ancestral fighting chief of Kāti Māmoe in the deep south
Te Whakatōhea	iwi name
Te Whānau a Apanui	tribal group from Maraenui to Tihirau on the East Coast, who descend from Apanui-waipapa
te whare tangata	house of the people
Te Whiti o Rongomai	of Ātiawa, he was one of the leaders who resisted the illegal taking of Taranaki land and who sought refuge in Parihaka
tekoteko	carved figure on gable of meeting house, figurehead of canoe
tēnā i takahia!	chant used to begin a haka
tēnā i whiua!	chant used to begin a haka
tēnā koe	'there you are', a greeting
tēnā koe e hoa	there you are, friend
tēnā koe te whiti	greetings to you, Te Whiti
tēnei te kupu o te Māori	here are the words of the Māori
tihei mauriora	the sneeze of life
tikanga	correct procedure; custom
Tikoraki	Tikoraki Point in Otago
tī-kōuka	cabbage tree
tino	very
tino mokemoke	very lonely
tino rangatiratanga	self-governance, self-determination, sovereignty
tipuna / tīpuna	ancestor, elder / ancestors, elders
tītī	muttonbird, sooty shearwater, gathered by Kāi Tahu people as a valued food source
titiro	to look
Tītokowaru	of Ngāti Ruanui, he fiercely resisted British troops sent to drive Māori off their land in Taranaki
toetoe	genus of tall native grasses with feathery blooms
tohorā	whale
tohu	sign, certificate
Tohu Kākahi	Parihaka chief
tohunga	skilled person, expert; priest

Tōia mai, te waka ki te urunga, te waka ki te moenga, te waka ki te takotoranga i takoto ai, te waka	a canoe-hauling chant used to welcome visitors on to the marae
Tokomaru	waka name; Te Ātiawa whakapapa back to this waka
tonga	the south wind
Tongariro	the senior mountain on the central plateau of the North Island; ancestral mountain of the iwi Tūwharetoa
tōnuitanga	prosperity; abundance, plenty
toroa	albatross
tōtara	New Zealand tree valued for building waka and for carving
Truganini	A woman widely considered to be the last full-blood Aboriginal Tasmanian. Her request to have her ashes scattered was not observed and her remains were exhumed by the Royal Society of Tasmania and later placed on display. Only in April 1976, approaching the centenary of her death, were Truganini's remains finally cremated and scattered according to her wishes.
Tū	to stand; or the shortened version of Tūmatauenga, the god of war
tū kākāriki	the stand of green parrots
Tū-tāwake	personal name; place name
tuakana	eldest sibling
tuarua	second
tuatahi	first
tuatara	New Zealand lizard
tuatua	New Zealand shellfish
Tūhoto Ariki	name of the tohunga who foresaw the Tarawera eruption
tūī	New Zealand songbird with distinctive white tuft of throat feathers
tukutuku	wall weaving; woven panels between poupou in wharenui
Tūmatauenga	the god of war
tūpuna wāhine	female elders/ancestors
tupuna / tūpuna	ancestor, elder / ancestors, elders
tūrangawaewae	the place where one has the right to stand; one's home territory
ture te haki	the law of the flag
tūtae	faeces, excrement
tūtara-kauika	leader of a pod of whales
Tūwharetoa	iwi name
tuwhera mai	open the doors
uenuku / Uenuku	rainbow; name of ancestor who lived in Hawaiki

umu	(Samoan) earth oven used in Samoa and some other Pacific Island societies
Unuhia te rito o te harakeke Kei hea te korimako e kō	If you cut out the heart of the flax Where will the bellbird sing
upoko	head; leader
urupā	burial grounds
waewae-koukou	climbing club moss found in scrubland
wahanui	loud mouth
waharoa	entrance to a pā, gateway, main entranceway
wāhi	location, locality, place
wahine / wāhine	woman / women
wahine toa	woman of strength/power
wai whenua	land water
Waiapu	'Swallowing waters', dangerous to cross. Waiapu Valley in the Gisborne region is significant to Ngāti Porou.
waiata	song; sung poem
waiata aroha	love song
waiata ringaringa	song accompanied by actions
waiata tangi	lament
waiata whaikōrero	song to accompany speech
waiho	to let be, leave alone; put, place, ignore
Waikaka	river in the Southland region
Waikato	North Island river and its surrounding region
wāina	vine; also type of kūmara
Waiōuru	a small town in the centre of the North Island, home to a military camp for the New Zealand Army
Wairaka	The ancestress who is said to have saved the Mātaatua waka. Whakatāne is named after her deed and translates 'to act like a man'.
wairua	spirit, soul, quintessence
Waitangi	place name meaning 'crying waters', where the Treaty of Waitangi was signed in 1840
waka	canoe; sailing vessel; in modern times any vehicle
waka rererangi	aeroplane
wētā	large endangered New Zealand insect
whaea	mother or aunt
whaikōrero	formal speeches

Whakaata, Taupare, Tūwhakairiora	hapū, tūpuna of Ngāti Porou
whakairo	carved; to carve
whakamā	shame; shyness; embarrassment; timidity
whakapapa	genealogy
whakapiri tonu	still clinging
whānau	immediate family
whanaungatanga	family relationhips
whare	house, building, dwelling
whare pōrangi	mental hospital
wharekai	house for preparation and eating of food
wharenui	large house, meeting house
wharepaku	lavatory, toilet
whāriki	woven mat
whawhai	fight, struggle
whenua	land; afterbirth, placenta
Whetūmatarau	pā site and escarpment near the East Cape where a massacre took place in 1820
Whina	Refers to Whina Cooper, who in 1975 instigated the famous hīkoi from Te Hāpua in the north to Wellington. She worked to stem the loss of Māori land and was the founding mother of the Māori Women's Welfare League.

ACKNOWLEDGEMENTS

We would like to acknowledge and thank those who encouraged and supported this project. Financial support was given by Creative New Zealand, who recognised the importance of bringing together more than one hundred and twenty years of poetry written in English by Māori. Auckland University Press willingly and enthusiastically accepted the challenge of publishing the anthology. Our special gratitude and thanks go to Anna Hodge, Damian Love and Louisa Kasza who spent many, many hours in putting the collection together and for their careful reading and expert knowledge in every aspect of the project. Special thanks also to Diane Pomare and Jane McRae for assisting with interpreting Māori words and phrases; any misinterpretations are entirely ours.

But the most important acknowledgements must go to the poets and copyright holders who allowed work to be published in this anthology. Many of the contributors are established poets who have published widely and it is a privilege to be allowed to include their work here. So our very grateful thanks to: Hiria Anderson; Te Awhina Arahanga; Hinemoana Baker and Victoria University Press; Roimata Baker; the estate of Hilary Baxter; Anton Blank; Marino Blank; the estate of Bub Bridger; Ben Brown and Anahera Press; Tania Butcher; Jacq Carter; Mark Dansey; Shelly Davies; Kim Eggleston; Amber Esau; Rangi Faith; Miria George; Marewa Glover; Briar Grace-Smith; Rowley Habib; Aroha Harris; John Hovell; Keri Hulme; Witi Ihimaera; Sam Jackson; Phil Kawana; Hinewirangi Kohu; Paula Kora; Dora Roimata Langsbury; Marama Laurenson; Abigail McClutchie; the whānau of Katerina Mataira; Larissa McMillan; Trixie Te Arama Menzies; Kelly Ana Morey; Paula Morris; Justine Murray; Deirdre Nehua; Moana Nepia; Michael O'Leary; Tru Paraha; Pare Paul; Kiri Piahana-Wong and Anahera Press; Brian Potiki; Roma Pōtiki; Maraea Rakuraku; Vaughan Rapatahana; Jean Riki; Reihana Robinson, Steele Roberts and Auckland University Press; Te Kahu Rolleston; Zane Scarborough; Bruce Stewart; Georgina Stewart; Michael Stevens; the estate of J. C. Sturm; Tracey Tawhiao; Apirana Taylor and Canterbury University Press; Ngahuia Te Awekotuku; Alice Te Punga Somerville; Norman Te Whata; Irena Brorens and Hinewairangi Tocker-Fenton; Rob Tuwhare for the estate of Hone Tuwhare; Tracy Watson; Haare Williams; Vernice Wineera; Briar Wood; and Rewa Worley. Every effort has been made to find the correct copyright holders and estates, but if there are omissions or oversights we apologise and in these cases we would welcome contact from the poets or their families.

Reina Whaitiri & Robert Sullivan, May 2014